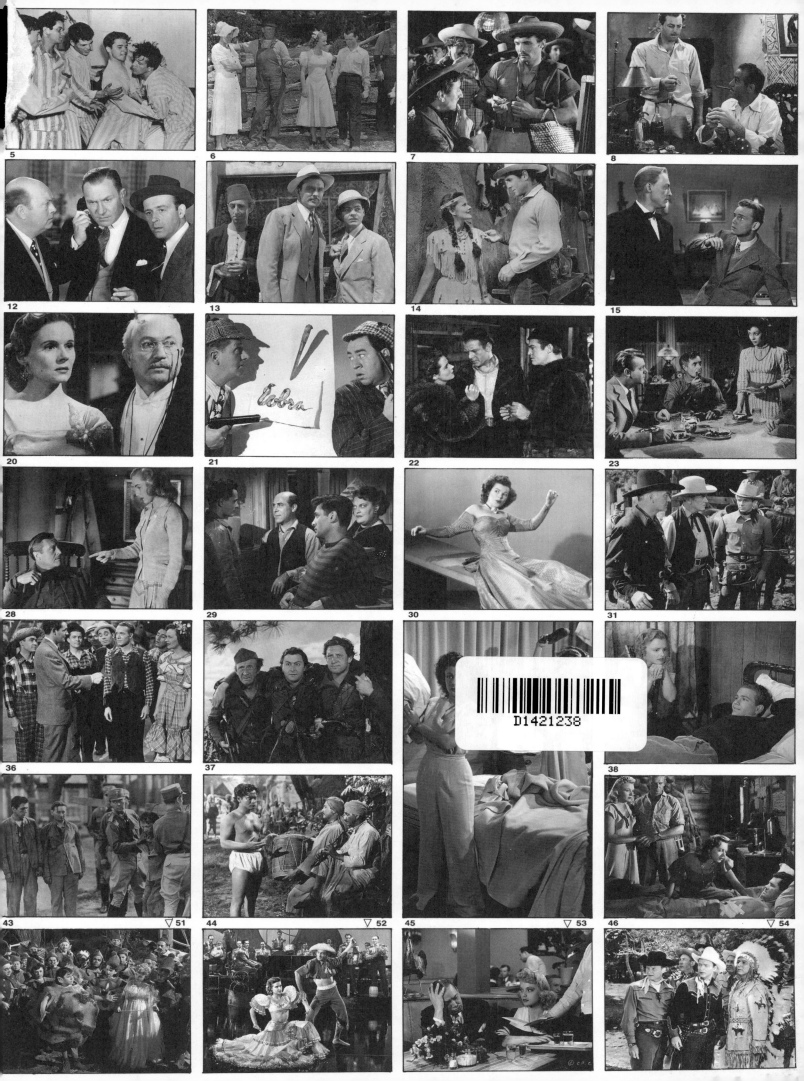

5

6

7

8

12

13

14

15

20

21

22

23

28

29

30

31

36

37

38

43 ▽ 51

44 ▽ 52

45 ▽ 53

46 ▽ 54

THE PICTUREGOER FILE

The Entertainment Years

THE STARS & FILMS OF THE 1940s

John Wayne in *Fort Apache* (RKO) 1948

THE PICTUREGOER FILE

The Entertainment Years

THE STARS & FILMS OF THE 1940s

Mark Lewis

Editor
Leonard Matthews

Consultant
Ken Sephton

WHSMITH
EXCLUSIVE
·BOOKS·

Key to illustrations inside front cover. 1. *Abe Lincoln in Illinois* (GB *Spirit of the People*) (RKO) 1940 **2.** *Angels in Disguise* (MoP) 1949 **3.** *Alias the Champ* (Rep) 1949 **4.** *Arson Inc* (LIP) 1949 **5.** *Bad Boy* (AA) 1949 **6.** *The Big Cat* (EL) 1949 **7.** *Border Incident* (MGM) 1949 **8.** *Call of the South Seas* (Rep) 1944 **9.** *Canyon Passage* (Univ) 1946 **10.** *Cheyenne* (WB) 1947 **11.** *City Across the River* (Univ) 1949 **12.** *Country Fair* (Rep) 1941 **13.** *Dark Streets of Cairo* (Univ) 1940 **14.** *Daughter of the West* (FC)1949 **15.** *Delinquent Daughters* (PRC) 1944 **16.** *The Dude Goes West* (AA) 1948 **17.** *The Farmer's Daughter* (Par) 1940 **18.** *The Shocking Miss Pilgrim* (Fox) 1947 **19.** *Fighting Fools* (MoP) 1949 **20.** *Gaiety George* (US *Showtime*) (Emb) 1946 **21.** *Genius at Work* (RKO) 1946 **22.** *Girl from God's Country* (Rep) 1940 **23.** *The Great Dan Patch* (UA) 1949 **24.** *The Guilty* (MoP) 1947 **25.** *Home of the Brave* (UA) 1949 **26.** *I'll Be Yours* (Univ) 1947 **27.** *The Imposter* (Univ) 1944 **28.** *Klondike Fury* (MoP) 1942 **29.** *Knock on Any Door* (Col) 1949 **30.** *Lady Luck* (RKO) 1946 **31.** *Lost Canyon* (UA) 1943 **32.** *The Mantrap* (Rep) 1943 **33.** *Murder by Invitation* (MoP) 1941 **34.** *My Kingdom for a Cook* (Col) 1943 **35.** *My Own True Love* (Par) 1948 **36.** *The National Barn Dance* (Par) 1944 **37.** *Northwest Passage* (MGM) 1940 **38.** *One Foot In Heaven* (WB) 1941 **39.** *The Princess and the Pirate* (SG) 1944 **40.** *The Red House* (UA) 1947 **41.** *The Runaround* (Univ) 1946 **42.** *Salome, Where She Danced* (Univ) 1945 **43.** *The Seventh Cross* (MGM) 1944 **44.** *Song of India* (Col) 1949 **45.** *What a Blonde* (RKO) 1945 **46.** *Spoilers of the North* (Rep) 1947 **47.** *Spring Song* (US *Springtime*) (BN) 1946 **48.** *Step Lively* (RKO) 1944 **49.** *Strange Journey* (Fox) 1946 **50.** *Thieves Highway* (Fox) 1949 **51.** *Three Wise Fools* (MGM) 1946 **52.** *The Time, The Place and The Girl* (WB) 1946 **53.** *Under Age* (Col) 1941 **54.** *Under Nevada Skies* (Rep) 1946

Key to illustrations inside back cover. 1. *Virginia City* (WB) 1940 **2.** *The Web* (Univ) 1947 **3.** *Another Part of the Forest* (Univ) 1948 **4.** *Beyond the Sacramento* (Col) 1941 **5.** *Call of the Forest* (LIP) 1949 **6.** *Campus Sleuth* (MoP) 1948 **7.** *Deep Waters* (Fox) 1948 **8.** *Do You Love Me?* (Fox) 1946 **9.** *Gas House Kids* (PRC) 1946 **10.** *Hot Cargo* (Par) 1946 **11.** *Jungle Man* (PRC) 1941 **12.** *Luck of the Irish* (Fox) 1948 **13.** *Too Young to Know* (WB) 1945 **14.** *Three of a Kind* (MoP) 1944 **15.** *You Were Meant For Me* (Fox) 1948 **16.** *Blonde Savage* (EL) 1947 **17.** *Bride of Vengeance* (Par) 1949 **18.** *Comin' Round the Mountain* (Par) 1940 **19.** *In Society* (Univ) 1944 **20.** *Mr Muggs Steps Out* (MoP) 1943 **21.** *Noose* (US *The Silk Noose*) (ED) 1948 **22.** *The Panthers Claw* (PRC) 1942 **23.** *Range Land* (MoP) 1949 **24.** *The Remarkable Andrew* (Par) 1942 **25.** *Remember the Night* (Par) 1940 **26.** *Santa Fe Marshal* (Par) 1940 **27.** *Santa Fe Trail* (WB) 1940 **28.** *Second Chorus* (Par) 1940 **29.** *Stick to Your Guns* (Fox) 1941 **30.** *Stork Bites Man* (UA) 1947 **31.** *Spirit of West Point* (FCL) 1947 **32.** *Shadow Valley* (EL) 1947 **33.** *Spooks Run Wild* (GB *Ghosts on the Loose*) (MoP) 1941 **34.** *The Devil Thumbs a Ride* (RKO) 1947 **35.** *The Long Night* (RKO) 1947 **36.** *Riders of the Dusk* (MoP) 1949 **37.** *Burma Convoy* (Univ) 1941 **38.** *Ginger* (MoP) 1946 **39.** *The Knockout* (MoP) 1947 **40.** *Red Stallion* (EL) 1947 **41.** *The Prime Minister* (WB) 1941 **42.** *Madonna of the Seven Moons* (G'boro) 1944 **43.** *So This is New York* (UA) 1948 **44.** *Shadow of a Woman* (WB) 1946 **45.** *Two Weeks to Live* (RKO) 1943 **46.** *Week-End in Havana* (Fox) 1941 **47.** *The Heiress* (Par) 1949 **48.** *Too Late for Tears* (UA) 1949 **49.** *Scott of the Antarctic* (EaS) 1948 **50.** *Ruthless* (EL) 1948 **51.** *Seven Days Leave* (RKO) 1942 **52.** *White Tie and Tails* (Univ) 1946 **53.** *Frisco Sal* (Univ) 1945 **54.** *It's a Pleasure* (RKO) 1945

Page 2 Gary Cooper in *The Westerner* (UA) 1940

The editor is pleased to acknowledge the generous help extended during the production of this book by John Hall of Edgbaston, Jim Tanner of Philadelphia, Moviefinds of London, Steve Sally of New York and Syndication International Ltd., London; also for their provision of several hundred movie stills.

This edition produced exclusively for W H Smith

Produced and edited by Martspress Limited

Published by
The Hamlyn Publishing Group Limited
part of Reed International Books
Michelin House, 81 Fulham Road, London SW3 6RB

Copyright © 1988, 1990 The Hamlyn Publishing Group Limited

Second impression

ISBN 0 600 55176 8

Printed in Yugoslavia

COVER ILLUSTRATIONS

From top right clockwise:
Bette Davis
Bob Hope in *The Princess and the Pirate* (RKO) 1944
Rita Hayworth
Humphrey Bogart and Dooley Wilson in *Casablanca* (WB) 1942

4

CONTENTS

Lana Turner

Jon Hall, Maria Montez, George Zucco and Andy Devine in *Sudan* (Univ) (1945)

John Mills, Freda Jackson and Bernard Miles in *Great Expectations* (Cine/IP) (1946)

INTRODUCTION

The decade opened with the Second World War and closed with the Cold War. It began with the box-office triumph of *Gone With the Wind* – the definitive Hollywood blockbuster – and ended with the birth of the television age and the dismemberment of Hollywood's vertically integrated studio empires. In the intervening years cinema had borne witness to a world in turbulent change and in the process underwent its own transformation. The sensation of 1940 was a 'Brazilian Bombshell' in a Tutti-Frutti hat – Carmen Miranda. In 1950 it was a charismatic young 'Method' actor playing a surly paraplegic – Marlon Brando.

At the beginning of the decade Hollywood reigned supreme as the most powerful medium of popular entertainment. It was the Dream Factory, a magnet for a million shopgirls who dreamed of stepping from behind a drug store counter into the movies – just like Lana Turner.

Wartime restrictions brought an end to the no-expenses-spared extravagance of the Thirties, but they were accompanied by a boom in cinema audiences, reaching a peak in 1946 when 90 million Americans went to the movies every week.

The Dream Factory required the minimum of conversion to meet the needs of war, effortlessly adapting all the stock genres – crime thrillers, musicals, even the B Western – to accommodate wartime themes. Combat films tended to reinforce romantic stereotypes of war, and it was only at the end of the conflict that Hollywood came to terms with its sombre reality in films like *A Walk in the Sun, The Story of GI Joe,* and *They Were Expendable* (all 1945).

The musical entered a golden age, emancipating itself from the stage and reaching a climax with MGM's *On the Town* (1949). Walt Disney pushed back the boundaries of animation in *Fantasia* (1940) and *Bambi* (1942). Universal revived the horror film and provided romance and escapism in the Technicolor 'Easterns' starring Maria Montez.

To wartime audiences each studio had its own style. MGM was the epitome of plush big-budget good taste; Twentieth Century-Fox's output was brash and brassy, typified by the musical extravaganzas of Carmen Miranda and Betty Grable; at Warner Brothers the keynotes were the sombre, low-key black-and-white photography of Sol Polito and Ernst Haller, and the drive and conviction which directors like Michael Curtiz and Jean Negulesco brought to the pulsating melodramas starring Bette Davis, Barbara Stanwyck and Joan Crawford.

In the Forties the art of studio film-making reached a peak, refined by technical advances which included the development of more sensitive finely grained film, portable power units and improved sound recording and mixing. These advances played an integral part in the shadowy lighting and virtuoso camerawork of the *film noir* cycle of the mid-Forties which launched such stars as Robert Mitchum, Burt Lancaster, Robert Ryan and Richard Widmark.

Nestor Paiva, Robert Barrat, Bing Crosby and Bob Hope in *Road to Utopia* (Par) (1945)

The second half of the decade marked a turning point in Hollywood's history. Changing leisure patterns caused a steady decline in audiences, a problem compounded by the arrival of television as a serious competitor. Labour disputes at the major studios and the onset of the Cold War, led to a witch-hunt for Communists by the House of un-American Activities Committee. In 1949 the Supreme Court's 'consent decree' forced the studios to split their theatre organizations from the production-distribution side of the business. The iron grip of the studio moguls had been steadily weakened. Like dinosaurs on the verge of extinction, they felt the first chill winds of a changing world in which they were ill-adapted to survive.

In Britain the Forties were a period of significant creative achievement, reflected in the critical and commercial successes on both sides of the Atlantic of wartime films like *In Which We Serve* (1942), *Henry V* (1944) and *The Way to the Stars* (US *Johnny in the Clouds*) (1945). Postwar classics like *Great Expectations* (1946), *The Red Shoes* (1948) and *The Third Man* (1949), testified to the vitality of British cinema, and the decade was rounded off by three great Ealing Studio comedies, *Passport to Pimlico* and *Whisky Galore* (US *Tight Little Island*) (1948), and *Kind Hearts and Coronets* (1949).

Barbara Stanwyck

▽ Fred MacMurray

By then world cinema had begun to re-assert itself. The Italian neo-realist movement had captured an international audience, and the stage was set for Japanese directors of the calibre of Akira Kurosawa and Kon Ichikawa to emerge as major talents. The days of the Dream Factory were numbered, but the memories remain: Judy Garland and Mickey Rooney in full flight in *Babes on Broadway* (1941); Hope and Crosby taking the *Road to Utopia* (1945); Barbara Stanwyck and Fred MacMurray locked in a death clinch in *Double Indemnity* (1944); Joan Crawford suffering mightily in *Mildred Pierce* (1945); in a darkened Viennese doorway a cat curling itself around Orson Welles' ankles in *The Third Man* (1949); and James Cagney making one of the most spectacular exits in film history in *White Heat* (1949). These truly were the Entertainment Years.

Two scenes from *Rebecca* (DS) (*Above:*) Laurence Olivier, Reginald Denny, Joan Fontaine, C Aubrey Smith and George Sanders. (*Below:*) Joan Fontaine.

CHAPTER ONE

1940

FILMS IN WARTIME

At 6.30 am on 1 September 1939, Germany invaded Poland. The last organized Polish resistance collapsed at the beginning of October. On the Western Front there followed six months of inactivity, dubbed the Phoney War. In April 1940, Hitler invaded Denmark and Norway, and on 10 May he unleashed his Blitzkrieg in the West. By September 1940, the tide of war had washed across Western Europe. Denmark and Norway had been occupied, the Low Countries overrun, France humiliated and the British Expeditionary Force bundled out of Europe. Massive Luftwaffe bomber formations droned across the English Channel daily as the Battle of Britain neared its height.

The USA remained neutral, but events in Europe had a serious effect in Hollywood, closing 11 countries to American films. In Belgium and Holland about 1400 cinemas had been immediately closed, representing a loss of about $2.5 million in annual revenue for American film companies. By the end of the year, with the exception of Sweden, Switzerland and Portugal, the whole of Continental Europe was closed to American films, slashing Hollywood's revenue by over a quarter.

This was a difficult time for Hollywood. A Gallup Poll of 1939 had revealed that although 84 per cent of Americans wanted an Allied victory, 96 per cent of them wanted the USA to stay out of the conflict. These contradictory messages induced a kind of paralysis in Hollywood. In the run-up to war, the major studios had shelved all their spy, refugee and anti-Nazi projects They were smartly dusted off when Germany invaded Poland, but the onset of the Phoney War, and the thin prospect of peace breaking out, had shunted these pictures back into limbo.

Warner Brothers, who had made the one explicitly anti-Nazi film of the pre-war period, *Confessions of a Nazi Spy* (1939), were unofficially told by the US government to hold back on similar movies. But in April 1940 rumours reached California that several Polish exhibitors who had shown *Confessions of a Nazi Spy* had been hanged in the foyers of their own cinemas.

Paul Lukas expresses fear in *Confessions of a Nazi Spy* released in April 1939, before the war in Europe commenced the following September.

Margaret Sullavan and Robert Young (l), Robert Stack and Bill Orr (r) in *The Mortal Storm* (MGM)

Charles Chaplin in *The Great Dictator* (UA)

Joel McCrea

American film-makers were now showing a commitment to the Allied cause, but caution still tempered their attacks on Nazism. At MGM, Louis B Mayer, fearful of economic and political reprisals, was reluctant to launch an all-out assault on fascism. There is a feeling of hedged bets about MGM's *The Mortal Storm.* Set in Germany in the early 1930s, it deals with the persecution of a Jewish professor (Frank Morgan), who is sent to a concentration camp. Morgan's wife (Irene Rich) ponders: 'Now that these people have come to power, what about people who think differently – people who are ... (long pause) ... non-Aryan?'

Hollywood's silence was now broken and there was a rush of dramas exposing the Nazis. John Cromwell's *So Ends Our Night,* based on a novel by Erich Maria Remarque, highlighted the plight of stateless people fleeing from the Nazis. The script did not shrink from using the word 'Jew' at a time when Hollywood preferred the euphemistic 'non-Aryan'.

Of doubly greater significance was Charlie Chaplin's *The Great Dictator,* for not only was this his verdict on fascism but also the first film in which he spoke dialogue; *Modern Times* (1936) contained only a gibberish song among the music and sound effects. In *The Great Dictator,* Chaplin played two parts: Adenoid Hynkel, the ranting vainglorious dictator of Ptomania; and his double, a little Jewish barber reminiscent of the Tramp. Inevitably, their identities are confused and it is the barber, rather than Hynkel, who delivers the long concluding speech to the world, pleading for an end to tyranny.

A rallying call for the beleaguered British was delivered in Alfred Hitchcock's *Foreign Correspondent,* an immensely stylish espionage thriller, with art direction by William Cameron Menzies, in which American newsman in Europe Joel McCrea uncovers an Axis spy ring headed by suave Herbert Marshall, chairman of the ironically named Universal Peace Party. *Foreign Correspondent* is crammed with classic Hitchcock set pieces: a superbly choreographed assassination in the rain under a canopy of bobbing umbrellas; McCrea's discovery of the killers in their creaking windmill hideout; mild little assassin Edmund Gwenn's death plunge from the tower of Westminster Cathedral; and a climactic 'plane crash in the Atlantic. The film ends with McCrea making a radio broadcast to America from London while an air raid rages overhead. He tells his audience: 'The lights are going out in Europe. Ring yourself around with steel, America!'

Walt Disney provided inspired fantasy in *Pinocchio,* his second full-length animated feature cartoon, which contrives to be both enchanting and truly terrifying in turns. He then capped this triumph with *Fantasia,* an ambitious marriage of image and music filmed at a cost of $2.3 million in Multiplane Technicolor and recorded with the advanced RCA Fantasound system.

Twentieth Century-Fox's *The Mark of Zorro,* directed by Rouben Mamoulian, was one of the most elegant of swashbucklers, with Tyrone Power in lithe form as the masked avenger of evil, duelling to the death with icy adversary Basil Rathbone and, as his foppish alter ego, romancing a shimmering Linda Darnell.

Errol Flynn starred as a devil-may-care Elizabethan privateer in Michael Curtiz' *The Sea Hawk,* for which Warner Brothers built two full-size galleons at a cost of $1.7 million. Brenda Marshall provided the romantic interest, Claude Rains and Henry Daniell silky villainy and Flora Robson repeated the role of Queen Elizabeth, which she had first played in Alexander Korda's *Fire Over England* (1937).

When *The Sea Hawk* was released, comparisons were drawn between Flora Robson's measured performance as Queen Bess and Bette Davis' more histrionic interpretation of the role in *The Private Lives of Elizabeth and Essex* (1939). However, Davis was utterly incomparable in William Wyler's *The Letter*, a Somerset Maugham colonial potboiler, in which she emptied a revolver into her lover, pleaded self-defence and very nearly got away with it. Davis sank her teeth into this portrayal of a bitch on wheels but was more restrained in *All This and Heaven Too,* in which she played a governess, fatally falling for aristocratic employer Charles Boyer.

Audiences were taken for an emotional roller coaster ride in RKO's *Kitty Foyle*, directed by Sam Wood, with Ginger Rogers in the title role as the working girl who runs into the vicious snobbery of the Philadelphia smart set. Artfully deglamourised with a brunette hairstyle, Rogers established her credentials as a 'straight' actress and won the Best Actress Oscar for 1940.

Best Picture of the Year was Alfred Hitchcock's *Rebecca*, chronologically his first film in Hollywood and a masterly exercise in romantic melodrama. Joan Fontaine, her shoulders hunched with anxiety, was Daphne du Maurier's mousy heroine and Laurence Olivier her darkly brooding husband Maxim de Winter, master of Manderley, the Old Dark House presided over by Judith Anderson's sinister housekeeper Mrs Danvers, drenched in the poisonous memory of Maxim's first wife. Also outstanding in a magnificent cast was George Sanders as the svelte blackmailer Jack Favell, his insinuating drawl seeming to linger in a room long after he left it.

Poverty turned ballerina Vivien Leigh into a prostitute in *Waterloo Bridge,* a move discreetly signalled by her choice of beret and black dress to greet the boys back from the front at the railway terminus of the title. Soldier boyfriend Robert Taylor, returns from the war ignorant of this sad turn of events but crusty Colonel C Aubrey Smith persuades Leigh to abandon Taylor for the sake of the regiment.

Romance was more delicately handled in Ernst Lubitsch's *The Shop Around the Corner*, set in a charmingly fantastic Budapest, where mutually antagonistic counter clerks James Stewart and Margaret Sullavan are unaware that they are lonely heart pen pals, a potential minefield of sentiment negotiated with affecting skill by the two stars.

Stewart followed *The Shop Around the Corner* with the all

Errol Flynn in *The Sea Hawk* (WB)

Bette Davis

James Stewart

Mae West and W C Fields in *My Little Chickadee* (Univ)

▽ Bob Hope

▽ Mickey Rooney

too appropriately named *No Time for Comedy,* as a naively serious playwright married to Broadway star Rosalind Russell. He redeemed himself at once in George Cukor's *The Philadelphia Story* as the unusually fast-talking (for Stewart) reporter smitten by prickly society beauty Katharine Hepburn. He lost the girl to her ex-husband Cary Grant – but although second-billed won the year's Best Actor Oscar.

Cary Grant was a conniving ex-husband again in Howard Hawks' *His Girl Friday,* in which he played a manipulative news editor, extorting headlines from his star reporter (and ex-wife) Rosalind Russell and sabotaging her engagement to dull dog Ralph Bellamy.

Wives, of the henpecking variety, were ever the curse of W C Fields, who was saddled with a nagging spouse (Cora Witherspoon) in his masterpiece, *The Bank Dick.* When his detestable little daughter suggests bouncing a rock off Fields' head, Mother replies: 'Respect your father,' adding quickly 'What sort of rock?'

Less happy was Fields' teaming with Mae West in *My Little Chickadee,* the comedy equivalent of *King Kong Versus Godzilla* in which they played competing con-artists in a spoof Wild West. Mae West's langorous deliberation and Fields' casual ad-libbing approach simply failed to mesh, a problem exacerbated by some heavy off-screen feuding. Mae observed, 'There is no one quite like Bill. And it would be snide of me to add "Thank God". A great performer. My only doubts about him come in bottles.' Fields sneaked the last laugh, ad-libbing West's immortal line, 'Come up and see me some time' and then annexing the sentiment for himself by adding, 'in Philadelphia'.

At Universal, Fields was allowed to do what he liked, provided it didn't cost too much. At Paramount a very different type of comedian, Bob Hope, was given more expensive packaging. He followed his 1939 hit *The Cat and the Canary,* (a lavishly mounted comedy version of Paul Leni's 1927 chiller) with *Ghost Breakers,* nervously investigating heiress Paulette Goddard's eerie Caribbean mansion. A big success, it was eclipsed by *The Road to Singapore,* the first of six amiable 'Road' films in which Bing Crosby ran lazy rings around the blustering Hope as they competed for sarong-girl Dorothy Lamour (in the seventh and last Joan Collins was the romantic interest.)

Hope was now established as one of Paramount's top stars. But Twentieth Century-Fox were about to lose one of their biggest gold mines of the 1930s, Shirley Temple, whose appearance in *Young People* was her last for the studio for nine years. Now 12, the little moppet was fast approaching the child star's equivalent of senility, and *Young People's* blend of sentimentality and clips from her past triumphs failed to restore her flagging fortunes at the box-office. The torch had passed to MGM's Judy Garland and Mickey Rooney, the latter No.1 at the box-office for the second year running. They were entrancingly teamed in Busby Berkeley's *Strike Up the Band,* a corny 'let's put on a show' musical animated by Rooney's ferocious energy and Garland's wistful charm, as Mickey's high school orchestra went for the big prize in a coast-to-coast band contest.

Fred Astaire and Eleanor Powell glided across a glittering mirrored floor to Cole Porter's 'Begin the Beguine' in MGM's *Broadway Melody of 1940*, the only film they made together. The studio's treatment of *Bitter Sweet* reportedly reduced Noel Coward to tears, of rage, the Master's ironic operetta having been inflated into a crassly plush vehicle for Jeanette MacDonald and Nelson Eddy.

The nominal stars of Twentieth Century-Fox's *Down Argentine Way* were Betty Grable and Don Ameche, but they were unceremoniously elbowed aside by the 'Brazilian Bombshell' Carmen Miranda. She had absolutely no connection with the plot (her musical numbers were filmed in New York) but sashayed through 'South American Way', eyes popping with excitement and several pounds of exotic fruit balanced precariously on her head, an extravagant form of headgear which became her trademark.

Miranda's arrival as one of the more engagingly dotty icons of the 1940s was no accident. With Europe all but closed to American films, Latin-America was now Hollywood's only strong foreign market. Carmen was in the vanguard of a concerted export drive.

Also making a big impression were radio comics Bud Abbott and Lou Costello, who made their movie debut in supporting roles in Universal's *One Night in the Tropics,* an adaptation of the Earl Derr Biggers' story *Love Insurance*, starring Allan Jones, Robert Cummings and Nancy Kelly. After *One Night in the Tropics* Abbott and Costello were signed on a long-term contract which gave them a percentage of their films' profits. This cost Universal a million dollars on their first four films alone.

Following the success of *Stagecoach* (1939), the big-budget Western swung back into fashion. Republic made a heavy investment in Raoul Walsh's *The Dark Command*, starring John Wayne and Walter Pidgeon, at $750,000 the most expensive prestige Western of the studio's early years.

German director Fritz Lang made his Western (and colour) debut with Twentieth Century-Fox's *The Return of Frank James*, a sequel to the hugely successful *Jesse James* (1939), with Henry Fonda in the title role, taking the law into his own hands to avenge the killing of his brother. *The Return of Frank James* had a beautiful feeling for American landscapes, seen at its best in the opening sequence showing Henry Fonda ploughing. The film also marked the debut of Gene Tierney, who, as a reporter wants to tell the true story of Frank James but predictably, winds up in his arms.

Also appearing for the first time on screen were Forrest Tucker and Dana Andrews, both well down the cast list in *The Westerner*, the year's outstanding Western and the last Sam Goldwyn production for United Artists. Confidently directed by William Wyler and magnificently photographed by Gregg Toland, *The Westerner* cast Walter

Carmen Miranda

Bud Abbott and Lou Costello

▽ Walter Pidgeon

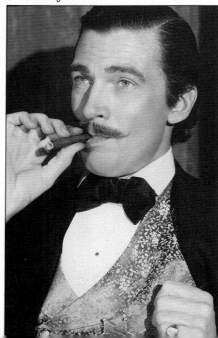

Walter Brennan in *The Westerner* (UA)

Charles Middleton

Raymond Massey in *Abe Lincoln in Illinois* (RKO)
(GB *Spirit of the People*) (RKO)

Brennan as the despotic Judge Roy Bean, sole source of law 'west of the Pecos' and besotted admirer of Lillie Langtry, a performance which won him the Best Supporting Actor Oscar.

Directed by Boris Ingster, RKO's *Stranger on the Third Floor*, was a forerunner of the *film noir* cycle of the mid 1940s, in which Peter Lorre stirred memories of *M* (1931) with his portrayal of an unhinged, disfigured murderer scuttling through the streets of Brooklyn. He was more relaxed in *Island of Doomed Men*, as a Pacific Island slave master unwinding to the strains of Chopin after a heavy work-out with the whip.

Universal raided their horror vaults and came up with *The Invisible Man Returns*, starring Vincent Price as the transparent one. The studio spared just about every expense in *The Mummy's Hand*, a cost-conscious sequel to the 1932 Boris Karloff classic *The Mummy*, which made up the running time of 67 minutes with generous use of flashbacks from the Karloff original. Karloff himself had embarked on a series of 'mad doctor' roles. In Columbia's *Before I Hang*, directed by Nick Grinde, he invented a 'cure for death' serum which had the predictable effect of turning him into a homicidal maniac.

At RKO Albert Dekker created a memorably deranged man of science, shaven-headed and pebble-spectacled Dr Thorkel, in Ernest B Schoedsack's *Dr. Cyclops*. Lurking in the Peruvian jungle he harnesses a radioactive deposit to shrink his victims. In a stirring climax a group of miniature scientists smash his glasses and lure him to his death in the mineshaft which provides him with his source of power.

A lovely young Rita Hayworth was showcased in *Blondie on a Budget*, a lively entry in the long-running Columbia series based on Chic Young's comic strip and starring Arthur Lake as the harassed Dagwood Bumstead and Penny Singleton as his airhead wife Blondie. In Universal's jaunty serial *Flash Gordon Conquers the Universe*, model rockets sputtered jerkily across the screen as Buster Crabbe's intergalactic hero Flash battled once more with Ming the Merciless (Charles Middleton), saving planet Earth from a cloud of Purple Death Dust.

Nearer home were a number of prestige biopics of eminent Americans. Dean Jagger took the title role in Twentieth Century-Fox's *Brigham Young*, a handsome account of the Mormon trek westward directed by Henry Hathaway. Raymond Massey repeated his stage role as *Abe Lincoln in Illinois*, which traced the Great Emancipator's progress from log cabin to White House with Massey giving a hugely dignified central performance in an otherwise dull film. Mickey Rooney was admirably restrained as the *Young Tom Edison*, which MGM shot simultaneously with *Edison The Man*. The latter, directed by Clarence Brown and starring Spencer Tracy as the Great Inventor, was the more successful of the two in spite of a strong sentimental streak and the whiskers under which Tracy was eventually camouflaged.

Young Tom Edison was Rooney's first flop as a star but he bounced back with *Andy Hardy Meets Debutante*, an above-par entry in the series – so dear to Louis B Mayer's heart – which celebrated the solid family virtues of a fantasy small-town America. A more tragic family, the Joads, were at the centre of Twentieth Century-Fox's *The Grapes of Wrath*, adapted from John Steinbeck's novel of dispossessed Oklahoma sharecroppers and directed by John Ford. This is a great film, with a fine script by Nunnally Johnson and immaculate photography by Gregg Toland. As Tom Joad, Henry Fonda gave one of the finest performances of his career, unshaven and hollow-cheeked and moving with a touchingly angular solemnity. Jane Darwell's resilient Ma Joad won her a deserved Oscar as the year's Best Supporting Actress. The film's ending, and the Joads' refusal to be 'licked', has an air of strain but this is a minor blemish on a moving document of American social history.

The year's newcomers included Anne Baxter, making her debut in a Wallace Beery vehicle, *20 Mule Team*; smooth Tom Conway, in real life George Sanders' brother; Marguerite Chapman, who was to become queen of Columbia's programmers in the mid Forties; Laird Cregar, shortly to be transformed into a memorably florid heavy at Twentieth Century-Fox; Maria Montez, soon to become the chief ornament of Universal's Technicolor 'Easterns', who turned up in a Western, *Boss of Bullion City*; Cornel Wilde, who had a small part in Warner Brothers' *The Lady with Red Hair*; and Arthur Kennedy, who appeared in *City for Conquest*. At Paramount, Preston Sturges made his directing debut with *The Great McGinty*, a scintillating satire on political graft and corruption.

Death took silent comedian Ben Turpin, and Marguerite Clark, who in her heyday had briefly rivalled Mary Pickford. Flamboyant cowboy star Tom Mix made a spectacular exit in a car crash. He was killed instantly, reputedly by a blow on the head from a suitcase crammed with silver dollars.

In Britain the outbreak of war had temporarily threatened to close down the film industry. A large amount of studio space was requisitioned for use in the 'shadow' factory programme and for storage. For two weeks in September 1939 the cinemas were shut, a measure prompted by fear of mass death at the height of an air raid. Like the nation itself, the British film industry underwent a kind of Phoney War before finding its feet and a fresh sense of purpose.

Michael Powell and Emeric Pressburger's *Contraband* was a sprightly spy thriller notable for the first use of the 'blackout' as a dramatic device. Carol Reed's *Night Train to Munich*, starring Rex Harrison and Margaret Lockwood, was a chase thriller in the mould of Hitchcock's *The Lady Vanishes* (1939), a resemblance reinforced by the presence of Basil Radford and Naunton Wayne, as the cricket-obsessed English clubmen, Charters and Caldicott. At one point they make delightfully symbolic use of a copy of Hitler's *Mein*

Mickey Rooney in *Young Tom Edison* (MGM)

Charley Grapewin

▽ Maria Montez

Harold Goodwin, Alf Goddard and John Carol in *Convoy* (EaS)

George Formby in *Spare a Copper* (EaS)

▽ Jean Gabin

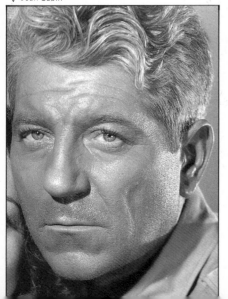

Kampf as a makeshift blindfold for a trussed-up Gestapo man.

Hitler turned up in the form of lookalike actor Billy Russell in Maurice Elvey's *For Freedom*, which recounted the scuttling of the German pocket battleship *Graf Spee*. The film's use of sailors from the British warships *Ajax* and *Exeter* gave a hint of the documentary influence which was to dominate the films of the mid-war years. Steaming cautiously in the same direction was Penrose Tennyson's *Convoy*, an Ealing Studios film made in collaboration with the British Ministry of Information (MOI). Tennyson also directed Ealing Studios' *The Proud Valley*, a Welsh mining drama which gave Paul Robeson his best screen role as the evocatively named David Goliath, a seaman who becomes a hewer of coal. Tragically the immensely talented Tennyson was killed in a plane crash in 1941.

Fifth columnists, mistaken identities and mysterious mid-European *femmes fatales* rapidly became the staples of wartime comedy. Popular comic George Formby stumbled across a Nazi spy ring in *Let George Do It* and a band of saboteurs in *Spare A Copper*.

The situation was grimmer in occupied France, where German films quickly replaced Hollywood movies as the main attractions on the Champs Elysées. The Paris offices of Tobis and Ufa were re-opened and Nazi propaganda chief Dr Josef Goebbels set up a puppet French company, Continental, to produce carefully monitored escapist entertainment. The Jewish interests in French cinema were taken over by the Germans.

In the so-called 'free zone' the Vichy government established the Comité d'Organisation Cinématographique, which immediately issued a list of Jewish personnel forbidden employment in films. With the exception of Marcel Carné, France's finest directors – René Clair, Julien Duvivier and Jean Renoir – were in Hollywood. Soon after the occupation they were joined by Jean Gabin and Michèle Morgan.

It was not until the outbreak of war that the German film industry produced specifically anti-Semitic tracts. But 1940 saw three major films identifying the Jews as the 'enemy within'. *Der Ewige Jude (The Eternal Jew)*, compiled by Dr Fritz Hippler, was a grisly 45-minute documentary denouncing every aspect of Jewry and blaming the Jews for every ill which had befallen Germany since 1918. *Die Rothschilds, (The Rothschilds)*, directed by Erich Waschneck, reached farther back into the past in a rambling account of the great banking family's rise to power in Regency Britain. As their victims were the British, now the 'enemy without', the propaganda effect was somewhat muted. Veit Harlan's *Jud Süss (Jew Süss)* was an insidiously brilliant orchestration of all the archetypes of Nazi hate propaganda against the Jews. Set in the 18th century it starred Ferdinand Marian as the Jewish finance minister of Württemberg and Werner Krauss in the double role of the Rabbi Loew and Süss' familiar. *Jud Süss* formed part of the evidence at the Nuremberg Trials.

Guinn 'Big Boy' Williams, Alan Hale and Errol Flynn in *Virginia City* (WB)

The start of a new decade and America, despite the forebodings of President Roosevelt, was determined on isolationism. Errol Flynn was now a Civil War Union officer in both *Virginia City* (WB) and *The Santa Fe Trail* (WB) and a future president named Ronald Reagan was a famous film star.

Fred MacMurray and Barbara Stanwyck in *Remember the Night* (Par)

Walter Brennan, Spencer Tracy and Robert Young in *Northwest Passage* (MGM)

Betty Grable, Jack Oakie and Alice Faye
in *Tin Pan Alley* (Fox) ▷

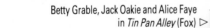

Joseph Calleia

Gene Autry, Ann Miller and Jerome Cowan in
Melody Ranch (Rep)

Ronald Reagan

Conrad Veidt in *The Thief of Bagdad* (UA)

Ronald Reagan, William Lundigan, Errol Flynn
and Olivia de Havilland in *Santa Fe Trail* (WB)

Edna Best, Terry Kilburn and Thomas Mitchell in *The Swiss Family Robinson* (RKO)

Joan Crawford

George Brent and Isa Miranda in *Adventure in Diamonds* (Par)
▽ Louis Hayward, Florence Bates, Joan Bennett and George Sanders in *The Son of Monte Cristo* (UA)

Jackie Cooper and Henry Fonda in *The Return of Frank James* (Fox)
▽ Charles Boyer and Bette Davis in *All This and Heaven, Too* (WB)

A scene from *Fantasia*   © 1940 Walt Disney Company

Poster for *Brother Orchid* (WB)

Picture Gallery for 1940

1. Robert Taylor and Vivien Leigh in *Waterloo Bridge* (MGM)
2. Spencer Tracy and Hedy Lamarr in *I Take This Woman* (MGM)
3. Irene Hervey
4. Ray Milland and Patricia Morison in *Untamed* (Par)
5. Henry Fonda
6. Lola Lane
7. Larry Crabbe
8. Jon Hall in *Kit Carson* (UA)

1

3

5

4

6

7

8

9

11

1. Tyrone Power
2. Jean Parker
3. Judy Canova in *Scatterbrain* (Rep)
4. Judy Canova
5. Lucille Ball
6. Frank Puglia, Ray Milland and Claudette Colbert in *Arise, My Love* (Par)
7. Sonja Henie
8. Joan Carroll and Tim Holt in *Laddie* (RKO)
9. Edward G Robinson and Humphrey Bogart in *Brother Orchid* (WB)
10. Edward G Robinson
11. Tim McCoy
12. Olympe Bradna and Pat O'Brien in *The Night of Nights* (Par)
13. Sigrid Gurie, Ralph Byrd, Yollande Mallot and Eddie Quillan in *Dark Streets of Cairo* (Univ)
14. Lola Lane and James Craig in *Zanzibar* (Univ)
15. Robert Coote and James Ellison in *You Can't Fool Your Wife* (RKO)
16. Lynn Bari and Lloyd Nolan in *Pier 13* (Fox)
17. Lee Bowman, Mary Nash, Ann Sothern, Virginia Weidler and Scotty Beckett in *Gold Rush Maisie* (MGM)
18. Preston Foster and Dorothy Lamour in *Moon Over Burma* (Par)
19. Dorothy Hyson and George Formby in *Spare a Copper* (EaS)
20. Ann Gillis in *Little Men* (RKO)
21. Edith Fellows, Mary Currier and Ben Taggart in *Nobody's Children* (Col)
22. Jean Arthur, Fred MacMurray, Harry Davenport and Melvyn Douglas in *Too Many Husbands* (GB *My Two Husbands*) (Col)
23. Charles Lane (l), Ken Howell and Jed Prouty in *Young As You Feel* (Fox)
24. Ferike Boros, Constance Moore and Dennis O'Keefe in *La Conga Nights* (Univ)

10 ▷

12

13

14

15

16

17

18

19

20
◁

21.

23.
▷

22

▽ 24

1

2

3

4

In *Northwest Passage* (MGM), Spencer Tracy was excellent in the role of Major Robert Rogers who in 1759 organised the famous Rogers Rangers. The film based on a best-selling novel by Kenneth Roberts, concerned itself with one exploit of the Rangers – their long trek from New Hampshire to the Canadian side of the border, to wipe out a band of merciless Indian raiders who had been wreaking havoc throughout the states of New York and New England. Robert Young is Langdon Towne, a fugitive who is wanted by the British for his scurrilous anti-British cartoons. He joins the Rangers and what followed added up to one of MGM's more successful films.

5

6

▽ **7**

8

10

9

11

12

1. Robert Young and Ruth Hussey
2. Robert Young
3. Spencer Tracy and Ruth Hussey
4. Spencer Tracy
5. Walter Brennan, Spencer Tracy and Robert Young
6. Spencer Tracy and Robert Young
7. Walter Brennan, Robert Young, Hugh Sothern and Regis Toomey
8. Robert Young, Walter Brennan and Nat Pendleton
9. Spencer Tracy, Walter Brennan and Robert Young
10. Walter Brennan and Robert Young
11. Spencer Tracy and Robert Young
12. Robert Young and Walter Brennan
13. Robert Young, Spencer Tracy and Walter Brennan
14. Walter Brennan, Robert Young, Donald MacBride and Andrew Pena
15. Robert Young and Spencer Tracy
16. Lester Matthews, Nat Pendleton and Robert Young

13

14

16

◁ 15

1. William Henry, Florence Rice and Richard Dix in *Cherokee Strip* (Par)
2. Charles King, Ken Maynard and Fay McKenzie in *Death Rides the Range* (Coy)
3. Ben Turpin and Oliver Hardy in *Saps at Sea* (HR/UA)
4. Louis Hayward, Joan Bennett and Florence Bates in *The Son of Monte Cristo* (ES)
5. Florence Bates and Joan Bennett in *The Son of Monte Cristo* (ES)
6. Louis Hayward and George Sanders in *The Son of Monte Cristo* (ES)
7. George Cleveland, Jackie Moran, Grant Withers and Marcia Mae Jones in *Tomboy* (MoP)
8. Ian Hunter in *Strange Cargo* (MGM)
9. George Sanders and Joan Bennett in *The Son of Monte Cristo* (ES)

1. Jean Cagney
2. Gene Raymond
3. Henry Wilcoxon, Irene Hervey and Edmund Lowe in *The Crooked Road* (Rep)
4. Frank Jenks, Virginia Grey and Thomas Mitchell in *Three Cheers for the Irish* (WB)
5. Kenne Duncan and Jack Randall in *Covered Wagon Trails* (MoP)
6. Francis Lederer
7. Joan Fontaine and Laurence Olivier in *Rebecca* (DS)
8. Jane Clayton, Russell Hayden and 'The King's Men' in *The Showdown* (Par)
9. Chick Hannon, Tris Coffin and Tex Ritter in *Rhythm of the Rio Grande* (MoP)
10. Lafe McKee, Nell O'Day and Dick Alexander in *Son of Roaring Dan* (Univ)

10 ▷

This film version of Johann David Wyss' famous classic *Swiss Family Robinson* (RKO) was a worthy attempt, not to be confused with Walt Disney's later commendable film of the same title that was produced in 1960. For Thomas Mitchell who played William Robinson, the head of a shipwrecked family, it was a completely different role from that of the drunken doctor of *Stagecoach* (UA) the previous year.

1. Edna Best and Thomas Mitchell
2. Thomas Mitchell and Edna Best
3. Terry Kilburn, Tim Holt and Freddie Bartholomew
4. Terry Kilburn, Edna Best, Freddie Bartholomew and Thomas Mitchell
5. Edna Best, Tim Holt and Thomas Mitchell
6. Thomas Mitchell and Terry Kilburn
7. Thomas Mitchell, Freddie Bartholomew and Terry Kilburn
8. Tim Holt, Freddie Bartholomew, Terry Kilburn and Thomas Mitchell
9. Edna Best and Thomas Mitchell
10. Tim Holt, Bobby Quillan, Edna Best, Terry Kilburn, Thomas Mitchell and Freddie Bartholomew
11. Freddie Bartholomew, Terry Kilburn, Edna Best and Tim Holt
12. Tim Holt, Bobby Quillan, Terry Kilburn and Freddie Bartholomew
13. Thomas Mitchell, Tim Holt and Freddie Bartholomew
14. Bobby Quillan and Edna Best
15. Freddie Bartholomew, Tim Holt, Thomas Mitchell, Edna Best and Terry Kilburn

10

11

12

13

14

15

1

2

As with all Errol Flynn actioners, it was once again a case of come one, come all, whether the location was *Virginia City* (WB) or *Dodge City* (WB) (1939). In both films he was flanked by Alan Hale and Guinn 'Big Boy' Williams. In *Dodge City* he was an ex-officer of the Confederate Army during the Civil War, while in *Virginia City* he was an under-cover officer of the Union. Both films depended much on the Flynn persona to attract cinema audiences. *Virginia City* had a good story to tell but both dialogue and acting were unfortunately somewhat stilted.

3

4

5

7

◁ 6

1. Dickie Jones, Errol Flynn, Miriam Hopkins and Alan Hale
2. Miriam Hopkins and Errol Flynn
3. Randolph Scott, Russell Hicks, Errol Flynn, Moroni Olsen and John Litel
4. Errol Flynn, Alan Hale and Guinn 'Big Boy' Williams
5. Alan Hale, Errol Flynn and Guinn 'Big Boy' Williams
6. Randolph Scott, Moroni Olsen, Miriam Hopkins and Dickie Jones
7. Miriam Hopkins and Randolph Scott
8. Miriam Hopkins, Randolph Scott, Charles Trowbridge, Howard Hickman, Brandon Tynan and Charles Middleton
9. Miriam Hopkins and Errol Flynn
10. Alan Hale, Guinn 'Big Boy' Williams and Moroni Olsen
11. Errol Flynn, Miriam Hopkins, Guinn 'Big Boy' Williams, Alan Hale and Frank McHugh
12. George Regas, Paul Fix, Humphrey Bogart, Moroni Olsen and Randolph Scott
13. Douglass Dumbrille, William Hopper and George Reeves

1

2

3

4

5

6

7

1. Irina Baronova

2. William Demarest, Richard Denning, Gertrude Michael and Tom Dugan in *The Farmer's Daughter* (Par)

3. Mae West and W C Fields in *My Little Chickadee* (Univ)

4. Henry Brandon, George O'Brien, Virginia Vale and Lloyd Ingraham in *The Marshal of Mesa City* (RKO)

5. Humphrey Bogart, Jessie Busley and Jeffrey Lynn in *It All Came True* (WB)

6. J Carrol Naish, Richard Denning, Blanche Yurka and James Seay in *Queen of the Mob* (Par)

7. Ann Miller, George 'Gabby' Hayes, Gene Autry and Jimmy Durante in *Melody Ranch* (Rep)

8. Marie Wilson

9. Renee Houston

10. Charles 'Buck' Jones

8

9

10

1

2

3

4

5

6

1. William Holden and Jean Arthur in *Arizona* (Col)
2. Robert Montgomery, Constance Cummings and Aubrey Mallalieu in *Busman's Honeymoon*
3. Ginger Rogers
4. Kay Francis and Frank Albertson (r) in *When the Daltons Rode* (Univ)
5. Danielle Darrieux in *Katia* (Univ)
6. Mary Carlisle
7. Dick Hogan, Chester Morris and Lucille Ball in *The Marines Fly High* (RKO)
8. Olivia de Havilland and David Niven in *Raffles* (SG)
9. Edward Arnold
10. Beulah Bondi, Fred MacMurray, Barbara Stanwyck and Elizabeth Patterson in *Remember the Night* (Par)
11. Fernandel, Josette Day and Raimu in *The Well Digger's Daughter* (FrF *La Fille du Puister*) (Siritzky)
12. Henry Wilcoxon.

7

8

10

9

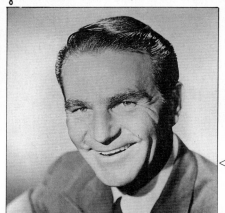

◁ 12

11

33

1. Charles Boyer and Bette Davis in *All This and Heaven, Too* (WB)
2. Bette Davis and Helen Westley in *All This and Heaven, Too* (WB)
3. John Justin
4. Irene Ware and Donald Briggs in *Outside the 3-mile Limit* (Col)
5. John Wayne in *The Long Voyage Home* (WaW)
6. Jeanette MacDonald and Nelson Eddy in *Bitter Sweet* (MGM)
7. Veda Ann Borg, George Sanders and Ian Hunter in *Bitter Sweet* (MGM)
8. Margaret Sullavan and Robert Young in *The Mortal Storm* (MGM)
9. Irene Rich and Frank Morgan in *The Mortal Storm* (MGM)
10. Linda Darnell in *Star Dust* (Fox)
11. John Payne and Roland Young in *Star Dust* (Fox)
12. Brenda and Cobina in *A Night at Earl Carroll's* (Par)
13. Roy Rogers
14. Tom Brown, Peggy Moran and Juanita Quigley in *Oh, Johnny, How You Can Love* (Univ)
15. Julieta Novis and Tony Martin in *Music In My Heart* (Col)

10

11

12

13

14

15

1

2

3

4

5

6

I. Donald Meek
2. Maureen O'Sullivan
3. Sydney Greenstreet
4. Harry Davenport
5. Ingrid Bergman
6. Evelyn Keyes
7. Lewis Stone
8. Ann Sothern
9. Robert Taylor
10. Sig Rumann
11. Anthony Caruso
12. William Lundigan
13. Alice Faye
14. Madeleine Carroll
15. Robert Preston
16. Pat O'Brien
17. James Hayter
18. Reginald Gardiner
19. Leif Erickson
20. Sylvia Sidney

7
◁
▷
8

9
▷

10

11

12

13

14

15

16

17

18

19

20

1. John Carradine, Henry Fonda and John Qualen
2. Eddie Quillan and Dorris Bowden
3. Henry Fonda and John Carradine
4. Henry Fonda and Jane Darwell
5. Grant Mitchell
6. Shirley Mills, Jane Darwell and Darryl Hickman
7. Eddie Quillan, Dorris Bowden, Henry Fonda, Jane Darwell, Russell Simpson, Frank Darien, O Z Whitehead and John Carradine
8. Henry Fonda and Dorris Bowden
9. Henry Fonda
10. Jane Darwell, Dorris Bowden, Henry Fonda, O Z Whitehead, Frank Darien and Russell Simpson
11. Frank Darien, Russell Simpson and Henry Fonda
12. Russell Simpson, Frank Darien, Jane Darwell and Dorris Bowden
13. Darryl Hickman, Henry Fonda and Shirley Mills
14. The Dance Band

Today, most people when the name of John Ford is mentioned, think of Westerns - *Stagecoach* (1939), *Fort Apache* (1948), *My Darling Clementine* (1946), *She Wore a Yellow Ribbon* (1949), for example. Few movie buffs though would not agree that *The Grapes of Wrath*, which he directed for Twentieth Century-Fox was a masterpiece. He won an Oscar for Best Direction and veteran actress Jane Darwell a similar award for Best Supporting Actress.

In Universal's *If I Had My Way* 12 year old Gloria Jean partnered Bing Crosby in an amiable story concerning the fortunes and misadventures of an orphan girl. With Charles Winninger, Allyn Joslyn and El Brendel contributing their joint comedy talents, the film, although failing to score heavily, was still enjoyed by cinema audiences.

1. Claire Dodd and Allyn Joslyn.
2. Bing Crosby, Gloria Jean and Moroni Olsen
3. Bing Crosby
4. Gloria Jean, El Brendel and Bing Crosby
5. Gloria Jean and Bing Crosby
6. Gloria Jean and Charles Winninger
7. Allyn Joslyn
8. Charles Winninger, Bing Crosby and Nana Bryant
9. Bing Crosby and Gloria Jean

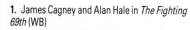

1. James Cagney and Alan Hale in *The Fighting 69th* (WB)
2. Lew Ayres, Joan Perry and Maureen O'Sullivan in *Maisie Was a Lady* (MGM)
3. William Frawley and Baby Sandy in *Sandy Gets Her Man* (Univ)
4. Sidney Blackmer
5. Bob Steele
6. Eve Arden in *Comrade X* (MGM)
7. Michael Redgrave
8. George Murphy, Brenda Joyce and Ralph Bellamy in *Public Deb No. 1.* (Fox)
9. Cesar Romero, Sheila Ryan and Janet Beecher in *The Gay Caballero* (Fox)

8 ▷
9 ▷

1. Billy Halop
2. Andy Devine and Richard Arlen in *Danger on Wheels* (Univ)
3. Andrea Leeds and Warner Baxter in *Earthbound* (Fox)
4. George Murphy
5. Robert Young and Helen Gilbert in *Florian* (MGM)
6. Frank Morgan, Spencer Tracy and Clark Gable in *Boom Town* (MGM)
7. Clark Gable and Claudette Colbert in *Boom Town* (MGM)
8. Maureen O'Hara, Louis Hayward and Lucille Ball in *Dance Girl Dance* (RKO)
9. Jeffrey Lynn in *A Child is Born* (WB)
10. Lynn Bari and Lloyd Nolan in *Charter Pilot* (Fox)
11. Helen Vinson, Barbara Read and Frank Faylen in *Curtain Call* (RKO)
12. Boris Karloff and Margaret Lindsay in *British Intelligence* (GB *Enemy Agent*) (WB)
13. Rosalind Russell
14. Johnny Russell, Shirley Temple and Helen Ericson in *The Blue Bird* (Fox)
15. John Loder, Isa Miranda and George Brent in *Adventure in Diamonds* (Par)
16. Hilda Vaughn, Sidney Toler and Victor Sen Yung in *Charlie Chan at the Wax Museum* (Fox)
17. Regis Toomey
18. Frank Morgan
19. Raymond Massey
20. Siegfried Arno and John Loder in *Diamond Frontier* (Univ)

9

10

13

11

12

15

14

16

17

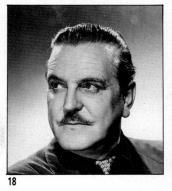

18

19
20

1

2

3

4

5

6

7

8

9

10

11

12

13

1. Willard Parker
2. Tyrone Power and Dorothy Lamour in *Johnny Apollo* (Fox)
3. Helen Parrish
4. John Payne, Allen Jenkins and Jack Oakie in *Tin Pan Alley* (Fox)
5. Jack Oakie, John Payne, Betty Grable and Alice Faye in *Tin Pan Alley* (Fox)
6. Robert Paige and Marjorie Gateson in *Parole Fixer* (Par)
7. Broderick Crawford, Ruth Terry, Douglas Dumbrille, Pat O'Brien and Edward Arnold in *Slightly Honorable* (WaW)
8. Ken Maynard
9. Tyrone Power in *The Mark of Zorro* (Fox)
10. Tyrone Power and Linda Darnell in *The Mark of Zorro* (Fox)
11. Anne Shirley
12. Ginger Rogers and Joel McCrea in *Primrose Path* (RKO)
13. Nelson Eddy and Jeanette MacDonald in *The New Moon* (MGM)
14. Anthony Quinn and Akim Tamiroff in *The Texas Rangers Ride Again* (Par)
15. Joel McCrea

14

15

1. William Gargan
2. Pat O'Brien and Frances Farmer in *Flowing Gold* (WB)
3. Ralph Forbes
4. Robert Sterling and Virginia Gilmore in *Manhattan Heartbeat* (Fox)
5. Akim Tamiroff
6. Glenn Strange (r) in *The Range Busters* (MoP)
7. Chester Morris and Charles Bickford in *The Girl from God's Country* (Rep)
8. Loretta Young, Ray Milland and Reginald Gardiner in *The Doctor Takes a Wife* (Col)
9. Frank Albertson, Jerome Cowan and Constance Moore in *Framed* (Univ)
10. Robert Lowery and Mary Beth Hughes in *Free, Blonde and 21* (Fox)
11. Penelope Dudley Ward, Helen Haye and Marius Goring in *The Case of the Frightened Lady* (US *The Frightened Lady*) (Penn)
12. Margaret Lindsay, Anne Gwynne and Edmund Lowe in *Honeymoon Deferred* (Univ)
13. Mirandy, Bob Burns and Una Merkel in *Comin' Round the Mountain* (Par)
14. Dennis Morgan
15. Helen Vinson
16. Jane Withers and Joe Brown Jr. in *High School* (Fox)
17. Don Ameche, George Ernest, Robert Lowery and Sig Rumann in *Four Sons* (Fox)
18. Lewis Howard (l), Tim Ryan (judge), and Dennis O'Keefe (r) in *I'm Nobody's Sweetheart Now* (Univ)

9

10

11

12

13

14

15

16

17

18

1. Mary Howard and Raymond Massey in *Abe Lincoln in Illinois* (GB *Spirit of the People*) (RKO)

2. Bernardine Hayes and Russell Hayden in *Santa Fe Marshal* (Par)

3. Raymond Massey in *Abe Lincoln in Illinois* (GB *Spirit of the People*) (RKO)

4. Roland Young, Zazu Pitts and Helen Broderick in *No No Nanette* (RKO)

5. Paulette Goddard and Charles Butterworth in *Second Chorus* (Par)

6. Jack Carson in *Lucky Partners* (RKO)

7. George Raft, Ann Sheridan, Humphrey Bogart, Gale Page and Roscoe Karns in *They Drive By Night* (GB *The Road to Frisco*) (WB)

8. Philip Dorn and John Arledge in *Ski Patrol* (Univ)

9. Brian Donlevy

10. Akim Tamiroff in *The Way of All Flesh* (Par)

11. Jon Hall and Olympe Bradna in *South of Pago Pago* (UA)

12. William 'Wild Bill' Elliott in *The Return of Wild Bill* (Col)

13. Roscoe Karns

14. Johnny Downs

15. Miriam Hopkins in *Lady with Red Hair* (WB)

16. Humphrey Bogart and George Raft in *Invisible Stripes* (WB)

8

9

10

11

12

13

14

15

16

49

1

Way back in 1924, Milton Sills celebrated movie idol of the day, starred in a film entitled *The Sea Hawk* which was based firmly on Rafael Sabatini's best-selling novel. It was produced by First National which later became part of Warner Brothers.

In 1940 Warners produced another movie with the same title but that was all that remained of the book. It was to prove one of Errol Flynn's best swashbucklers, a fitting successor to his previous film of freebooters of the Spanish Main, *Captain Blood* (1935), also a Warner Brothers epic.

2

3

4

◁ 5

7

1. Brenda Marshall and Errol Flynn
2. Errol Flynn
3. Una O'Connor, Claude Rains, Brenda Marshall, Alan Hale and Errol Flynn
4. Errol Flynn
5. David Bruce and Errol Flynn
6. Claude Rains, Brenda Marshall, Una O'Connor and Errol Flynn
7. Henry Daniell and Errol Flynn
8. Brenda Marshall and Errol Flynn
9. Errol Flynn
10. Alan Hale, Julien Mitchell, Errol Flynn and Charles Irwin

6

8

9

1. Cary Grant
2. Fred Astaire and Eleanor Powell in *Broadway Melody of 1940* (MGM)
3. Bob Burns
4. Charles Coburn, Spencer Charters, Sigrid Gurie and John Wayne in *Three Faces West* (Rep)
5. Robert Morley in *You Will Remember* (JRP)
6. Edward Arnold in *Lillian Russell* (Fox)
7. Tullio Carminati
8. Hedy Lamarr
9. Margaret Lockwood and Irene Handl in *The Girl in the News* (Fox)
10. Richard Tucker

A scene from *Pinocchio* © 1940 Walt Disney Company

Judy Garland and Mickey Rooney in *Strike up the Band* (MGM)

In his lifetime Charles Chaplin acted in more than 80 films but none grossed the money that *The Great Dictator* made for United Artists.

It received five Motion Picture Academy nominations for the year – for Chaplin Best Picture, Best Actor and Best Original Screenplay; for Jack Oakie Best Supporting Actor; lastly for Best Original Score. In the event the film did not achieve any of these awards but that did not prevent it from being a huge box-office success.

1. Charles Chaplin
2. Henry Daniell, Charles Chaplin and Jack Oakie
3. Paulette Goddard and Charles Chaplin
4. Paulette Goddard
5. Reginald Gardiner and Charles Chaplin
6. Charles Chaplin and Eddie Gribbon
7. Charles Chaplin and Reginald Gardiner
8. Charles Chaplin and Jack Oakie

1. Paul Cavanagh
2. Leo Genn
3. Doris Weston, Forrest Taylor and Johnny Mack Brown in *Chip of the Flying U* (Univ)
4. Ann Rutherford, John Shelton and Virginia Weidler in *Keeping Company* (MGM)
5. Eduardo Ciannelli
6. Olympe Bradna
7. Olivia de Havilland, Errol Flynn and Ronald Reagan in *Santa Fe Trail* (WB)
8. William Lundigan, Henry O'Neill, Olivia de Havilland and Errol Flynn in *Santa Fe Trail* (WB)
9. Van Heflin and Raymond Massey in *Santa Fe Trail* (WB)
10. Van Heflin, Errol Flynn and Alan Baxter in *Santa Fe Trail* (WB)

1

2

3

6

◁ 7

1. Chico, Harpo and Groucho Marx
2. G P Huntley Jr in *Private Affairs* (Univ)
3. Tom Conway, Laraine Day and Robert Young in *The Trial of Mary Dugan* (MGM)
4. Laraine Day and Henry O'Neill in *The Trial of Mary Dugan* (MGM)
5. Laurence Olivier and Greer Garson in *Pride and Prejudice* (MGM)
6. Marsha Hunt and Laraine Day in *The Trial of Mary Dugan* (MGM)
7. Rita Johnson in *Congo Maisie* (MGM)
8. George 'Gabby' Hayes
9. Lew Ayres in *Dr. Kildare's Crisis* (MGM)
10. Marjorie Main and Robert Young in *The Trial of Mary Dugan* (MGM)

4

5

8   9

10

Spring Parade from Universal was another resounding success for Deanna Durbin, now leaving behind forever her juvenile roles. In this film she was partnered by Robert Cummings in the role of an army drummer in Vienna, with pretensions to becoming a composer. The score was melodious, Deanna was in magnificent form and cinema audiences flocked to be enchanted by this mirthful music-packed movie.

1. Robert Cummings and Deanna Durbin
2. Deanna Durbin, Robert Cummings and Peggy Moran
3. Mischa Auer
4. Deanna Durbin
5. S Z Sakall and Deanna Durbin
6. Robert Cummings

58

1. John Justin in *The Thief of Bagdad* (UA)
2. Conrad Veidt and June Duprez in *The Thief of Bagdad* (UA)
3. Charles Ruggles
4. Frank Albertson
5. Glenn Ford
6. Johnny Downs (c) in *Sing, Dance, Plenty Hot* (Rep)
7. Henry Hull and Gene Tierney in *The Return of Frank James* (Fox)
8. Donald Woods
9. Lionel Stander
10. Herbert Rawlinson
11. Ann Miller

Orson Welles

CHAPTER TWO
1941
ISOLATIONISM ENDS IN HOLLYWOOD

Orson Welles and Joseph Cotten in *Citizen Kane* (RKO)

Veronica Lake

The year began with Hollywood sunk deep in economic gloom and ended with the USA at war. The closure of the rich Continental markets, and currency restrictions with the embattled United Kingdom and Commonwealth, had made a big dent in profits. In the Far East, where Japanese expansion continued unchecked, revenues were on the slide. At home the US Government's anti-trust laws forced the Hollywood majors to abandon the practice of compelling exhibitors to book 'blind' a studio's entire product. From the autumn of 1941 movies were to be sold only in blocks of five. Hollywood responded by tightening its purse strings; studio personnel were laid off and all but the biggest stars were obliged to take a cut in salary.

Despite all the drawbacks, Hollywood enjoyed a year of renewed profit and significant creative achievement which included Orson Welles' *Citizen Kane,* Preston Sturges' *The Lady Eve,* John Huston's *The Maltese Falcon* and William Wyler's *The Little Foxes.* Hollywood regained the confidence to meet the challenge of war, which broke out on 7 December 1941 when, without warning, the Japanese attacked the great US Pacific naval base at Pearl Harbor.

America's military preparedness had already been hymned in Paramount's *I Wanted Wings,* directed by Mitchell Leisen, forerunner of a host of service movies which followed a group of recruits through the trials and tribulations of training. This time around it was a smug rich boy Ray Milland, dumb but willing Wayne Morris and grease monkey William Holden undergoing the rigours of air force training. Romantic interest was the attractive blonde newcomer Veronica Lake, seventh on the cast list and signed by the studio on a seven-year contract starting at $75 a week.

In Warners' *Dive Bomber,* made in co-operation with the Naval Air Corps, Errol Flynn played a surgeon fighting to eliminate pilot 'blackout' after a power dive. Cocky American aviator Tyrone Power travelled to London to join up and impress torch singer Betty Grable in the Twentieth Century-Fox film *A Yank in the RAF,* directed by Henry King. The film used some impressive footage of aerial combat and reached a climax over the beaches at Dunkirk, splicing news-reel material into studio set-ups which clashed jarringly with the real thing.

Warners aimed higher with Howard Hawks' *Sergeant York,* starring Gary Cooper as the pacifist Tennessee farm boy who became a war hero in 1918, capturing 132 Germans single-handed. *Sergeant York's* rural passages are positively toe-curling, but the combat sequences, supervised by York himself, are well mounted and Cooper's natural dignity salvages the film from bathos and won him the year's Best Actor Oscar.

Cooper was equally well cast in Frank Capra's *Meet John Doe,* also for Warner Brothers, in which he played a drifter taken up by journalist Barbara Stanwyck and fashioned into a fraudulent mouthpiece for a corrupt political campaign with undertones of fascism. Cooper rebels and is casually destroyed by his vengeful backers. Renewed destitution and despair are, however, mitigated by the waiting arms of a remorseful Stanwyck. Capra filmed five different endings to the film, later claiming that if he had found the right one, *Meet John Doe* would have been a masterpiece.

Which brings us to an unquestionable masterpiece, Orson Welles' *Citizen Kane.* In 1939, amid much ballyhoo, the boy wonder Welles had been signed by RKO, who gave him almost complete artistic freedom and $100,000 for one film a year, the budget of which was not to exceed $500,000. The much-delayed result was *Citizen Kane,* around whose authorship controversy has raged ever since. However, the presiding genius was Welles, whose overpowering energy galvanized all those around him into making his purposes manifest. Indeed, *Citizen Kane* is not only a thinly disguised portrait of the newspaper baron William Randolph Hearst, but also a self-portrait of the artist as self-destructive talent, and an uncannily accurate prediction of the melancholy trajectory which Welles himself would describe.

Citizen Kane's immediate fate was to suffer the wrath of William Randolph Hearst, egged on by his familiar, gossip columnist Louella Parsons. Hearst newspapers barred all advertising from RKO, which at the time was near bankruptcy, and many circuits refused to book the film. Where it was shown, the public's response was lukewarm. Nominated for several Oscars, *Citizen Kane* received just one, for the Best Screenplay. The Academy's Best Picture of the Year was the Twentieth Century-Fox film *How Green Was My Valley,* a lavishly mounted but lachrymose adaptation of Richard Llewellyn's best-selling novel of a Welsh mining community which also won the Best Director Award for John Ford. It was about as Welsh as Hollywood Boulevard, but it also won Donald Crisp the Oscar for Best Supporting Actor.

The year's second sensational directing debut was made at Warners by John Huston with *The Maltese Falcon,* the definitive version of the Dashiell Hammett novel, previously filmed by the studio in 1931 and 1936. It also gave Sydney Greenstreet his first screen role at the age of 61.

Gary Cooper

Donald Crisp and Maureen O'Hara in *How Green Was My Valley* (Fox)

▽ Humphrey Bogart in *The Maltese Falcon* (WB)

Peter Lorre and Mary Astor in *The Maltese Falcon* (WB)

Willie Best, Ida Lupino and Humphrey Bogart in *High Sierra* (WB)

Bette Davis and Mary Astor in *The Great Lie* (WB)

Joan Fontaine, Billy Bevan and CaryGrant in *Suspicion* (RKO)

Humphrey Bogart was the shopsoiled private eye Sam Spade, world-weary but retaining a streak of integrity. Sydney Greenstreet's Caspar Gutman, with his menacing bulk, rumbling laugh and floridly bogus Edwardian bon-homie, was very close to Hammett's original creation. His pairing with Peter Lorre's Joel Cairo was one of Hollywood's happiest strokes of casting. Elisha Cook Jr was the hapless gunman Wilmer, perpetually surprised by Bogart and tossed to the wolves when the going gets rough. Finally, Mary Astor was Miss Wunderly, the demure snake in the grass, her lips puckering with greed. At the end of the film she almost, but not quite, keeps a hold on our sympathy as the lift doors close over her face and she is carried away from a regretful Bogart.

The year marked a turning point in Bogart's career. In Raoul Walsh's superb *High Sierra* he emerged as an actor of stature, playing Roy 'Mad Dog' Earle, the hunted killer wearily resigned to his fate. Bogart's co-star in *High Sierra* was Ida Lupino, who gave a fine steely performance as a homicidal housekeeper in Columbia's *Ladies in Retirement*, directed by Charles Vidor.

MGM provided Joan Crawford with a supercharged veh-icle in George Cukor's *A Woman's Face,* a quintessential 1940's melodrama in which she suffered mightily as a scar-red criminal who falls under the spell of reptilian Svengali Conrad Veidt.

In William Wyler's *The Little Foxes,* adapted from Lillian Hellman's play, Bette Davis returned to the rank landscape of steamy Southern passions which she had explored in *Jezebel* (1938). She unsheathed her claws as the ruthless Re-gina – passionate, thwarted and tyrannical – watching the death of her husband Herbert Marshall with a chilling expression in which malevolence, satisfaction and fear struggled for supremacy.

Davis left the bitchery to Mary Astor in *The Great Lie.* When bland explorer George Brent goes missing in the jungle, he leaves his concert-pianist ex-wife Astor pregnant and new spouse Davis determined to bring up the child as her own. Astor was superb as the venomously chic pianist – a part built up on Davis' insistence – and won the year's Best Supporting Actress Oscar.

The suffering spouse in Alfred Hitchcock's *Suspicion* was Joan Fontaine, assailed by the growing conviction that her feckless playboy husband Cary Grant is plotting to kill her. The film has a feeble ending – RKO refused to countenance Grant as a cold-blooded murderer – but nevertheless reveals the darker side of its leading man's screen persona. Fon-taine's performance won her the Best Actress Oscar, but it is Grant we remember, walking soundlessly upstairs to his tor-mented wife carrying an eerily lit glass of hot milk.

The supremely professional Barbara Stanwyck starred in two of the decade's best comedies, Howard Hawks' *Ball of Fire* and Preston Sturges' *The Lady Eve.* The first was an in-genious variation on the theme of Snow White and the Seven

Dwarfs, scripted by Billy Wilder and Charles Brackett, with Stanwyck as the burlesque dancer moving in with a team of stuffy professors (led by Gary Cooper) to explain 'slang' for their new encyclopedia. In *The Lady Eve* she was a cardsharp, working the North Atlantic liner beat with father Charles Coburn. Over the horizon sails tangle-footed brewery heir Henry Fonda whose only passion is rare snakes, until he meets Stanwyck over a marked deck of cards.

Barbara Stanwyck and Gary Cooper in *Ball of Fire* (RKO)

Bette Davis revealed a deft comic touch in *The Man Who Came to Dinner*. W C Fields' *Never Give a Sucker an Even Break* was his calculatedly incoherent farewell to the insanities of Hollywood. *Buck Privates*, a $90,000 Universal programmer, was a huge hit, establishing Abbott and Costello as two of the studio's top money earners.

The Marx Brothers said farewell to MGM with *The Big Store*. So did Greta Garbo in *Two-Faced Woman*, directed by George Cukor. The studio attempted to Americanize her in a chic comedy of sexual manners or bury her career, according to your point of view. Garbo had always been more popular in Europe than in the USA, but this market was now closed to her. After the critical and commercial failure of *Two-Faced Woman*, she withdrew into a temporary retirement which, with the passing of the years, became permanent.

Laurence Olivier and Vivien Leigh made a handsome couple in Alexander Korda's *That Hamilton Woman*, (GB *Lady Hamilton*) playing Admiral Nelson and his mistress. At MGM Greer Garson and Walter Pidgeon were teamed for the first time in *Blossoms in the Dust*. Mickey Rooney and Judy Garland continued their triumphant progress in *Babes on Broadway*, directed by Busby Berkeley, in which Rooney gave a famous impersonation of Carmen Miranda, wickedly precise down to the last bobbling banana. Berkeley also handled the production numbers in *Ziegfeld Girl*, a feast for the eyes whose endless parade of ever so slightly camp costumes prompted Tony Martin to croon 'You Stepped Out of a Dream' to Hedy Lamarr.

Bud Abbott and Lou Costello

Errol Flynn played General George Armstrong Custer to the manner born in Warners' *They Died With Their Boots On*, Raoul Walsh's vigorous, highly romanticized account of the flamboyant cavalryman's career and one of the few films to deal cohesively with the Civil War, its aftermath and the gradually increasing conflict between the Indians and the White Man.

Gene Tierney was less happy as the guntotin' heroine of Twentieth Century-Fox's *Belle Starr*, while Robert Taylor was a decidedly over-age *Billy the Kid*, an anodyne MGM addition to a Western legend. Fritz Lang, however, made the most of his big budget in Twentieth Century-Fox's *Western Union*, magnificently photographed in Utah by Edward Cronjager, in which Randolph Scott battled outlaw brother Barton MacLane and swarms of Indians as the telegraph wires were laid between Omaha and Salt Lake City.

Universal's horror factory delivered *The Wolf Man*, directed by George Waggner, an everyday tale of werewolves

Errol Flynn in *They Died With Their Boots On* (WB)

Spencer Tracy and Lana Turner in *Dr Jekyll and Mr Hyde* (MGM)

Evelyn Keyes and Peter Lorre in *The Face Behind the Mask* (Col)

Rochelle Hudson and Chester Morris in *Meet Boston Blackie* (Col)

▽ Patricia Dane and Robert Taylor in *Johnny Eager* (MGM)

starring Lon Chaney Jr as the luckless Larry Talbot, hulking scion of the British aristocracy who sprouts hair and fangs 'when the wolfbane blooms and the autumn moon is bright'.

Less emphasis was placed on the make-up in MGM's stylish remake of *Dr Jekyll and Mr Hyde*. Spencer Tracy was revealingly menacing as the stricken man of science, turning into his demoniacal alter ego in a symbolic surrealist montage created by Peter Ballbusch.

Low-budget delights included Republic's *Sis Hopkins,* in which pert young Susan Hayward was a snobbish city girl playing reluctant host to raucous hayseed cousin Judy Canova. Hayward also turned up in Paramount's excellent *Among the Living,* terrorized by Albert Dekker in the double role of a homicidal maniac and his innocent twin brother.

In Columbia's *The Face behind the Mask,* directed by the sadly neglected Robert Florey, Peter Lorre gave a richly sinister performance as a disfigured mobster hiding under a layer of contoured rubber.

Columbia cast Chester Morris as Boston Blackie, the jewel thief turned sleuth, in *Meet Boston Blackie,* the first in a snappy series of 13. And Paramount launched newcomer Jimmy Lydon as a low-budget rival to Andy Hardy in *Henry Aldrich for President.* Eight more Henry Aldrich adventures followed in a modest but well-crafted series.

New faces in Hollywood included Dan Duryea and exotic leading man Turhan Bey; Lloyd Bridges and Larry Parks, who both made their debuts in *Honolulu Lu;* Czech skating star Vera Hruba Ralston, who became the queen of the Republic lot after marrying the boss, Herbert Yates; and June Havoc, sister of Gypsy Rose Lee, who turned up in *Four Jacks and a Jill* as a torch singer called Opal.

Jean Renoir directed his first film in Hollywood, Twentieth Century-Fox's *Swamp Water,* (GB *The Man Who Came Back*) a tale of the Georgia backwoods starring Walter Brennan, Anne Baxter and Dana Andrews. Van Heflin secured a breakthrough role in MGM's slick melodrama *Johnny Eager,* as racketeer Robert Taylor's pathetic drunken sidekick. Laird Cregar also made his substantial presence felt for the first time as the psychopathic cop hounding Betty Grable and Victor Mature in H Bruce Humberstone's *I Wake Up Screaming,* (GB *Hot Spot*) a compellingly creepy portrait of highly strung menace and fastidious grossness.

The most successful British film of the year was Michael Powell and Emeric Pressburger's *49th Parallel,* (US *The Invaders*) financed by the Ministry of Information (MoI) and aimed at the North American market. Given considerable freedom, Powell and Pressburger were able to indulge their delight in paradox by placing Germans at the centre of the action as a group of enemy submariners flee across Canada after their U-boat is sunk in the Gulf of St Lawrence. In a star-studded cast (Laurence Olivier, Anton Walbrook, Leslie Howard, Raymond Massey) Eric Portman gave an outstanding performance as the Germans' grimly fanatical leader.

Leslie Howard directed himself in *Pimpernel Smith,* (US

The Fighting Pimpernel and Mister V) playing the very model of the absent-minded English academic whose secret alter ego is a modern version of the Scarlet Pimpernel (a role he had played in 1934) who runs an escape line for scientists threatened with imprisonment in pre-war Germany. *Pimpernel Smith* was a deft celebration of the superiority of the genteel English 'amateur' over the blinkered thuggery of the Nazis but its whimsical spirit was out of touch with the demands now made by the waging of Total War.

Nearer the mark was Harry Watt's *Target for Tonight,* the first documentary to show the British 'hitting back' at the enemy. It followed a Wellington bomber, 'F for Freddie', and its crew during the planning and execution of a raid over Germany.

Romance and escapism were provided by the immensely popular *Dangerous Moonlight,* (US *Suicide Squadron*) directed by Brian Desmond Hurst, in which Anton Walbrook played an exiled Polish concert pianist who becomes a Battle of Britain fighter pilot. This was a better commercial formula than studied attempts to raise patriotic consciousness with stiff historical dramas like *The Young Mr. Pitt,* starring Robert Donat in the title role and *The Prime Minister,* with John Gielgud as Benjamin Disraeli and Fay Compton as Queen Victoria.

Deborah Kerr was given her first starring role in John Baxter's clumsy but affecting *Love on the Dole,* adapted from Walter Greenwood's novel of the Depression, struggling gamely with a wavering Lancashire accent as headstrong working girl Sally Hardcastle. Will Hay kept audiences in stitches in *Black Sheep of Whitehall.*

In Germany, Josef Goebbels had a hand in the script of *Ohm Krüger,* directed by Hans Steinhoff, an ambitious piece of anti-British propaganda set in South Africa during the Boer War. Emil Jannings played Paul Krüger, a heroically monolithic and all-seeing patriarch leading the peace-loving Boer farmers in their resistance to the grasping British imperialists, represented by a whiskey-sodden Queen Victoria and a bloated Winston Churchill strutting round a concentration camp whose inmates are dying of starvation. This shred of historical truth – the British did indeed introduce a system of internment camps in the Boer War – is the basis for an exercise in breathtaking cynicism, as the Nazis now had concentration camps of their own.

In France the flood of German films which followed the occupation had been boycotted by French audiences. In contrast receipts for French films rose steadily, ironically placing the home industry on a firmer footing. Much French production was now replacing the escapist entertainment previously supplied by Hollywood. The Continental company, established by the Germans in 1940, was now producing a stream of 'American-style' features, among them Henri Decoin's comedy *Le Premier Rendezvous* and Georges Lacombe's thriller *Le Dernier de Six (The Last Six)* scripted by Henri-Georges Clouzot.

Owen Nares (l) and John Gielgud (r) in *The Prime Minister* (WB)

Deborah Kerr, George Carney and Mary Merrall in *Love on the Dole* (BN)

Will Hay

Buck Jones, Tim McCoy and Raymond Hatton in *Arizona Bound* (MoP)

Dean Jagger, Minor Watson, Chill Wills and Robert Young in *Western Union* (Fox)

Virginia Bruce and Herbert Marshall in *Adventure in Washington* (Col)

William Gargan and Martha Scott in *Cheers For Miss Bishop* (UA)

Film Favourites 1941

The drums of war were beating furiously all over Europe and North Africa and the United States were now taking a more than passing interest in the mounting hostilities. Even so, Hollywood was still strong for whimsies such as Tarzan and routine musicals such as *Week-End in Havana* (Fox).

Johnny Weissmuller, Maureen O'Sullivan and Johnny Sheffield in *Tarzan's Secret Treasure* (MGM)
Ethel Griffies and Sidney Toler in *Dead Men Tell* (Fox)

Deanna Durbin and Robert Stack in *Nice Girl* (Univ)

W C Fields and Leon Errol in *Never Give a Sucker an Even Break* (Univ)

William Powell and Henry O'Neill in *Shadow of The Thin Man* (MGM)

Ingrid Bergman and Warner Baxter in *Adam Had Four Sons* (Col)

Henry Fonda and Barbara Stanwyck in *You Belong To Me* (GB *Good Morning, Doctor*) (Col)

Nancy Coleman and John Garfield in *Dangerously They Live* (WB)

Spencer Tracy in *Men of Boys' Town* (MGM) ▷

Madeleine Carroll and Fred MacMurray in *One Night In Lisbon* (Par)

Herbert Marshall, Spring Byington, Joan Crawford, Rafael Storm and Robert Taylor in *When Ladies Meet* (MGM)

Joseph Schildkraut, Ellen Drew, Paul Hurst, Phillip Terry and ▷ Charles Ruggles in *The Parson of Panamint* (Par)

Guy Kibbee, John Archer, Joseph Crehan and Edward Earle in *Scattergood Baines* (RKO)

John Hubbard in *Road Show* (UA)

John Payne, George Barbier and Cobina Wright Jr in *Weekend In Havana* (Fox)

Joan Crawford, William Farnum and Melvyn Douglas in *A Woman's Face* (MGM)

Errol Flynn in *They Died With Their Boots On* (WB) ▽

Walter Pidgeon and Joan Bennett in *Man Hunt* (Fox)

Albert Dekker and Susan Hayward in *Among The Living* (Par)

Robert Montgomery and Claude Rains in *Here Comes Mister Jordan* (Col)

Dorothy Lamour and Bob Hope in *Caught in the Draft* (Par)
▽ Myrna Loy and William Powell in *Love Crazy* (MGM)

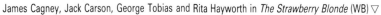

Charles Boyer, Olivia de Havilland and Nestor Paiva in *Hold Back the Dawn* (Par)

Joseph Cotten, Orson Welles and Everett Sloane in *Citizen Kane* (RKO)

James Cagney, Jack Carson, George Tobias and Rita Hayworth in *The Strawberry Blonde* (WB) ▽

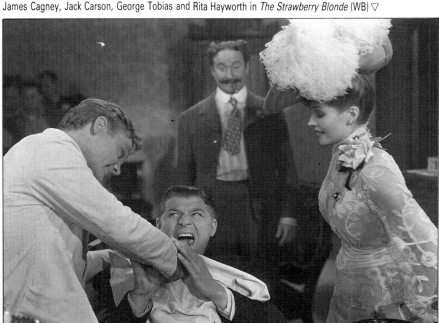

1

2

3

4

5

Picture Gallery for 1941

1. Lynn Bari in *Blood and Sand* (Fox)
2. Herbert Anderson and David Bruce in *The Body Disappears* (WB)
3. Frank Sully (r) in *Let's Go Collegiate* (MoP)
4. Greta Garbo
5. James Ellison and Dorothy Lewis in *Ice-Capades* (Rep)
6. Marion Martin
7. Robert Cummings and Margaret Tallichet in *It Started With Eve* (Univ)
8. Leon Ames in *No Greater Sin* (UNV)

6

7

8

1

2

3

4

5

6

5

1. Fredric March and Loretta Young in *Bedtime Story* (Col)
2. Dennis Morgan in *Bad Men of Missouri* (WB)
3. Wayne Morris, Dennis Morgan and Arthur Kennedy in *Bad Men of Missouri* (WB)
4. Buster Crabbe and Sheila Darcy in *Jungle Man* (PRC)
5. Regis Toomey and Jeffrey Lynn in *Law of the Tropics* (WB)
6. Richard Carlson
7. Charles Boyer and Margaret Sullavan in *Back Street* (Univ)
8. Frank Jenks and Margaret Sullavan in *Back Street* (Univ)
9. Lynne Overman and Jon Hall in *Aloma of the South Seas* (Par)

7

8

9

70

Anton Walbrook and Sally Gray in *Dangerous Moonlight* (RKO)

A scene from *Dumbo* © 1941 Walt Disney Company

Douglas Fairbanks Jr in *The Corsican Brothers* (UA)

1. Mickey Rooney, Spencer Tracy and Sidney Miller in *Men of Boys Town* (MGM)
2. Ken Murray, Frances Langford and Hanley Stafford in *Swing It, Soldier* (Univ)
3. Lou Costello and Bud Abbott in *In the Navy* (Univ)
4. Frank Sinatra
5. Betty Field
6. Roberta Huby
7. Boris Karloff and Amanda Duff in *The Devil Commands* (Col)
8. Bette Davis and James Cagney in *The Bride Came C O D* (WB)
9. J Carrol Naish, Ruth Warrick and Douglas Fairbanks Jr in *The Corsican Brothers* (UA)
10. Bob Crosby and Susan Hayward in *Sis Hopkins* (Rep)
11. Don Ameche and Joan Bennett in *Confirm or Deny* (Fox)
12. Maris Wrixon, Paul Cavanagh and William Lundigan in *The Case of the Black Parrot* (WB)
13. Alan Mowbray, Lynn Bari, Dan Dailey and John Sutton in *Moon Over Her Shoulder* (Fox)
14. Frank Albertson, Peggy Moran, William Gargan and Edmund Lowe in *Flying Cadets* (Univ)

13 ▷

1. John Halliday in *Lydia* (UA)
2. Nils Asther in *Night of January 16th* (Par)
3. Sidney Blackmer and William Powell in *Love Crazy* (MGM)
4. Ann Sheridan, Herbert Anderson and Howard da Silva (r) in *Navy Blues* (WB)
5. Robert Warwick
6. Dick Foran
7. Richard Dix
8. Jerome Cowan
9. Noah Beery Sr
10. Victor Kilian
11. Spencer Charters
12. Leo Carrillo

10
11

1

2

3

4

5

6

7

8

9

10

11

1. Ann Sheridan and George Brent in *Honeymoon for Three* (WB)
2. Ann Sheridan, George Brent and Osa Massen in *Honeymoon for Three* (WB)
3. Harvey Stephens
4. John Wayne, Ona Munson and Dorothy Dandridge in *Lady From Louisiana* (Rep)
5. Donald Woods, Kathryn Adams, Edward Everett Horton and Raymond Walburn in *Bachelor Daddy* (Univ)
6. Harold Huber, Sen Yung, Sidney Toler and Victor Jory in *Charlie Chan in Rio* (Fox)
7. Carole Lombard
8. John Barrymore and Kay Kyser in *Playmates* (RKO)
9. Bela Lugosi in *Invisible Ghost* (MoP)
10. Randolph Scott and Elizabeth Bergner in *Paris Calling* (Univ)
11. Lupe Velez and Kay Kyser in *Playmates* (RKO)
12. Andrew Tombes, Peggy Moran, Rand Brooks, Una Merkel and Edmund Lowe in *Double Date* (Univ)
13. Edward Arnold and Lionel Barrymore in *The Penalty* (MGM)
14. Margaret Lockwood and A E Matthews in *Quiet Wedding* (Conqueror)
15. W C Fields

14
▷◁
▽
15

12

13

75

The Young Mr Pitt (Fox) was produced in Britain in 1941 and shown in the US one year later. The story was inclined to be laborious but the film fulfilled the wartime requirements of the cinemagoers because it was devised as timely propaganda against the Nazis viz: for Hitler read Napoleon Bonaparte (as played by Herbert Lom).

1. Leslie Bradley and Robert Donat
2. Jean Cadell, John Mills and Robert Donat
3. Raymond Lovell and Agnes Laughlan
4. Bromley Davenport and Robert Morley
5. Phyllis Calvert and Robert Donat
6. Albert Lieven and Robert Donat
7. Robert Donat
8. Robert Donat
9. Robert Donat, James Harcourt and Ian MacLean
10. Albert Lieven and Herbert Lom

9
◁
▷
10

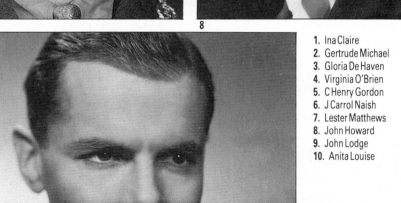
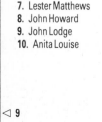

1. Ina Claire
2. Gertrude Michael
3. Gloria De Haven
4. Virginia O'Brien
5. C Henry Gordon
6. J Carrol Naish
7. Lester Matthews
8. John Howard
9. John Lodge
10. Anita Louise

◁ 9

1. Gene Tierney and Charley Grapewin in *Tobacco Road* (Fox)
2. Marian Marsh
3. George Irving
4. Ernest Cossart and Jack Benny in *Charley's Aunt* (Fox)
5. Lionel Barrymore and Lew Ayres in *Dr Kildare's Wedding Day* (MGM)
6. Sonja Henie, John Payne and Lynn Bari in *Sun Valley Serenade* (Fox)
7. John Beal, Florence Rice and Edward Norris in *Doctors Don't Tell* (Rep)
8. Lloyd Nolan, Alexis Smith and Gene Lockhart in *Steel Against the Sky* (WB)
9. Mary Martin and Don Ameche in *Kiss the Boys Goodbye* (Par)
10. Rufe Davis, Robert Livingston and Bob Steele in *Pals of the Pecos* (Rep)
11. Rosemary Lane, Lola Lane, Gale Page and Priscilla Lane in *Four Mothers* (WB)
12. Frances Neal and Dennis O'Keefe in *Lady Scarface* (RKO)
13. Jane Wyman, Phil Silvers and Jimmy Durante in *You're in the Army Now* (WB)
14. Philip Reed, Edward Everett Horton, Jane Wyatt and Dennis O'Keefe in *Weekend for Three* (RKO)
15. Ruth Hussey and Robert Cummings in *Free and Easy* (MGM)

14
▷
▷
15

1. Glenn Strange
2. Patric Knowles
3. Louis Hayward
4. Clarence Kolb
5. William Henry
6. Jean Arthur
7. Robert Sterling
8. Constance Bennett
9. John Miljan
10. Dale Evans
11. Ann Sheridan
12. Steffi Duna
13. Charles Farrell
14. Herbert Marshall

1

2

3

4

5

6

7

8

9

10

11

12

13

14

15

1. Bing Crosby, Una Merkel and Bob Hope in *The Road to Zanzibar* (Par)
2. Gary Cooper and Margaret Wycherley in *Sergeant York* (WB)
3. Burgess Meredith and Ginger Rogers in *Tom, Dick and Harry* (RKO)
4. James Ellison, Buddy Ebsen and Maureen O'Hara in *They Met in Argentina* (RKO)
5. Frank Morgan in *The Vanishing Virginian* (MGM)
6. Tyrone Power and John Sutton in *A Yank in the RAF* (Fox)
7. George Murphy, Ann Sothern, Robert Sterling, Natalie Thompson and Maxie Rosenbloom in *Ringside Maisie* (MGM)
8. Harry Cording and Johnny Mack Brown in *Rawhide Rangers* (U)
9. Warren William, Henry Fonda and Ona Munson in *Wild Geese Calling* (Fox)
10. Patricia Morison and Pedro de Cordoba in *Romance of the Rio Grande* (Fox)
11. Robert Young and Randolph Scott in *Western Union* (Fox)
12. Neil Hamilton in *Federal Fugitives* (PRC)
13. Richard Arlen, Andy Devine and Linda Hayes in *Raiders of the Desert* (Univ)
14. Diana Wynyard and John Gielgud in *The Prime Minister* (WB)
15. Sarah Padden and Wallace Ford in *Murder By Invitation* (MoP)
16. Paul Fix and Billy Halop in *Mob Town* (Univ)
17. Phillip Terry, Frank Puglia, Ellen Drew and Charles Ruggles in *The Parson of Panamint* (Par)
18. Elizabeth Risdon and Robert Armstrong in *Mr. Dynamite* (Univ)
19. Carol Hughes, Forrest Tucker and Evelyn Brent in *Emergency Landing* (PRC)
20. Geraldine Fitzgerald and Jeffrey Lynn in *Flight from Destiny* (WB)
21. Victor Kilian and Donald Woods in *I Was a Prisoner on Devil's Island* (Col)
22. Nelson Eddy
23. Anna Lee and Charles Winninger in *My Life With Caroline* (RKO)

16

17

18

19

20

21

22

▷

23

83

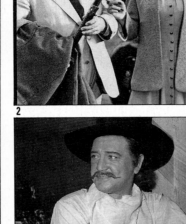

1. Gene Raymond and Jeanette MacDonald in *Smilin' Through* (MGM)
2. Cecil Kellaway, Evelyn Ankers, Charles Bickford and C Montague Shaw in *Burma Convoy* (Univ)
3. Richard Dix in *Badlands of Dakota* (Univ)
4. Ray Milland, Brian Aherne and Claudette Colbert in *Skylark* (Par)
5. Philip Reed
6. Robert Stack and Broderick Crawford in *Badlands of Dakota* (Univ)
7. Andy Devine, Broderick Crawford and Lon Chaney Jr in *Badlands of Dakota* (Univ)
8. Hugh Herbert and Frances Farmer in *Badlands of Dakota* (Univ)
9. Hugh Herbert, Broderick Crawford and Robert Stack in *Badlands of Dakota* (Univ)
10. Marie Wilson and Ruth Terry in *Rookies on Parade* (Rep)

9
▷ ◁
10

1. Jean Hersholt, Walter Woolf King and Fay Wray in *Melody for Three* (RKO)
2. Douglas Kennedy
3. Frank Morgan and Irene Rich in *The Wild Man of Borneo* (MGM)
4. Barbara Stanwyck in *Ball of Fire* (SG)
5. Isabel Jeans
6. Johnny Mack Brown
7. Everett Sloane, Orson Welles and Joseph Cotten in *Citizen Kane* (RKO)
8. Dorothy Comingore in *Citizen Kane* (RKO)
9. Orson Welles in *Citizen Kane* (RKO)
10. Orson Welles and George Coulouris in *Citizen Kane* (RKO)

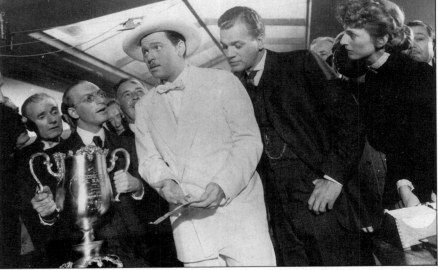

85

1. Sally Payne, George 'Gabby' Hayes, Roy Rogers and Gale Storm in *Jesse James at Bay* (Rep)
2. Joan Woodbury and Roy Rogers in *In Old Cheyenne* (Rep)
3. William Boyd, Minna Gombell and Georgia Hawkins in *Doomed Caravan* (Par)
4. Jacqueline Wells, Smiley Burnette and Gene Autry in *Back in the Saddle* (Rep)
5. Tim Holt and Betty Jane Rhodes in *Along the Rio Grande* (RKO)
6. Gene Autry and Carol Hughes in *Under Fiesta Stars* (Rep)
7. Smiley Burnette, Fay McKenzie and Gene Autry in *Sierra Sue* (Rep)
8. Sally Payne, Roy Rogers and Marjorie Reynolds in *Robin Hood of the Pecos* (Rep)
9. Elyse Knox, Sally Payne, and Roy Rogers in *Sheriff of Tombstone* (Rep)
10. Evelyn Brent, William Boyd, Morris Ankrum, Bernice Kay and Russell Hayden (r) in *Wide Open Town* (Par)
11. Fuzzy Knight, Dick Curtis, Johnny Mack Brown and Nell O'Day in *Arizona Cyclone* (Univ)
12. Gene Autry, Maris Wrixon and Smiley Burnette in *Sunset in Wyoming* (Rep)
13. Don Barry and Lynn Merrick in *The Apache Kid* (Rep)
14. Bob Steele, Robert Livingston and June Johnson in *Gangs of Sonora* (Rep)
15. Triss Coffin (stg l) and Tim McCoy (std) in *Forbidden Trails* (MoP)
16. Betty Miles, Tom Keene, Sugar Dawn and Frank Yaconelli in *Lone Star Law Men* (MoP)
17. Robert Livingston and Bob Steele (r) in *Prairie Pioneers* (Rep)
18. George Houston (c) in *The Lone Rider Fights Back* (PRC)
19. Andy Devine, Luane Walters, Leo Carrillo and Anne Gwynne in *Road Agent* (Univ)
20. Ray Corrigan, Max Terhune and John King in *The Kid's Last Ride* (MoP)

The role of George Armstrong Custer seemed tailor-made for Errol Flynn who played the swashbuckling cavalryman to the life, in Warner Brothers *They Died With Their Boots On.* The true facts of Custer's life, however, were altered somewhat to provide Flynn with a part that was one hundred per cent hero whereas Custer himself was an iron disciplinarian, inclined to over-reach himself at times – and ultimately tragically for him and for his command who died with him on the banks of the Little Big Horn River in 1876

1. Errol Flynn and G P Huntley Jr
2. Charley Grapewin and Errol Flynn
3. Sydney Greenstreet
4. Gene Lockhart, Olivia de Havilland and Errol Flynn
5. Arthur Kennedy (c) and Errol Flynn
6. Errol Flynn
7. Arthur Kennedy and Joe Sawyer
8. Walter Hampden, Arthur Kennedy, Errol Flynn and Olivia de Havilland

1

2

3

4

5

6

7

8 ▷

1   2   3   4

5

7   8   9

1. Grant Withers

2. Otto Kruger (r) in *The Big Boss* (Col)

3. Jack Carson

4. Susanna Foster in *There's Magic in Music* (Par)

5. Allan Jones and Susanna Foster in *There's Magic In Music* (Par)

6. Rand Brooks

7. Edgar Buchanan and William Holden in *Texas* (Col)

8. William Gargan and Carol Bruce in *Keep 'Em Flying* (Univ)

9. Ellen Drew

10. Lloyd Nolan, Richard Whorf and Betty Field in *Blues in the Night* (WB)

10 ▷

1

2

3

4

5

6

7

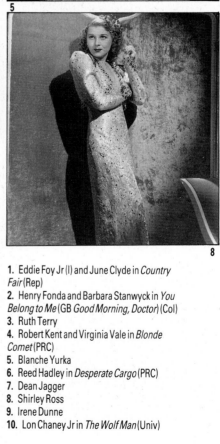

8

9

10 ▷

1. Eddie Foy Jr (l) and June Clyde in *Country Fair* (Rep)
2. Henry Fonda and Barbara Stanwyck in *You Belong to Me* (GB *Good Morning, Doctor*) (Col)
3. Ruth Terry
4. Robert Kent and Virginia Vale in *Blonde Comet* (PRC)
5. Blanche Yurka
6. Reed Hadley in *Desperate Cargo* (PRC)
7. Dean Jagger
8. Shirley Ross
9. Irene Dunne
10. Lon Chaney Jr in *The Wolf Man* (Univ)

1

2

3

4

5

6

7

8

1. Jane Withers and Richard Clayton in *A Very Young Lady* (Fox)
2. Shirley Ross and Dennis Morgan in *Kisses for Breakfast* (WB)
3. Martha Raye
4. Zoya Fyodorova in *Musical Story* (Lenfilm-Russian)
5. Ginny Simms
6. James Craig
7. Lee Bowman
8. Elsa Lanchester, Ida Lupino and Louis Hayward in *Ladies in Retirement* (Col)
9. Tony Martin, Harpo Marx, Douglas Dumbrille, Chico Marx, Virginia Grey, Groucho Marx and Margaret Dumont in *The Big Store* (MGM)

9 ▷

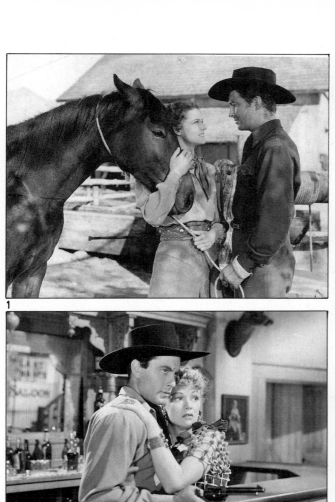

1

2

4

5

3

6

7

8

9

11

◁ 10

1. Mary Howard and Robert Taylor in *Billy The Kid* (MGM)

2. Leif Erickson, Florence Rice and Gordon Jones in *The Blonde From Singapore* (Col)

3. George Montgomery and Lynne Roberts in *Last of the Duanes* (Fox)

4. William Frawley

5. Franchot Tone

6. Jean Arthur and Robert Cummings in *The Devil and Miss Jones* (RKO)

7. Rise Stevens and Nelson Eddy in *The Chocolate Soldier* (MGM)

8. Sterling Holloway

9. Frieda Inescort

10. Jack Hulbert

11. Lyle Talbot

1

2

3

4

5

6

7

8

9

10

11

12

13

14

15

16

17

1. Donald Douglas and Nan Wynn in *A Shot in the Dark* (WB)

2. Cecil Kellaway, Charles Boyer and Ruth Terry in *Appointment for Love* (Univ)

3. Francis McDonald, Stanley Ridges, John Garfield and Barry Fitzgerald in *The Sea Wolf* (WB)

4. Randolph Scott in *Belle Starr* (Fox)

5. Laraine Day, Tom Conway, Lionel Barrymore, Henry Travers and Ronald Reagan in *The Bad Man* (MGM)

6. John Payne, Alice Faye, Carmen Miranda and Cesar Romero in *Weekend in Havana* (Fox)

7. Richard Lane, Lynne Roberts, Ted North and Edgar Kennedy in *The Bride Wore Crutches* (Fox)

8. Robert Cummings, Ann Sheridan and Ronald Reagan in *King's Row* (WB)

9. Lynn Bari, Lloyd Nolan and Mary Beth Hughes in *Sleepers West* (Fox)

10. Evelyn Knapp, Henry Wilcoxon (c) and Warren William (on floor) in *The Lone Wolf takes a Chance* (Col)

11. Jane Darwell, Jackie Searl and Jane Withers in *Small Town Deb* (Fox)

12. Hardie Albright, George Barbier, Brenda Joyce and Bruce Edwards in *Marry The Boss's Daughter* (Fox)

13. Andy Devine, Anne Nagel and Richard Arlen in *Mutiny in the Arctic* (Univ)

14. Don Ameche and Betty Grable in *Moon Over Miami* (Fox)

15. Bette Davis in *The Little Foxes* (RKO)

16. Bette Davis and Monty Woolley in *The Man Who Came to Dinner* (WB)

17. Manton Moreland, Frankie Darro, Keye Luke and Jackie Moran in *Let's Go Collegiate* (MoP)

18. Gary Cooper and Barbara Stanwyck in *Meet John Doe* (WB)

19. Marlene Dietrich in *Manpower* (WB)

18

◁ 19

93

1. Vera Lewis, Clem Bevans, Roger Pryor and Eve Arden in *She Couldn't Say No* (WB)

2. Barbara Stanwyck, Henry Fonda and Charles Coburn in *The Lady Eve* (Par)

3. Alexis Smith, Wayne Morris and Brenda Marshall in *The Smiling Ghost* (WB)

4. Walter Catlett, Iris Adrian, Johnny Downs, George Barbier and Mischa Auer in *Sing Another Chorus* (Univ)

5. Dick Purcell, Joan Perry, Roger Pryor and Anthony Quinn in *Bullets for O'Hara* (WB)

6. John Hubbard, Franchot Tone and Joan Bennett in *She Knew All the Answers* (Col)

7. Victor McLaglen, Marjorie Woodworth, Leonid Kinsky and Dennis O'Keefe in *Broadway Limited* (UA)

8. Conrad Veidt and Loretta Young in *The Men in Her Life* (Col)

9. Ruth Warrick, Robert Smith and Joan Carroll in *Obliging Young Lady* (RKO)

10. George Montgomery, Carole Landis and Shepperd Strudwick in *Cadet Girl* (Fox)

11. Bela Lugosi in *Devil Bat* (PRC)

12. Pauline Moore and Roy Rogers in *Arkansas Judge* (Rep)

11 ▷

1. Kent Taylor
2. Norman Foster
3. Boris Karloff
4. Frances Dee
5. David Niven
6. Jane Wyatt
7. Lee Tracy
8. Landis
9. Michael O'Shea
10. John Wayne
11. Errol Flynn

1

2

3

1. Jean Parker and Richard Arlen in *Power Dive* (Par)
2. Marjorie Reynolds and Tim Holt in *Cyclone on Horseback* (RKO)
3. Binnie Barnes in *Tight Shoes* (Univ)
4. Ricardo Cortez, John Barrymore and Virginia Dale in *World Premiere* (Par)
5. Cliff Edwards and Charles Starrett in *Thunder Over the Prairie* (Col)
6. Barton MacLane, Evelyn Ankers, Gladys George, Billy Halop, Bernard Punsley, Huntz Hall, Gabriel Dell and Bobs Watson in *Hit the Road* (Univ)
7. Marjorie Gateson, Leo Carrillo and Lupe Velez in *Honolulu Lu* (Col)
8. Key Luke, Evelyn Ankers and Charles Bickford in *Burma Convoy* (Univ)
9. Basil Rathbone and George Brent in *International Lady* (UA)
10. Eddie Albert, John Garfield, Ida Lupino, George Tobias and Bernard Gorcey in *Out of the Fog* (WB)
11. Buck Jones, David O'Brien and Christine McIntyre in *The Gunman From Bodie* (MoP)
12. Jim Jordan, Lucille Ball, Edgar Bergen and Marian Jordan in *Look Who's Laughing* (RKO)

4

6

9

11

12

◁ 10

1. Brian Donlevy (l), Bing Crosby (c), Mary Martin and Harry Barris (Double Bass) in *Birth of the Blues* (Par)
2. Ruth Hussey in *Free and Easy* (MGM)
3. Joan Blondell and Dick Powell in *Model Wife* (Univ)
4. Brian Aherne and Kay Francis in *The Man Who Lost Himself* (Univ)
5. Jane Frazee and Johnny Downs in *Moonlight in Hawaii* (Univ)
6. Patricia Morison in *The Round-Up* (Par)
7. Leon Errol, Helen Parrish, Charles Lang and William Frawley in *Six Lessons From Madame La Zonga* (Univ)
8. Jerome Cowan, Helen Parrish and Rudy Vallee in *Too Many Blondes* (Univ)
9. Cesar Romero and William Henry in *Dance Hall* (Fox)
10. Anne Nagel and Hugh Herbert in *Meet the Chump* (Univ)
11. John Wayne and Frances Dee in *A Man Betrayed* (GB *Citadel of Crime*) (Rep)

10 ▷
▷ ◁
11

1

2

3

4

5

6

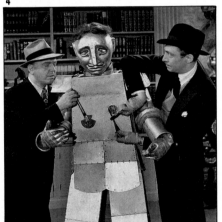

7

8

9

10

11

1. Binnie Barnes and Gilbert Roland in *Angels With Broken Wings* (Rep)

2. Mona Barrie, Ralph Bellamy, Charley Grapewin, Olin Howland, Edward Gargan and Margaret Lindsay in *Ellery Queen and the Murder Ring* (Col)

3. Astrid Allwyn and John Archer in *I'll Sell My Life* (SeP)

4. Gene Tierney and Bruce Cabot in *Sundown* (UA)

5. Merle Oberon, Dennis Morgan, Rita Hayworth and Ralph Bellamy in *Affectionately Yours* (WB)

6. Elliott Sullivan, John Litel, William Gargan and Anne Nagel in *Sealed Lips* (Univ)

7. William Frawley and Mischa Auer in *Cracked Nuts* (Univ)

8. Madeleine Carroll and Sterling Hayden in *Bahama Passage* (Par)

9. Lewis Howard, Walter Catlett, Dick Foran, Peggy Moran, John Eldredge, Hobart Cavanaugh and Rolf Harolde in *Horror Island* (Univ)

10. Paul Kelly, Don Costello, Robert Sterling, Fay Holden, Marsha Hunt and Henry Travers in *I'll Wait for You* (MGM)

11. Joan Leslie, Humphrey Bogart, Eddie Albert and Sylvia Sidney in *The Wagons Roll at Night* (WB)

CHAPTER THREE

1942
THE MOVIE
WORLD MOBILIZES

Humphrey Bogart and Peter Lorre in *All Through the Night* (WB)

Hollywood threw itself into the war effort, demonstrating in the process that patriotism could also be profitable. Paramount recorded profits of $13 million, followed by MGM with $12 million, Twentieth Century-Fox with $10.5 million and Warner Brothers with $8.5 million. Films were seen as a powerful instrument of national policy, and the major studios remained relatively unaffected by wartime shortages. In return they willingly submitted to the Office of War Information's guidelines on how best to present the various aspects of the war on the screen.

Initially the results were neither very thoughtful nor very original. Stock themes were rapidly manipulated into wartime settings of varying degrees of plausibility and tricked out at appropriate moments with lengthy anti-Nazi speeches. In Warner Brothers' *All Through the Night*, Humphrey Bogart played a New York mobster, 'Gloves' Donohue, who rounds up a gang of Nazi saboteurs led by Peter Lorre and Conrad Veidt. In *Sherlock Holmes and the Voice of Terror* Universal updated Conan Doyle's *His Last Bow* to the second World War, unleashing Basil Rathbone's aquiline master sleuth on a nest of enemy agents. In the Republic Western *Valley of Hunted Men*, The Three Mesquiteers (Bob Steele, Tom Tyler and Jimmie Dodd) saved a vital formula from falling into enemy hands.

The Hollywood backlots swarmed with spies and secret agents. In Universal's *The Invisible Agent,* jauntily scripted by Curt Siodmak, Jon Hall was the transparent spy, parachuting into Berlin, foiling Sir Cedric Hardwicke's plans to invade America, and driving dastardly Japanese assassin Peter Lorre to commit hara-kiri. Cultured Japanese agent Sydney Greenstreet lost his nerve when contemplating a similar fate in *Across the Pacific,* when his plans to block the Panama Canal ended in ruins. Directed by John Huston and starring Humphrey Bogart and Mary Astor, this efficient Warners' thriller has something of the feel of *The Maltese Falcon*. Its original location had been Hawaii, but the Japanese attacked Pearl Harbor during

Nigel Bruce and Basil Rathbone in *Sherlock Holmes and the Voice of Terror* (Univ)

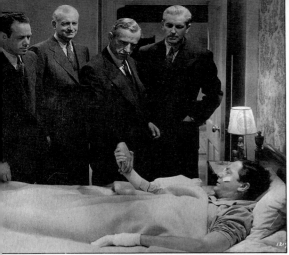

Harvey Stephens, Russell Hicks, Jonathan Hale, William Forrest and Robert Young in *Joe Smith, American* (GB *Highway to Freedom*) (MGM)

Greer Garson

Teresa Wright

filming, obliging Warners to shift the action south of the border. The honour of being the first film to incorporate the attack on Pearl Harbor into its storyline went to an MGM B feature, *A Yank on the Burma Road* (GB *China Caravan*), in which New York taxi driver Barry Nelson led a caravan of medical supplies to China.

Alfred Hitchcock directed *Saboteur* for Universal, a bravura chase thriller, full of quirky touches, in which munitions worker Robert Cummings played the fall guy in a fifth columnist plot.

In the same mould was *Joe Smith, American* (GB *Highway to Freedom*,) in which aircraft mechanic Robert Young's knowledge of a secret bombsight condemns him to torture at the hands of Nazi agents. Air plant workers did not normally lead such hazardous lives. Warners' *Wings for the Eagle* was set in the giant Lockheed plant in California, with 'Oomph Girl' Ann Sheridan providing a wisecracking distraction from the hardware on display.

MGM channelled the upsurge of sentiment towards the British into *Mrs Miniver,* directed by William Wyler, which within five weeks of its opening had been seen by over 1.5 million people. In North America it took $6 million, making it the highest-grossing film up to that time. *Mrs Miniver* swept the board at the Academy awards, where it took the Oscars for Best Film, Best Director, Best Actress (Greer Garson), Best Supporting Actress (Teresa Wright), Best Screenplay from Another Source (Arthur Wimperis and James Hilton, among others) and Cinematography (Joseph Ruttenberg).

Mrs Miniver is an artfully glossy Hollywood fantasy of a middle-class Albion – full of flower shows, comic servants and crusty aristocrats with hearts of gold. Greer Garson's Mrs M reads *Alice in Wonderland* to the children in their air raid shelter and pluckily rounds up a downed German flier (Helmut Dantine) in her garden. Walter Pidgeon's tweedily reliable Mr M sucks his pipe gravely and sails his little boat across the Channel to rescue British soldiers from the beaches at Dunkirk. The film ends in the bombed village church with RAF bombers roaring overhead and 'Land of Hope and Glory' thundering over the soundtrack.

Combat features too, found it difficult to struggle free from cardboard cut-out images of war. In Warners' *Captains of the Clouds* James Cagney was a bumptious recruit to the Royal Canadian Air Force, who proves his mettle under fire before making the inevitable act of self-sacrifice. In Universal's *Eagle Squadron,* a baby-faced Robert Stack, Eddie Albert and Jon Hall were Yanks in the RAF, hijacking a Nazi mystery 'plane from a French air base. John Wayne growled his way through Republic's *Flying Tigers*, a tribute to the volunteer US pilots who had joined the Chinese fight against Japan before Pearl Harbor. Warners' *Desperate Journey* plumbed depths of implausibility as Errol Flynn led a group of downed airmen across Occupied Europe.

At this stage in the war the Japanese were still gorging

themselves on victory in the Pacific, a grim fact recognized in Paramount's *Wake Island,* directed by John Farrow. This was a relatively sober attempt to tell the story of a heavily outnumbered Marine garrison holding a former Pan American fuelling base. *Wake Island* had its share of stereotypes and clichés but it established one of the abiding motifs of the Second World War combat film: a disparate group of men bonded together by common adversity and a yearning for a fondly remembered civilian life.

Michèle Morgan and Paul Henreid made their Hollywood debuts in RKO's *Joan of Paris,* a Resistance drama, which also featured Alan Ladd in a small role as an RAF airman. The most acutely observed war film of 1942 – and the most controversial – was Ernst Lubitsch's *To Be Or Not To Be,* starring Jack Benny and Carole Lombard as a husband-and-wife acting team, Joseph and Maria Tura, who use their wits and stage skills to outwit the Gestapo in Occupied Poland. Critics, unnerved by this biting burlesque, accused the film of gross tastelessness.

To Be Or Not To Be's release was accompanied by extremely hostile press notices but was overshadowed by the death of Lombard, killed in an air crash on a war bonds tour. She was irreplaceable. Her death was an emotional shock for millions. Her husband Clark Gable, whom she had married in 1939, was never the same man again.

Meanwhile Warners had a lucky escape. They had lined up Dennis Morgan and Ann Sheridan to star in an espionage melodrama based on an unproduced play, *Everybody Goes to Rick's.* Before the cameras rolled a number of other players floated in and out of the frame, among them Ronald Reagan, George Raft and Hedy Lamarr. Happily for posterity 'Rick's Café Americain' was presided over by Humphrey Bogart and the film – *Casablanca* directed by Michael Curtiz – became arguably the studio's most enduring legacy.

Bogart was the disillusioned gun runner Rick Blaine, an idealist turned cynical Casablanca nightclub owner, still haunted by a bitter-sweet Paris romance with Ingrid Bergman. Now the wife of Resistance hero Victor Laszlo (Paul Henreid), she walks into Rick's and persuades a reluctant Dooley Wilson to play 'As Time Goes By', a request calculated to bring a tremor even to Bogie's legendary stiff upper lip. Swirling around the starcrossed lovers are enough subplots and salty character actors to sustain at least half-a-dozen lesser movies: Peter Lorre as the cringing little black marketeer Ugarté; Claude Rains as the dapper amoral French Chief of Police, Conrad Veidt's thin-lipped Nazi emissary Major Strasser; and Sydney Greenstreet's Senor Ferrari, the acceptable face of corruption, basking in the shadows of the Blue Parrot Café. Time has gone by, but has done nothing to dim the brilliance of *Casablanca's* ensemble playing.

Spencer Tracy and Katharine Hepburn began a magical screen partnership at MGM in George Stevens' *Woman of the*

Arthur Kennedy, Errol Flynn and Ronald Reagan in *Desperate Journey* (WB)

Robert Stack and Carole Lombard in *To Be Or Not To Be* (UA)

Paul Henreid, Ingrid Bergman and Humphrey Bogart in *Casablanca* (WB)

Spencer Tracy in *Woman of the Year* (MGM)

Bette Davis and Paul Henreid in *Now Voyager* (WB)

Gary Cooper

Year. He is a grizzled sports writer, she is a briskly omniscient political pundit, an urbane combination of opposites which approximately reflected their off-screen personalities.

MGM had originally slated Tracy for *Random Harvest*, adapted from James Hilton's novel. But Ronald Colman took the role of the amnesiac ex-serviceman who contrives to marry Greer Garson twice. This was romance at its most glutinous, and set in an English never-never land which made *Mrs Miniver* look like a masterpiece of documentary realism. But its absurdities were smoothed away by Colman's tact, timing and incomparable restraint, a remarkable feat of legerdemain which won him an Oscar nomination and re-established him as a major star.

Bette Davis wallowed in the wish-fulfilment of *Now Voyager,* directed by Irving Rapper, in which she played a dowdy, disturbed spinster transformed by psychiatrist Claude Rains into the chic recipient of Paul Henreid's lighted cigarettes.   A new star emerged in the form of tiny, glacial Alan Ladd, locked in the miniature blonde embrace of Veronica Lake in Paramount's *This Gun for Hire,* directed by Frank Tuttle. In one of those occasional strokes of haphazard Hollywood flair, Ladd was perfectly cast as Graham Greene's feline, unsmiling killer, carrying himself with a slender ferocity which marked him out as the first Hollywood actor to portray a gunman as a cold angel. Paramount immediately rushed Ladd and Lake into *The Glass Key,* a pacy adaptation of a Dashiell Hammett thriller, in which her sultry, teasing style - emphasized by her peek-a-boo hairstyle – neatly complemented his coolly underplayed tough guy persona.

At the age of 30 Gene Kelly made a comparatively late start in movies after starring on Broadway in 'Pal Joey'. MGM cast him as a similar heel-hero in Busby Berkeley's *For Me and My Gal,* a sentimental stroll through vaudeville's memory lane animated by the charming rapport between Kelly and his co-star Judy Garland.

MGM star Norma Shearer made her last film, *Her Card-board Lover,* a title which might have referred to the less than supple acting talents of co-star Robert Taylor. Singing cowboy Gene Autry left Republic for the Army, ceding top-spot on the backlot to Roy Rogers.

RKO's *Pride of the Yankees,* a Sam Goldwyn production directed by Sam Wood, starred Gary Cooper as Lou Gehrig, the New York Yankee first baseman felled by an incurable disease. A crucial film in the Cooper canon of shy, self-effacing heroes, it concluded with Gehrig's moving speech to his fans: 'People all say I've had a bad break. But today – today I consider myself the luckiest man on the face of the Earth'. Luck ran out for Orson Welles. His adaptation of a Booth Tarkington family saga, *The Magnificent Ambersons*, was mangled by RKO and released on a double bill with *Mexican Spitfire Sees A Ghost.*

Jean Gabin made his Hollywood debut in Twentieth Cen-

Jean Gabin and Claude Rains in *Moon Tide* (Fox)

tury-Fox's *Moontide,* a fog-bound waterfront melodrama in which director Archie Mayo tried hard to echo Gabin's pre-war triumph in *Quai des Brumes* (US *Port of Shadows*) (1938). In RKO's *The Falcon's Brother,* suave Tom Conway stepped into the shoes of his real-life brother George Sanders, as the elegant ladies' man sleuth The Falcon.

After completing *Somewhere I'll Find You,* co-starring Lana Turner, Clark Gable followed James Stewart into the USAAF (United States Army Air Force). Swimming star Esther Williams made her debut opposite Mickey Rooney in *Andy Hardy's Double Life.*

Billy Wilder made his solo directing debut at Paramount with *The Major and the Minor,* in which Ginger Rogers' unconventional bid to avoid paying a train fare led to romantic complications with Ray Milland. She also appeared in RKO's *Once Upon A Honeymoon* and Twentieth Century-Fox's *Tales of Manhattan.* She confirmed her talent as a comedienne in *Roxie Hart,* (Fox) a much-underrated film directed by William Wellman, playing a brassy Jazz Age showgirl who confesses to a murder as a publicity stunt.

Jane Randolph and Tom Conway in *The Falcon's Brother* (RKO)

Fred Zinnemann made a striking directorial debut at MGM with a polished B movie, *Kid Glove Killer,* starring Van Heflin. Preston Sturges continued his triumphant progress with *The Palm Beach Story,* a deliciously amoral marital comedy, starring Claudette Colbert and Joel McCrea. Bing Crosby crooned 'Moonlight Becomes You' – one of his biggest hits – in Paramount's *Road to Morocco.*

Curvaceous Maria Montez launched her brief career as a star in Universal's *Arabian Nights,* the studio's first three-colour Technicolor production. Hedy Lamarr provided a heady dose of exotica in MGM's *White Cargo,* playing the dusky South Seas nymphomaniac Tondelayo, slinking all over Walter Pidgeon in her revealing 'lurong'.

Paramount put its back into the war effort with *Star Spangled Rhythm,* a musical showcase for its stars with a patriotic finale in which Bing Crosby sang 'Old Glory'. Classier fare was provided by Fred Astaire and Rita Hayworth in Columbia's *You Were Never Lovelier.* And indeed Rita never was as she danced 'I'm Old Fashioned' with Fred across a romantically moonlit terrace.

Hedy Lamarr

George M Cohan

Paramount's *The Fleet's In* launched newcomer Betty Hutton, singing 'Build a Better Mousetrap'. Then the studio paired Crosby and Astaire for the first time in Mark Sandrich's *Holiday Inn,* a huge hit which gave Bing the chance to warble 'White Christmas'.

1942 saw the death of George M Cohan, the ultra-patriotic song-and-dance man on whose life Warner's had based their fabulous success *Yankee Doodle Dandy,* starring James Cagney. Other deaths that year were those of Buck Jones, killed in the Coconut Grove Club fire in Boston and John Barrymore.

The changing mood of the British people in wartime was caught by Noel Coward's *In Which We Serve,* (Two Cities) which he wrote, produced and co-directed with David Lean.

HMS *Torrin* sinks in *In Which We Serve* (TC)

Noel Coward star of *In Which We Serve* (TC)

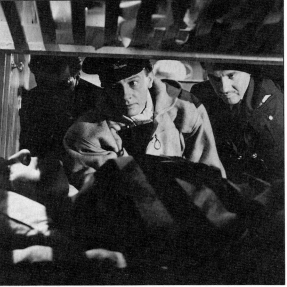

Roland Culver and Eric Portman in *One of Our Aircraft is Missing* (BN)

Using a flashback framework, *In Which We Serve* tells the story of a warship, *HMS Torrin,* from her commissioning, through action in the North Sea and at Dunkirk to her sinking during the evacuation of Crete. *In Which We Serve* broke new ground by devoting equal time to officers and men. Previously it had been the latter lived and died conveniently offscreen while the officers got on with the heroics. The film remains very conscious of class distinctions but nevertheless presents *HMS Torrin* as a community working together for the same end, like the nation. British National's *One Of Our Aircraft is Missing* was a Powell and Pressburger film which also showed how people from different classes were living and fighting together.

Thorold Dickinson's *Next of Kin* rammed home the wartime message that 'Careless Talk Costs Lives'. A series of casual indiscretions enables the Germans to piece together the details of a British commando raid on the French coast. They are waiting when the raid goes in, and the commandos suffer heavy casualties. By sheer coincidence, Churchill was given a screening of the film two weeks before the raid on St. Nazaire. He noted with alarm that in *Next of Kin* an officer indicates a spot on the map of France not far from St Nazaire. He ordered the film to be withdrawn until after the raid and insisted that when it was released fewer British casualties should be shown.

In 1942, France produced two of the most notable films of the Occupation, *L'Eternel Retour* (GB *Love Eternal,* US *The Eternal Return*) and *Les Visiteurs du Soir* (*The Devil's Envoys*). The first, written by Jean Cocteau and directed by Jean Delannoy, was a version of the story of Tristan and Isolde, revamped to provide a showcase for Cocteau's close friend Jean Marais.

The pressures of censorship channeled the efforts of many French film-makers into politically neutral 'poetic romanticism'. Set in the Middle Ages, *Les Visiteurs du Soir* was a guarded allegory of the Occupation in which the Devil (Jules Berry) despatches two emissaries (Arletty and Alain Cuny) to make mischief at a feast, only to find his evil designs thwarted by the course of true love.

This kind of fantasy was greatly influenced by the costume epics of the Italian director Alessandro Blasetti. In complete contrast was Luchino Visconti's first film, *Ossessione,* based on James C Cain's thriller *The Postman Always Rings Twice* and filmed in the bleak marshy flatlands of the Ferrarese region in northern Italy. Massimo Girotti was the drifter who finds casual work with a couple who run a roadhouse, seduces the young wife (Clara Calamai) and is then drawn into a plot to kill her middle-aged husband. This was a deliberate gesture of defiance against the Fascist regime, which had fatuously banned criminal activity and sexual immorality from the screen on the grounds that the government had brought an end to these social evils. *Ossessione* has often been hailed as the first example of what later became known as neo-realism. In truth, it was the most outstanding of a number of films of the period which drew their inspiration from everyday settings and emphasized sexual candour.

Errol Flynn in *They Died With Their Boots On* (WB)

James Cagney in *Captains of the Clouds* (WB)

Stan Laurel in *A-Haunting We Will Go* (Fox)

Bruce Cabot and Priscilla Lane in *Silver Queen* (UA)

Three weeks before the start of a new year, Japan struck a deadly blow at Pearl Harbour and the war was now world-wide. Britain was already producing war films such as *One of Our Aircraft is Missing* (BN) and Hollywood was also now clearing the flight decks for action.

Esther Howard, Bob Hope and Madeleine Carroll in *My Favourite Blonde* (Par)

Vera Vague, Broderick Crawford, Ed Brophy, Edward G Robinson, Jack Carson and Jane Wyman in *Larceny Inc* (WB)

Ida Lupino and Monty Woolley in *Life Begins at Eight-Thirty* (GB *The Light of Heart*) (Fox)

◁ Cary Grant and Ginger Rogers in *Once Upon A Honeymoon* (RKO)

Jack Carson, Olivia de Havilland and Henry Fonda in *The Male Animal* (WB)

Richard Haydn, Betty Field, Phillip Terry, Patricia Morison, Ray Milland and Leif ▽ Erickson in *Are Husbands Necessary?* (Par)

Marsha Hunt, Kathryn Grayson and Van Heflin in *Seven Sweethearts* (MGM)

Fay Bainter and Clem Bevans in *Mrs Wiggs of the Cabbage Patch* (Par)

Spencer Tracy in *Woman of the Year* (MGM)

Humphrey Bogart and Ingrid Bergman in *Casablanca* (WB)

Alan Ladd and Helen Walker in *Lucky Jordan* (Par)

Robert Stack and Broderick Crawford in *Men of Texas* (Univ)

Bernard Miles, Eric Portman and Hugh Burden in *One of Our Aircraft Is Missing* (BN)

Preston Foster and Gene Tierney in *Thunder Birds* (Fox)
◁ Richard Quine and Rosalind Russell in *My Sister Eileen* (Col)

Spencer Tracy and Richard Whorf in *Keeper of the Flame* (MGM)
▽ Helen Parrish and John Wayne in *In Old California* (Rep)

▽ Melvyn Douglas, Norma Shearer and Gail Patrick in *We Were Dancing* (MGM)

1

2

3

4

5

6

7

1. Virginia Bruce
2. Otto Kruger
3. Nils Asther
4. Celia Johnson
5. Harold Huber
6. Humphrey Bogart in *All Through the Night* (WB)
7. Tina Thayer and Rick Vallin in *Secrets of a Co-Ed* (PRC)
8. Alan Baxter (l) and Ernest Dorian (r) in *Prisoner of Japan* (PRC)
9. Ilona Massey
10. Lena Horne in *Panama Hattie* (MGM)
11. James Gleason in *My Gal Sal* (Fox)
12. Joe Sawyer and William Tracy in *About Face* (UA)

8

9

10
▷◁
11

12
▷

1

2

3

4

5

6

In the last month of 1942, cinema audiences were regaled for the first time with *Casablanca,* one of Hollywoods 'Greats'. Michael Curtiz, the director, managed to assemble a splendid cast of actors with Humphrey Bogart turning in one of his finest performances as Rick Blaine, a disenchanted ex-arms smuggler, determined if possible now to stay on the right side of the law. Will anyone who has seen the film ever forget Dooley Wilson's rendering of 'As Time Goes By'? *Casablanca* took the 1943 Oscar awards for Best Film, Best Direction and Best Screenplay.

◁ 7

8

9

10

11

12

◁13

14

1. Lana Turner
2. Jeff Corey, Dorothy Granger, Monte Blue, Evelyn Ankers, Andy Devine and Keye Luke in *North to the Klondike* (Univ)
3. Henry Wilcoxon in *Lady Hamilton* (US *That Hamilton Woman*) (LF)
4. Vivien Leigh and Laurence Olivier in *Lady Hamilton* (US *That Hamilton Woman*) (LF)
5. James Mason and Joyce Howard in *The Night Has Eyes* (US *Terror House*) (ABPC)
6. Dan Dailey, Grace McDonald and Charles Butterworth in *Give Out, Sisters* (Univ)
7. Hugh Burden, Hay Petrie (st. with pipe), Pamela Brown and Eric Portman in *One of our Aircraft is Missing* (BN)
8. Celia Johnson in *In Which We Serve* (TC)
9. Yvonne De Carlo

9 ▷

1. Clifford Severn, Hans Schumm, John Beal (std) and Victor Kilian in *Atlantic Convoy* (Col)
2. Hugh Williams and Patricia Medina in *The Day Will Dawn* (US *The Avengers*) (NF)
3. Humphrey Bogart and Mary Astor in *Across the Pacific* (WB)
4. Alan Mowbray, Douglas Fowley and Marjorie Woodworth in *The Devil With Hitler* (UA)
5. Fred MacMurray.
6. Macdonald Carey
7. Reginald Denny
8. Katharine Hepburn (st) in *Woman of the Year* (MGM)
9. Richard Barthelmess
10. Katharine Hepburn in *Woman of the Year* (MGM)
11. Spencer Tracy in *Woman of the Year* (MGM)

10
▷ ◁
▷ ◁
11

113

1. Raymond Massey (I) and Robert Preston in *Reap the Wild Wind* (Par)
2. Lorna Gray
3. Paulette Goddard in *Reap the Wild Wind* (Par)
4. John Wayne and Randolph Scott in *The Spoilers* (Univ)
5. Ruth Hussey and Bruce Cabot in *Pierre of the Plains* (MGM)
6. Reginald Owen in *Reunion* (MGM)
7. James Dunn
8. Anne Revere
9. Lewis Howard
10. Henry Fonda and Gene Tierney in *Rings On Her Fingers* (Fox)
11. Thurston Hall and Frank Albertson in *Shepherd of the Ozarks* (Rep)
12. John Carradine and Tyrone Power in *Son of Fury* (Fox)

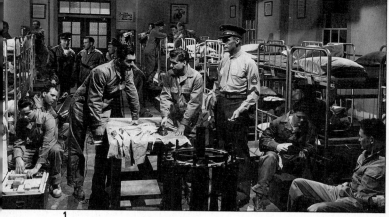

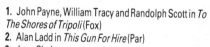

1. John Payne, William Tracy and Randolph Scott in *To The Shores of Tripoli* (Fox)
2. Alan Ladd in *This Gun For Hire* (Par)
3. June Clyde
4. Charles Butterworth
5. John Payne and Betty Grable in *Springtime in the Rockies* (Fox)
6. Minna Gombell
7. Cesar Romero and Betty Grable in *Springtime in the Rockies* (Fox)
8. Betty Rhodes
9. John Kimbrough and Paul Hurst in *Sundown Jim* (Fox)
10. Leo Carrillo, Dan Dailey, Marjorie Lord and Andy Devine in *Timber* (Univ)
11. Victor Jory, Edgar Buchanan and Richard Dix in *The Town Too Tough To Die* (Par)

11 ▷

1

2

3

4

5

6

7

8

1. Alexis Smith
2. Ray Milland
3. Greer Garson
4. Ann Rutherford
5. Mona Maris
6. Ludwig Donath
7. Ann Dvorak
8. Hillary Brooke
9. Edmund Lowe
10. Joan Davis
11. Rosemary Lane
12. Cornel Wilde

9

10

11

12 ▷

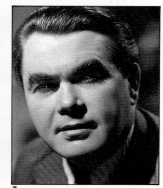

1. Wallace Beery in *Jackass Mail* (MGM)
2. Marjorie Main, William Haade, Wallace Beery and Esther Howard in *Jackass Mail* (MGM)
3. Hedy Lamarr in *White Cargo* (MGM)
4. Barbara Britton, Fay Bainter and John Archer in *Mrs Wiggs of the Cabbage Patch* (Par)
5. Anne Nagel
6. Franchot Tone and Allyn Joslyn (r) in *The Wife Takes a Flyer* (GB *A Yank in Dutch*) (Col)
7. Oscar Homolka
8. John Howard and Heather Angel in *The Undying Monster* (GB *The Hammond Mystery*) (Fox)
9. Irving Bacon
10. Irving Bacon, Robert Wilde, Jane Withers and Ben Carter in *Young America* (Fox)
11. Lou Costello, Bud Abbott and Patric Knowles in *Who Done It?* (Univ)

10
▷
11

1. Ian Wolfe
2. Nelson Eddy and Jeanette MacDonald in *I Married An Angel* (MGM)
3. Reginald Owen in *I Married An Angel* (MGM)
4. Queenie Leonard and Eddie Albert in *Eagle Squadron* (Univ)
5. Frederick Valk and Lilli Palmer in *Thunder Rock* (CF)
6. Katherine DeMille
7. Lilli Palmer
8. Mickey Rooney, Cecilia Parker, Lewis Stone, Fay Holden and Sara Haden in *The Courtship of Andy Hardy* (MGM)
9. Edmond O'Brien in *Powder Town* (RKO)
10. Pat O'Brien, Glenn Ford, William Forrest and Jonathan Hale in *Flight Lieutenant* (Col)
11. Lionel Atwill (r) in *Cairo* (MGM)

1. Richard Fraser, John Loder, Marian Hall and Lumsden Hare in *The Gorilla Man* (WB)

2. Olivia de Havilland, Bette Davis and John Hamilton in *In This Our Life* (WB)

3. Julie Bishop, Tom Stevenson, Ruth Ford, Roland Drew, Frank Wilcox and Marian Hall in *The Hidden Hand* (WB)

4. Diana Lewis, Guy Kibbee, Celia Travers, Red Skelton, Ann Rutherford, Rags Ragland and George Bancroft in *Whistling In Dixie* (MGM)

5. Fay McKenzie, Gene Autry, Smiley Burnette and Cecil Cunningham in *Cowboy Serenade* (Rep)

6. Brian Donlevy, Janet Blair, Sig Arno and Pat O'Brien in *Two Yanks in Trinidad* (Col)

7. Bela Lugosi and Joan Barclay in *Black Dragons* (MoP)

8. Donald Mayo (Boy), Larry 'Buster' Crabbe, Rochelle Hudson, Milt Kibbee and Vince Barnett in *Queen of Broadway* (PRC)

9. Mary Howard, Donald Woods and Jerome Cowan in *Through Different Eyes* (Fox)

10. Kay Harris, Edward Norris and George McKay in *Sabotage Squad* (Col)

11. Sidney Miller, Huntz Hall, Leo Gorcey, Douglas Fowley and the East Side Kids in *Mr Wise Guy* (MoP)

12. Don Terry, Lionel Royce, Frederick Giermann, Irene Hervey, Leo Carrillo and Turhan Bey in *Unseen Enemy* (Univ)

13. Jackie Cooper and Bonita Granville in *Syncopation* (RKO)

14. Gail Patrick and Richard Denning in *Quiet Please, Murder* (Fox)

15. Burgess Meredith and Claire Trevor in *Street of Chance* (Par)

1

2

3 4

5

6

1. Ann Gillis in *Tough As They Come* (Univ)
2. Billy Halop and Paul Kelly in *Tough As They Come* (Univ)
3. Peter Lorre
4. Albert Lieven
5. Kay Kyser
6. Deborah Kerr
7. Elizabeth Allan in *The Great Mr Handel* (IP)
8. Charles Laughton, Jon Hall, Jody Gilbert and Ernie Adams in *The Tuttles of Tahiti* (RKO)
9. Clark Gable in *Somewhere I'll Find You* (MGM)
10. Richard Arlen and Dick Purcell in *Torpedo Boat* (Par)
11. Sen Yung and Sidney Toler in *Castle In The Desert* (Fox)

7

8

9

10
11

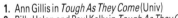

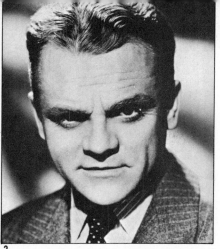

1. William Boyd in *Undercover Man* (UA)
2. James Cagney
3. Adele Mara
4. John Sutton
5. Janis Carter in *Girl Trouble* (Fox)
6. Spencer Tracy
7. *Yankee Doodle Dandy* (WB)
8. James Cagney and Joan Leslie in *Yankee Doodle Dandy* (WB)
9. Patricia Medina
10. Michael 'Sunset' Carson
11. Bette Davis and Paul Henreid in *Now Voyager* (WB)

◁ 8

9

10

11 ▷

1

2

4

3

6

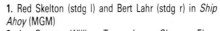

9

8

1. Red Skelton (stdg l) and Bert Lahr (stdg r) in *Ship Ahoy* (MGM)

2. Joe Sawyer, William Tracy, James Gleason, Elyse Knox and Noah Beery Jr in *Hay Foot* (UA)

3. Freddie Mercer, Jane Darwell, Roddy McDowall, Katharine Alexander and Don Douglas in *On the Sunny Side* (Fox)

4. Corinna Mura, Edmund Lowe and Marion Martin in *Call Out the Marines* (RKO)

5. Jack La Rue, Richard Deane and Mary Hull in *Swamp Woman* (PRC)

6. Bobby Breen, Jane Withers and Patrick Brook in *Johnny Doughboy* (Rep)

7. Joseph Cotten, Everett Sloane (c) and Ruth Warrick in *Journey Into Fear* (RKO)

8. Elyse Knox and Don Terry in *Top Sergeant* (Univ)

9. Edward Norris, Nell O'Day and Maria Ouspenskaya in *The Mystery of Marie Roget* (Univ)

10. Neil Hamilton, George Davis and Joyce Compton in *Too Many Women* (PRC)

11. Florence Rice and Jackie Gleason in *Tramp, Tramp, Tramp* (Col)

12. Robert Sterling and Ann Rutherford in *This Time For Keeps* (MGM)

13. Jerry Colonna, Johnny Johnston, Vera Vague and Betty Rhodes in *Priorities on Parade* (Par)

14. Chick Chandler and Gale Storm in *Rhythm Parade* (MoP)

15. Ray Corrigan (in gorilla costume) and Anne Gwynne in *The Strange Case of Doctor RX* (Univ)

16. Van Heflin, Lee Bowman, Marsha Hunt and Cliff Clark in *Kid Glove Killer* (MGM)

14
▷

▷
15

16
▷

Ray Milland and Paulette Goddard in *Reap the Wild Wind* (Par)

A scene from *Bambi* © 1942 Walt Disney Company

1

2

3

1. Spencer Tracy, Allen Jenkins, Frank Morgan and John Qualen in *Tortilla Flat* (MGM)
2. Roy Rogers, Linda Hayes and George 'Gabby' Hayes in *South of Santa Fe* (Rep)
3. Bob Nolan (l) and Roy Rogers (r) in *Man from Cheyenne* (Rep)
4. Tom Tyler, Rufe Davis and Bob Steele in *Code of the Outlaw* (Rep)
5. Fred Burns, Roy Rogers and George 'Gabby' Hayes in *Sunset on the Desert* (Rep)
6. Marjorie Manners, George Chesebro and Bill (Cowboy Rambler) Boyd in *Tumbleweed Trail* (PRC)
7. Gene Autry and James Seay in *Home In Wyomin'* (Rep)
8. John King, David Sharpe and Max Terhune in *Trail Riders* (MoP)
9. George Chesebro, Ray Corrigan and Ted Mapes in *Thunder River Feud* (MoP)
10. Don Barry and Lynn Merrick in *Jesse James Jr* (Rep)
11. Al 'Fuzzy' St John, Don Barry and Lynn Merrick in *Arizona Terror* (Rep)
12. Andy Devine
13. Ruth Hussey, Evelyn Ankers, Phil Brown, Pat McVey, John Carroll, Bruce Cabot and Sheldon Leonard (on floor) in *Pierre of the Plains* (MGM)
14. Walter Catlett, Warren William, Constance Bennett and Ward Bond in *Wild Bill Hickok Rides* (WB)

4

5

6

7

8

9

12

11

10

13

14

1

2

3

4

5

6

7

8

9

10

1. Lydia Bilbrook, Elizabeth Risdon, Leon Errol and Walter Reed in *Mexican Spitfire's Elephant* (RKO)
2. Simone Simon and Kent Smith in *Cat People* (RKO)
3. S Z Sakall, Pat O'Brien and Anne Gwynne in *Broadway* (Univ)
4. Robert Paige and Gloria Jean in *Get Hep To Love* (Univ)
5. Kay Francis, Robert Cummings, Diana Barrymore and John Boles in *Between Us Girls* (Univ)
6. John Boles in *Road to Happiness* (MoP)
7. Eddie Bracken and June Preisser in *Sweater Girl* (Par)
8. John Litel, William Gargan and Margaret Lindsay in *A Desperate Chance for Ellery Queen* (Col)
9. (Std l to r) Buddy Ebsen, Dorothy Lovett, Patsy Kelly and Bert Lahr in *Sing Your Worries Away* (RKO)
10. Hugh Herbert, Mischa Auer, Robert Paige and Jane Frazee in *Don't Get Personal* (Univ)
11. Phil Brown, Donna Reed, Lionel Barrymore and Philip Dorn in *Calling Dr Gillespie* (MGM)
12. Richard Arlen, Arline Judge and Arthur Hunnicutt in *Wildcat* (Par)
13. Walter Sande, Richard Lane, Chester Morris and George E Stone in *Boston Blackie Goes to Hollywood* (Col)
14. George Murphy and Carole Landis in *The Powers Girl* (UA)
15. Bonita Granville and James Craig in *Seven Miles from Alcatraz* (RKO)
16. Ronald Colman and Jean Arthur in *The Talk of the Town* (Col)

11

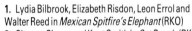

12

15

13

14

16 ▷

Rafael Sabatini, who wrote *Captain Blood*, also penned another rousing book about the pirates of the Spanish Main. This was *The Black Swan*, in which that roistering buccaneer Henry Morgan played a big part. Twentieth Century-Fox filmed the book in Technicolor, with Tyrone Power as the swashbuckling hero and Laird Cregar as Morgan. The movie was an all-round success, one of the best of its genre.

1. Edward Ashley and Maureen O'Hara
2. Laird Cregar
3. Maureen O'Hara and Tyrone Power
4. Tyrone Power and Thomas Mitchell
5. Tyrone Power
6. Tyrone Power, Laird Cregar, Thomas Mitchell and Maureen O'Hara
7. George Zucco and Tyrone Power
8. Tyrone Power, Anthony Quinn, George Sanders, Laird Cregar and Thomas Mitchell

8 ▷

1

2

3

4

5

6

7

8

9

10

128

11

12

13

14

15

16

1. Lynn Bari, Joseph Allen Jr and Mary Beth Hughes in *The Night Before the Divorce* (Fox)
2. Preston Foster, Leo Carrillo and Richard Dix in *American Empire* (UA)
3. John Payne, Betty Grable and Jimmy Gleason in *Footlight Serenade* (Fox)
4. Fred MacMurray, Paulette Goddard and Susan Hayward in *The Forest Rangers* (Par)
5. Andy Devine, Don Terry and Leo Carrillo in *Danger in the Pacific* (Univ)
6. Dick Foran and Carol Bruce in *Behind the Eight Ball* (Univ)
7. William Demarest and The Ritz Brothers in *Behind the Eight Ball* (Univ)
8. Harry Morgan, George Montgomery and Ann Rutherford in *Orchestra Wives* (Fox)
9. George Murphy (l) Richard Barthelmess and Rex Downing (r) in *The Mayor of 44th Street* (RKO)
10. Turhan Bey, Lloyd Corrigan and William Gargan in *Bombay Clipper* (Univ)
11. Sabu in *Arabian Nights* (Univ)
12. Jon Hall, Leif Erickson and Maria Montez in *Arabian Nights* (Univ)
13. Ann Sheridan and Jack Benny in *George Washington Slept Here* (WB)
14. Nat Pendleton, Elisabeth Risdon and Robert Paige in *Jail House Blues* (Univ)
15. Jean Gabin and Ida Lupino in *Moontide* (Fox)
16. Robert Cummings and Priscilla Lane in *Saboteur* (Univ)
17. Richard Whorf, Gene Lockhart and Alan Hale in *Juke Girl* (WB)
18. Arline Judge and John King in *Law of the Jungle* (MoP)
19. Dean Jagger in *The Omaha Trail* (MGM)
20. Guy Kibbee and Shirley Temple in *Miss Annie Rooney* (UA)

17

18

19

20

129

1

2

3

4

5

6

7

9

8

11

10

13

1. Walter Woolf King
2. Norman Willis (in doorway), George Eldredge, Jan Wiley, Edna Johnson, Paul McVey and James Dunn in *The Living Ghost* (GB *Lend Me Your Ear*) (MoP)
3. William Gargan, Lou Costello, Bud Abbott and William Bendix in *Who Done It?* (Univ)
4. Brenda Marshall, George Brent, Roscoe Karns and Fred Kelsey in *You Can't Escape Forever* (WB)
5. Florence Rice and Tom Brown in *Let's Get Tough* (MoP)
6. Lynn Bari, Leyland Hodgson and Preston Foster in *Secret Agent of Japan* (Fox)
7. Robert Preston and Martha O'Driscoll in *Pacific Blackout* (Par)
8. Stan Laurel and Oliver Hardy in *A-Haunting We Will Go* (Fox)
9. Walter Huston and Gloria Warren in *Always In My Heart* (WB)
10. Carole Landis and Lloyd Nolan in *Manila Calling* (Fox)
11. Adele Mara, Chester Morris and Paul Fix in *Alias Boston Blackie* (Col)
12. The Ink Spots and Robert Paige in *Pardon My Sarong* (Univ)
13. Elizabeth Patterson, Helen Gilbert, Gerald Oliver Smith, Jack Haley and Richard Denning in *Beyond the Blue Horizon* (Par)
14. Glenn Ford

14 ▷

1

2

3

4

5

6

7

1. George 'Gabby' Hayes, Bob Nolan, Hugh Farr, Sally Payne, Carl Farr and Roy Rogers with Trigger in *Romance on the Range* (Rep)

2. Don Barry and Slim Andrews in *The Cyclone Kid* (Rep)

3. Al 'Fuzzy' St John, Lynn Merrick, Robert Kent, Guy Kingsford and Don Barry in *Stagecoach Express* (Rep)

4. Ruth Terry, Bob Nolan, Hugh Farr and Gene Autry in *Call of the Canyon* (Rep)

5. Roy Rogers, Jack Rockwell and Helen Parrish in *Sunset Serenade* (Rep)

6. William 'Wild Bill' Elliott (r) in *The Devil's Trail* (Col)

7. Pat Brady, Roy Rogers and George 'Gabby' Hayes in *Sons of the Pioneers* (Rep)

8. George Houston and I Stanford Jolley in *Border Roundup* (PRC)

9. Ed Cassidy (l), Tom Tyler (r), Bob Steele and Rufe Davis in *The Phantom Plainsmen* (Rep)

10. James Seay, Lorna Gray, Hal Taliaferro and Addison Richards in *Ridin' Down the Canyon* (Rep)

11. Walter Abel, Bing Crosby and Fred Astaire in *Holiday Inn* (Par)

12. Abner Biberman, Brenda Joyce and Preston Foster in *Little Tokio, USA* (Fox)

13. Preston Foster and Patricia Morison in *A Night in New Orleans* (Par)

9

12

8

10

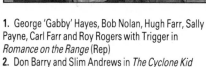

11

13 ▷

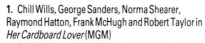

1. Chill Wills, George Sanders, Norma Shearer, Raymond Hatton, Frank McHugh and Robert Taylor in *Her Cardboard Lover* (MGM)

2. Ray Milland, Paulette Goddard and Addison Richards in *The Lady Has Plans* (Par)

3. Dennis Morgan, Jack Carson and Ida Lupino in *The Hard Way* (WB)

4. Lynn Bari and George Montgomery in *China Girl* (Fox)

5. Lionel Barrymore, Van Johnson and Susan Peters in *Dr Gillespie's New Assistant* (MGM)

6. John Wayne, Anna Lee and John Carroll in *Flying Tigers* (Rep)

7. Brian Donlevy and Barbara Stanwyck in *The Great Man's Lady* (Par)

8. Fredric March and Veronica Lake in *I Married a Witch* (UA)

9. Eric Blore, Hillary Brooke and Warren William in *Counter-Espionage* (Col)

10. Marjorie Lord, Frank Puglia, Don Terry, Andy Devine, Leo Carrillo and Chester Gann in *Escape From Hong Kong* (Univ)

11. Lester Matthews and Roddy McDowall in *The Pied Piper* (Fox)

12. Kent Taylor, Jane Wyatt and James Ellison in *Army Surgeon* (RKO)

13. Patricia Dane and John Carroll in *Rio Rita* (MGM)

1. Pat Flaherty, Errol Flynn and James Flavin in *Gentleman Jim* (WB)
2. Ralph Byrd, Sheila Ryan, James Ellison, Virginia Bruce and Aubrey Mather in *Careful, Soft Shoulders* (Fox)
3. Johnny Mack Brown and Fuzzy Knight in *The Boss of Hangtown Mesa* (Univ)
4. Nancy Coleman, Geraldine Fitzgerald and Barbara Stanwyck in *The Gay Sisters* (WB)
5. Kay Linaker, Edward Norris, Ralph Morgan and Margaret Lindsay in *A Close Call for Ellery Queen* (Col)
6. Donald Stewart and Richard Greene in *Flying Fortress* (WB)
7. Robert Frazer, Betty Blythe and Raymond Hatton in *Dawn on the Great Divide* (MoP)
8. Peter Lorre, Jeff Donnell, Boris Karloff and Larry Parks in *The Boogie Man Will Get You* (Col)
9. Hans Conried, Penny Singleton and Arthur Lake in *Blondie's Blessed Event* (Col)
10. James Monks, Jack Briggs, Richard Fraser, Alan Ladd and Paul Henreid in *Joan of Paris* (RKO)
11. Joseph Calleia, Frank Puglia and John Qualen in *The Jungle Book* (UA)
12. Van Heflin and Virginia Grey (I) in *Grand Central Murder* (MGM)
13. Forrest Tucker, John Hubbard, George McKay, Stanley Brown and Chester Morris in *Canal Zone* (Col)

John Garfield, Gig Young, Harry Carey, Murray Alper, Moroni Olsen and George Tobias in *Air Force* (WB)

James Flavin, Paulette Goddard, Bill Goodwin and Claudette Colbert in *So Proudly We Hail* (Par)

Marsha Hunt, Heather Angel and Ann Sothern in *Cry Havoc* (MGM)

In June 1942 the Japanese had suffered their first major defeat, at the Battle of Midway. In the winter of 1942-43 the initiative was wrested from the Axis. In North Africa, Rommel's Afrika Korps was thrown back from the gates of Cairo in the Second Battle of El Alamein. On the Eastern Front a German army was surrounded in the snows of Stalingrad. In the Pacific the US Marines secured Guadalcanal after a struggle of the utmost ferocity, a crucial psychological and material victory over the Japanese.

In Hollywood the number of films dealing either directly or indirectly with the war reached a peak. Combat films moved away from the reinforcement of popular preconceptions to more honest depictions of the realities of battle.

MGM's *Bataan*, directed by Tay Garnett, was a gritty drama, celebrating an American platoon's sacrificial rearguard action during the withdrawal from the Philippines. The group motif loomed large in Twentieth Century-Fox's *Guadalcanal Diary*, a watered-down version of war correspondent Richard Tregaskis' hard-hitting account of one of the Pacific war's most hard-fought campaigns.

The Pacific war took to the air in Warner Brothers' *Air Force*, a $3 million epic directed by Howard Hawks which followed the progress of a B-17 bomber, 'Mary Ann', from her first flight through action in the Philippines and the Battle of the Coral Sea to a battle-damaged landing on an Australian beach.

Two films concentrated on the part played by women in the front line. In Paramount's *So Proudly We Hail*, directed by Mark Sandrich, Veronica Lake, Paulette Goddard and Claudette Colbert were glamorously dishevelled combat nurses on the besieged island fortress of Corregidor. The same theme was taken up by MGM's *Cry Havoc*, directed by Richard Thorpe, whose strong cast included Margaret Sullavan, Joan Blondell, Ann Sothern and Marsha Hunt.

Twentieth Century-Fox focussed on the war at sea in *Crash*

Dive, a submarine drama which was Tyrone Power's last film before he left Hollywood to join the Marines. Universal's *Corvette K-225* (GB *The Nelson Touch*) produced by Howard Hawks and directed by B movie veteran Richard Rosson, was a grimly realistic picture of life aboard a cramped convoy escort and one of the few films of this period accurately to convey the combination of boredom, discomfort and sudden fear which was the lot of servicemen everywhere.

A similar feature was Warners' *Action in the North Atlantic,* set on a Liberty ship whose captain and mate — Raymond Massey and Humphrey Bogart — play a cat-and-mouse game with a U-boat in the chilly waters ploughed by the Arctic convoys.

The action moved to North Africa in Columbia's *Sahara,* directed by Zoltan Korda, in which American sergeant Humphrey Bogart and assorted Tommies defended a desert oasis against a battalion of thirsty Germans.

Paramount cast Erich von Stroheim as General Rommel in Billy Wilder's *Five Graves to Cairo,* in which British agent Franchot Tone cracked the secret of Rommel's vital desert supply dumps. In Twentieth Century-Fox's *The Immortal Sergeant,* Henry Fonda was a Canadian serving with the 8th Army in the Libyan desert whose jellied backbone is stiffened by the rough, tough old sergeant of the title, Thomas Mitchell.

The depiction of 'the nature of the enemy' ranked high in the Office of War Information's guidelines to the Hollywood studios. When dealing with the psychology of Nazism, Hollywood found it all but impossible to resist a mixture of sensationalism and prurience. In Steve Sekely's *Women in Bondage,* shortsighted Nancy Kelly was deemed unfit to marry her Nazi sweetheart and then condemned to enforced sterilization.

Bonita Granville underwent a public flogging in RKO's *Hitler's Children,* directed by Edward Dmytryk.

Universal's *The Strange Death of Adolf Hitler,* was a lurid exploitation melodrama starring Ludwig Donath in the dual role of the Führer and a Viennese double. The latter is shot by his wife Gale Sondergaard, who mistakes him for the real thing. In *Hitler's Madman,* (GB *Hitler's Hangman*) an independent cheapie directed by Douglas Sirk and released by MGM, John Carradine chewed up the flimsy sets as Reinhard Heydrich, Reich Protector of Occupied Czechoslovakia.

A more chilling glimpse of the unspeakable Heydrich — a cruel vignette played entirely in German by Hans von Twardowski — was seen in Fritz Lang's *Hangmen Also Die.* Scripted by Bertolt Brecht, this was the story of the Gestapo terror which followed Heydrich's assassination by Czech patriot Brian Donlevy. The film is notable for having contributed a famous line to the language — 'Ve haf vays of making you talk'.

An attempt to give a more shaded picture of the enemy

Dana Andrews and Tyrone Power in *Crash Dive* (Fox)

Humphrey Bogart and Dane Clark in *Action in the North Atlantic* (WB)

Erich Von Stroheim, Ian Keith and Miles Mander in *Five Graves to Cairo* (Par)

Alan Curtis, John Carradine and Patricia Morison in *Hitler's Madman* (MGM)

Kent Smith, Maureen O'Hara and Charles Laughton in
This Land is Mine (RKO)

Henry Victor, Ann Harding, Walter Huston and Eleanor
Parker in *Mission to Moscow* (WB)

Ann Ayars and Mickey Rooney in *The Human Comedy*
(MGM)

was made in Twentieth Century-Fox's *The Moon is Down*, from John Steinbeck's novel, in which Sir Cedric Hardwicke played a civilized German commander, reluctant to use extreme measures against the inhabitants of a small Norwegian mining village.

Hollywood was also edging towards a more considered approach to the plight of ordinary citizens in Occupied Europe. RKO's *This Land is Mine*, directed by Jean Renoir, ventured into the moral minefield of resistance, passivity in the face of the occupiers, and active collaboration. Charles Laughton was a cowardly, mother-fixated schoolteacher who speaks out against the Nazis when he is tried for a murder of which he is innocent.

However, there was still no shortage of simple-minded cloak-and-dagger actioners set in a fanciful pasteboard Europe, full of sturdy peasants with Bronx accents, furtive collaborators and square-jawed Resistance heroes. The tone of these films was caught in MGM's *Above Suspicion,* in which the redoubtable Joan Crawford resisted Gestapo chief Basil Rathbone's interrogation methods with the stirring cry, 'I've already told you I don't know – and if you bring in Göring, Goebbels and Himmler my answer will still be the same!' Sadly, *Above Suspicion* was the last film made by Conrad Veidt, who died shortly afterwards from a heart attack.

The Soviet Union was now an ally to be saluted rather than a bogeyman to be feared. RKO's *The North Star* (AKA *Armored Attack*) was a big-budget Goldwyn epic, scripted by Lillian Hellman and directed by Lewis Milestone, which narrowed its focus to the tide of war washing over a small Russian village whose inhabitants included such sturdy Soviet peasant types as Anne Baxter, Walter Brennan and (making his debut) Farley Granger.

Warners celebrated the alliance with the Soviet Union in *Mission to Moscow,* based on a book by the former US ambassador to Russia Joseph E Davies. Directed with immense flair by Michael Curtiz, *Mission to Moscow* has few wartime equals for manipulative brilliance but embarrassed the studio in the late 1940s when the political wind changed direction.

The problems of war widows were tackled in RKO's saccharine *Tender Comrade,* in which Ginger Rogers pluckily kept her chin up after husband Robert Ryan's death on the battlefield. Bizarrely, in the late 1940s *Tender Comrade* was seen as dangerous Communist propaganda, principally because Ginger and her colleagues at the Douglas factory pooled their salaries and lived together collectively in a rented house: not the American Way.

The domestic virtues of Middle America were cloyingly hymned in MGM's *The Human Comedy,* based on a story written by William Saroyan and directed with insinuating skill by Clarence Brown. It chronicled the lives, thoughts and emotions of a small-town family, the Macauleys. Even by the standards of Louis B Mayer, sentimentality has seldom been laid on so thick. Alternately beguiling and maddening, this is a fantasy America in which your birthday greetings, or the dreaded War Department telegram, are brought to you by telegraph boy Mickey Rooney and lonely soldiers get taken to the movies by his kindhearted teenage sis, Donna Reed. Rooted more firmly in reality was Columbia's *The More the Merrier,* a charming comedy which cleverly exploited the wartime housing shortage in Washington.

Musicals reached a peak of popularity, and from 1943 accounted for 40 per cent of all production. Warners' contribution to the war effort was *This is the Army,* a tribute to the American soldier based on Irving Berlin's stage smash and containing no fewer than 18 of his songs. It raised nearly $2 million for Army Emergency relief.

The same studio's *Thank Your Lucky Stars,* was a typical wartime divertissement, boasting a star-packed grand finale.

At Twentieth Century-Fox, Busby Berkeley's *The Gang's All Here,* (GB *The Girls He Left Behind*), was his first in colour and Alice Faye's last musical before she retired into motherhood. Loosely built around a war bond fund-raising show, *The Gang's All Here* featured Carmen Miranda singing 'The Lady in the Tutti Frutti Hat' while 60 chorus girls did suggestive things with bananas.

United Artists' *Stage Door Canteen* was a tribute to the American Theatre Wing and its servicemen's entertainment centre in New York. Among the non-stop parade of stars was Katherine Cornell (making her only screen appearance), and Franklin Pangborn and Johnny Weissmuller (in his Tarzan loincloth) lending a hand with the washing up. Twentieth Century-Fox's *Stormy Weather* showcased America's top black artists – an indication of the segregation still enforced in Hollywood – in a revue format tracing the evolution of black music in the 20th century. Lena Horne is unforgettable singing the title song.

Lena Horne also appeared, singing 'Honeysuckle Rose', in *Thousands Cheer,* MGM's big-budget morale-booster in which soldier Gene Kelly was confined to quarters and danced enchantingly with his only companion, a mop.

By 1943 Betty Grable was firmly established as one of the biggest stars on Twentieth Century-Fox's lot, and the favourite pin-up of millions of servicemen. She entered the peak years of her career with *Coney Island,* a typical Fox extravaganza set at the turn of the century, in which she played a singer pursued by Cesar Romero and George Montgomery.

Vincente Minnelli made his directing debut at MGM with *Cabin in the Sky,* an all-black musical fantasy which once again allowed the camera to dwell gloriously on Lena Horne. At Columbia, Gregory Ratoff's *Something To Shout About* marked the debut of a young dancer Lily Norwood (real name Tula Finklea) who subsequently became Cyd Charisse. The Andrews Sisters went to work in a shell factory in Universal's *Swingtime Johnny,* but contrived to make

Lena Horne

Betty Grable

John Bubbles and Ethel Waters in *Cabin in the Sky* (MGM)

Fred Astaire and Joan Leslie in *The Sky's the Limit* (Col)

Rags Ragland (c) and Mickey Rooney in *Girl Crazy* (MGM)

Ingrid Bergman and Gary Cooper in *For Whom the Bell Tolls* (Par)

Irene Dunne and Spencer Tracy in *A Guy Named Joe* (MGM)

more music than munitions. Fred Astaire sang 'One For My Baby (And One More For the Road)' in *The Sky's the Limit*, playing an incognito fighter ace who falls for Joan Leslie. Mickey Rooney and Judy Garland were joyously teamed for the eighth time in MGM's *Girl Crazy,* joining forces with Tommy Dorsey and his Orchestra for the 'I Got Rhythm' finale.

Hollywood's continuing ambivalence about the earlier conflict in Spain was demonstrated in Paramount's *For Whom the Bell Tolls*, directed by Sam Wood and starring Gary Cooper and Ingrid Bergman as Hemingway's ill-fated lovers. Described by Darryl F Zanuck as a 'film without any political connotation', this failed to mollify General Franco, who banned the film in Spain. The only beneficiary was Katina Paxinou, whose performance as the guerrilla fighter Pilar won her the year's Best Supporting Actress Oscar.

Alfred Hitchcock directed Universal's *Shadow of a Doubt* which was a cunning blend of Americana and *film noir* with a disturbingly effective central performance from Joseph Cotten as a small-town family's rakish, beloved Uncle Charlie, who might be the 'Merry Widow' killer whose exploits dominate the headlines.

Greer Garson discovered radium in the title role of MGM's *Madame Curie,* teamed with Walter Pidgeon in an attempt to give the Miniver treatment to scientific research. Newcomer Jennifer Jones won the Best Actress Oscar for her portrayal of the teenage visionary Bernadette Soubirous in Twentieth Century-Fox's *The Song of Bernadette.*

The horror film was given a new twist in *The Phantom of the Opera,* which Universal turned into an opulent ersatz musical hampered by the presence of Nelson Eddy and Susanna Foster as the romantic leads. Claude Rains, as the hideously scarred Phantom, gave one of the few bad performances of his career. At RKO, Jacques Tourneur's *Cat People* launched a classic series of low-budget chillers stamped with the literary flair of their producer Val Lewton.

The Devil, in the bulky form of Laird Cregar, appeared at the beginning of Ernst Lubitsch's sprightly *Heaven Can Wait,* amiably denying Don Ameche admittance to Hell and redirecting him to Heaven. And it was from Heaven that God (Lionel Barrymore) despatched dead fighter pilot Spencer Tracy to Earth in MGM's *A Guy Named Joe.* His mission, improbably, to guide young airman Van Johnson through the pitfalls of service life and into the arms of Tracy's old flame Irene Dunne. Outstanding Western of the year was Twentieth Century-Fox's *The Ox-bow Incident*, directed by William Wellman, a sombre indictment of lynch law.

RKO's *The Outlaw,* was a pet project of Howard Hughes who fashioned it for his busty young discovery, Jane Russell. Hughes designed a brassiere specifically engineered to enhance Miss Russell's natural 'assets.' *The Outlaw,* an off beat Western much of which was directed by Howard

Hawks, opened briefly in San Francisco before becoming the subject of extended litigation over its suitability to be granted a Code Seal of Approval.

Paul Lukas won the year's Best Actor Oscar, repeating his stage success as the anti-Nazi Resistance leader Kurt Müller in Warners' *Watch on the Rhine,* adapted by Dashiell Hammett from Lillian Hellman's play.

In Britain the wartime documentary reached its peak with Humphrey Jennings' *Fires Were Started,* a tribute to fire-fighters in the Blitz. Documentary influence can be seen at work in films like *Nine Men, San Demetrio, London* and *Millions Like Us,* Launder and Gilliat's moving populist epic set in a munitions factory.

The Gentle Sex, (Two Cities) adroitly directed by Leslie Howard, told the stories of seven young women serving in the Auxiliary Territorial Service with quiet tact and documentary-tinged restraint. Tragically this was Howard's last film project. Returning from Lisbon where he had ostensibly been lecturing on theatre, his 'plane was shot down by Luftwaffe fighters.

Now that the British had real military victories to celebrate, the interest in war films waned. Filmgoers craved escapism, and this was provided by Gainsborough's *The Man in Grey,* directed by Leslie Arliss, a full-blooded Regency melodrama starring Margaret Lockwood, Phyllis Calvert, Stewart Granger and James Mason. The film was a huge success, launching Mason as a star.

The most spectacular German film of the year was *Titanic,* another slice of history refashioned to show the British at their most spineless and grasping. In this version of one of the great maritime disasters, the doomed liner's first officer was an heroic German whose attempts to avert catastrophe were thwarted by the machinations of corrupt British capitalists. *Titanic's* director, Herbert Selpin, went down with the ship, being liquidated on Goebbels' orders after complaining about the lecherous behaviour of a number of Army officers who were acting as extras. Such were the perils of film-making in the Third Reich.

In Occupied France the film industry was nourishing new talents. Director Robert Bresson made his debut with *Les Anges du Pêche,* (US *Angels of the Streets*), set in a nunnery and exploring the austere metaphysical concerns which have preoccupied Bresson throughout his career. Jacques Becker directed *Goupi Mains Rouges* (GB *It Happened at the Inn*) a rich portrait of French rural life.

In Henri-Georges Clouzot's *Le Corbeau,* (US *The Raven*) Pierre Fresnay played a provincial doctor who becomes the victim of a poison-pen campaign. The film's baleful picture of a village torn apart by hatred and intrigue was gleefully used as anti-French propaganda by the Germans throughout Occupied Europe. After the Liberation *Le Corbeau* was banned and Clouzot denied work by the film industry until 1947.

Jane Russell

James Mason

Hollywood was churning out war movies of the *Bombardier* (RKO) and *Bomber's Moon* (Fox) type but were also continuing with escapist films such as *Lassie Come Home* (MGM) and *Lady of Burlesque* (GB *Striptease Lady*) (UA) in which Barbara Stanwyck played a strip-tease dancer revealing, apart from her leggy charms, the identity of a cunning murderer.

Donald Crisp in *Lassie Come Home* (MGM)

Eric Roberts, Paul Lukas, Donald Buka, Bette Davis and Janis Wilson in *Watch on the Rhine* (WB)

Charles Bickford and Jennifer Jones in *The Song of Bernadette* (Fox)

Claude Rains in *The Phantom of the Opera* (Univ)

Christine Gordon and James Ellison in *I Walked With a Zombie* (RKO)

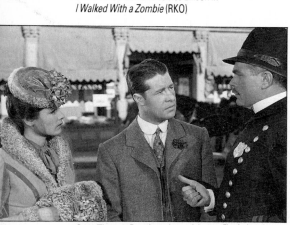

Gene Tierney, Don Ameche and James Flavin in *Heaven Can Wait* (Fox)

140

SEVEN MILES FROM ALCATRAZ

THE PURPLE V

A REPUBLIC PICTURE

Frank Sinatra

Joel McCrea and Jean Arthur in *The More the Merrier* (Col)

Ingrid Bergman in *For Whom the Bell Tolls* (Par)

Teresa Wright and Macdonald Carey in
Shadow of a Doubt (Univ)

Fred MacMurray and Claudette Colbert in
No Time for Love (Par)

Robert Young, Ina Claire and Dorothy McGuire in
Claudia (Fox)

Loretta Young, Brian Aherne and Lee Patrick in *A Night to Remember* (Col)

William Terry, Cheryl Walker, Margaret Early, Lon
McCallister, Michael Harrison and Marjorie Riordan
in *Stage Door Canteen* (UA)

143

Marjorie Lord, Margaret Hamilton, George Cleveland,
Grace George and James Cagney in *Johnny Come
Lately* (GB *Johnny Vagabond*) (UA)
▽ Randolph Scott and Pat O'Brien in *Bombardier* (RKO)

Robert Ryan and Ginger Rogers in *Tender Comrade*
(RKO)

George Montgomery and Annabella in *Bombers' Moon*
(Fox)

▽ Otto Preminger and Joan Bennett in
Margin For Error (Fox)

Barbara Stanwyck and Michael O'Shea in *Lady of
Burlesque* (GB *Striptease Lady*) (UA)
▽ George Raft and Sydney Greenstreet in
Background to Danger (WB)

1. Marguerite Chapman and Charles Coburn in *My Kingdom for a Cook* (Col)

2. The Ritz Brothers and Frances Langford in *Never a Dull Moment* (Univ)

3. John Carradine and Acquanetta in *Captive Wild Woman* (Univ)

4. Bill Henry and Jean Parker in *Alaska Highway* (Par)

5. Ellen Drew, Robert Preston, Otto Kruger and Steven Geray in *Night Plane From Chungking* (Par)

6. Morris Ankrum, Lucille Ball and Henry O'Neill in *Best Foot Forward* (MGM)

7. Barry Sullivan, Rand Brooks and Jean Parker in *High Explosive* (Par)

8. Willard Parker, Brian Aherne and Rosalind Russell in *What a Woman* (Col)

1. Rosemary La Planche in *Around the World* (RKO)
2. Virginia Mayo
3. Jose Iturbi
4. James Brown, Helen Walker, Cecil Kellaway and Diana Hale in *The Good Fellows* (Par)
5. William Hartnell
6. Louise Allbritton and Robert Paige in *Fired Wife* (Univ)
7. Gary Cooper and Ingrid Bergman in *For Whom the Bell Tolls* (Par)
8. David Bruce, Walter Sande and Noah Beery Jr in *Gung Ho* (Univ)
9. Robert Paige and Harriet Hilliard in *Hi Buddy* (Univ)
10. Robert Mitchum and William Boyd in *False Colors* (UA)
11. Douglas Dumbrille, Red Skelton and Donald Meek in *Du Barry Was a Lady* (MGM)

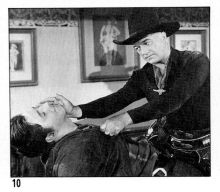

146

1

2

3

4

5

6

7

8

9

1. Louise Allbritton and Lon Chaney Jr in *Son of Dracula* (Univ)
2. Ina Claire in *Claudia* (Fox)
3. Jean-Pierre Aumont
4. Cyd Charisse
5. William Boyd, Andy Clyde, Jay Kirby and Claudia Drake in *Border Patrol* (UA)
6. Edward G Robinson, Marguerite Chapman and Regis Toomey in *Destroyer* (Col)
7. Albert Dekker (cl) and Richard Dix (cr) in *Buckskin Frontier* (UA)
8. Byron Foulger and George Zucco in *The Black Raven* (PRC)
9. Phil Silvers and George Montgomery in *Coney Island* (Fox)
10. Don Douglas (fg) and Robert Ryan (r) in *Behind the Rising Sun* (RKO)
11. Eduardo Ciannelli, Charles Boyer, Joyce Reynolds and Joan Fontaine in *The Constant Nymph* (WB)
12. John Hodiak

11

12

◁ 10

147

1. Bonita Granville
2. Samuel Goldwyn
3. Jane Frazee
4. Bela Lugosi and Lon Chaney Jr in *Frankenstein Meets The Wolf Man* (Univ)
5. William Bendix in *China* (Par)
6. Errol Flynn in *Northern Pursuit* (WB)
7. Phyllis Brooks and Dick Purcell in *No Place For A Lady* (Col)
8. Marjorie Gateson, Ernest Truex and Jane Frazee in *Rhythm of the Islands* (Univ)
9. Robert Paige and Elyse Knox in *Mr Big* (Univ)
10. Kenny Baker and Patricia Morison in *Silver Skates* (MoP)
11. Roddy McDowall and Preston Foster in *My Friend Flicka* (Fox)
12. Peggy Ryan, Elyse Knox and Donald O'Connor in *Mr Big* (Univ)

1. Philip Dorn and Anna Sten in *Chetniks* (Fox)
2. John Shepperd, Philip Dorn, Frank Lackteen and Harry Cording in *Chetniks* (Fox)
3. Kathryn Grayson and John Boles in *Thousands Cheer* (MGM)
4. Rita Hayworth
5. Martha O'Driscoll
6. Mary Clare, Joyce Howard and James Mason in *They Met In The Dark* (IP)
7. Cary Grant in *Destination Tokyo* (WB)
8. Richard Fraser and Brenda Joyce in *Thumbs Up* (Rep)
9. Dana Andrews, Paul Burns and Henry Fonda in *The Ox-Bow Incident* (Fox)
10. Inez Cooper, Edward Norris, Montagu Love and Ernie Adams in *Wings Over The Pacific* (MoP)
11. David Bruce and Grace McDonald in *She's For Me* (Univ)

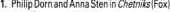

1

2

3

4

1. Patricia Collinge, Charles Bates, Joseph Cotten, Henry Travers and Edna May Wonacott in *Shadow of a Doubt* (Univ)
2. Macdonald Carey, Wallace Ford, Teresa Wright and Joseph Cotten in *Shadow of a Doubt* (Univ)
3. Hume Cronyn and Henry Travers in *Shadow of a Doubt* (Univ)
4. Teresa Wright and Joseph Cotten in *Shadow of a Doubt* (Univ)
5. Reginald Gardiner in *Sweet Rosie O'Grady* (Fox)
6. Simone Simon and Dennis O'Keefe in *Tahiti Honey* (Rep)
7. Steven Geray in *Hostages* (Par)
8. Eddie Albert in *Lady Bodyguard* (Par)
9. Halliwell Hobbes, Leo Gorcey (c) and the East Side Kids in *Mr Muggs Steps Out* (MoP)
10. John Archer and Peter Lawford in *The Purple V* (Rep)
11. James Flavin (3rd l), John Loder, Joan Winfield and William B Davidson (r) in *Murder On The Waterfront* (WB)
12. William Lundigan (l) in *Headin' for God's Country* (Rep)

5

6

7

8

9

10

11

12

1

2

3

4

5

6

1. Ann Savage and Tom Neal in *Klondike Kate* (Col)
2. Sheldon Leonard, Tom Neal and Glenda Farrell in *Klondike Kate* (Col)
3. Jack Oakie, Alice Faye and John Payne in *Hello, Frisco, Hello* (Fox)
4. Alice Faye in *Hello, Frisco, Hello* (Fox)
5. Monty Woolley, Gracie Fields and Ian Wolfe in *Holy Matrimony* (Fox)
6. Raymond Walburn
7. Gracie Fields and Monty Woolley in *Holy Matrimony* (Fox)
8. Frank Faylen and Jean Porter in *That Nazty Nuisance* (UA)
9. Preston Foster
10. Ian Keith (l), Henry Victor, Bobby Watson (Hitler) and Johnny Arthur (r) in *That Nazty Nuisance* (UA)

7

9

◁ 8

10 ▷

1. Jane Russell in *The Outlaw* (HH)
2. Laraine Day and Edward Fielding in *Mr Lucky* (RKO)
3. John Beal, Dorothy Ann Seese, Bert Gordon and Margaret Lindsay in *Let's Have Fun* (Col)
4. Bill Boyd, Tony Ward and Robert Mitchum in *Riders of the Deadline* (UA)
5. Mel Torme and Dooley Wilson in *Higher and Higher* (RKO)
6. Esther Williams
7. Paul and Grace Hartman in *Higher and Higher* (RKO)
8. Michele Morgan in *Higher and Higher* (RKO)
9. Guy Kibbee
10. Keenan Wynn

152

1

8

1. Jinx Falkenburg in *She Has What It Takes* (Col)
2. Thelma White, Catherine Craig, Bill Hunter and Richard Travis in *Spy Train* (MoP)
3. Janis Carter and Bob Haymes in *Swing Out the Blues* (Col)
4. Jimmy Rogers, Mike Mazurki, Noah Beery Jr and Jack Norton in *Prairie Chickens* (UA)
5. Dick Powell, Mary Martin and Rudy Vallee in *Happy Go Lucky* (Par)
6. Erville Anderson, Carl Esmond, Merle Oberon and Brian Aherne in *First Comes Courage* (Col)
7. Buster Crabbe and Al 'Fuzzy' St John in *The Renegade* (PRC)
8. Walter Reed in *Bombardier* (RKO)
9. William Boyd

3

4

6

5

2

9

◁ 7

153

1. Ann Rutherford, Red Skelton and Jean Rogers in *Whistling in Brooklyn* (MGM)
2. Lois Collier and David Bruce in *She's For Me* (Univ)
3. Ann Harding, Dean Jagger, Anne Baxter and Ann Carter in *The North Star* (RKO)
4. Edgar Kennedy in *The Girl From Monterey* (PRC)
5. Frances Langford and Walter Catlett in *Cowboy In Manhattan* (Univ)
6. Donald O'Connor and Gloria Jean in *It Comes Up Love* (Univ)
7. Billy Halop, Gabriel Dell, Bernard Punsley, Huntz Hall and Dick Hogan in *Mug Town* (Univ)
8. Harriet Hilliard and Tom Conway in *The Falcon Strikes Back* (RKO)
9. Rosalind Russell and Herbert Marshall in *Flight for Freedom* (RKO)

9 ▷

1. Dick Powell and Dorothy Lamour in *Riding High* (GB *Melody Inn*) (Par)
2. John Hubbard, Ann Miller and Eddie 'Rochester' Anderson in *What's Buzzin', Cousin?* (Col)
3. Billy Gilbert, Edith Barrett and Charles Butterworth in *Always a Bridesmaid* (Univ)
4. Lon Chaney Jr and Patricia Morison in *Calling Dr Death* (Univ)
5. Leon Ames, Ruth Warrick and Pat O'Brien in *The Iron Major* (RKO)
6. Wendy Barrie, Doris Nolan and William Harrigan in *Follies Girl* (PRC)
7. Eleanor Parker, Bruce Lester and John Loder in *The Mysterious Doctor* (WB)
8. Joe Devlin, Mike Mazurki, Grace Bradley, Sheldon Leonard and William Bendix in *Taxi, Mister* (UA)
9. Barry Sullivan and Claire Trevor in *The Woman of the Town* (UA)

1

2

3

4

5

6

7

1. Morton Lowry, Melville Cooper, Henry Fonda, Alyn Joslyn, Thomas Mitchell and Bramwell Fletcher in *The Immortal Sergeant* (Fox)

2. Francis Pierlot, William Terry, Fred Brady, Michael Harrison, Dorothea Kent and Lon McCallister in *Stage Door Canteen* (UA)

3. Rita Corday and Tom Conway in *The Falcon and the Co-eds* (RKO)

4. Douglas Fowley and Joe Sawyer in *Sleepy Lagoon* (Rep)

5. Marguerite Chapman, Edmund Lowe and Veda Ann Borg in *Murder In Times Square* (Col)

6. Richard Martin, Dennis O'Keefe and James Bell in *The Leopard Man* (RKO)

7. Marguerite Chapman and Warren William in *One Dangerous Night* (Col)

8. Robert Ryan (r) in *Gangway For Tomorrow* (RKO)

9. Scotty and Lulubelle with Vera Vague in *Swing Your Partner* (Rep)

10. Terry 'Curly' Howard, Moe Howard and Larry Fine (The Three Stooges)

9

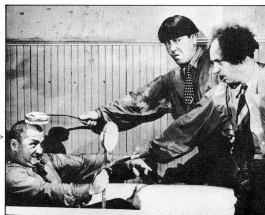

10 ▷

1. Greer Garson and Walter Pidgeon in *Madame Curie* (MGM)
2. William Farnum, William Haade, Charles Middleton and Brian Donlevy in *Hangmen Also Die* (UA)
3. Evelyn Brent and Tom Conway in *The Seventh Victim* (RKO)
4. Noah Beery Jr, Mary Brian and Jimmy Rogers in *Calaboose* (UA)

◁ 4

Claudette Colbert

1. Mickey Rooney (c) in *Girl Crazy* (MGM)
2. Mickey Rooney in *Girl Crazy* (MGM)
3. Judy Garland and Guy Kibbee in *Girl Crazy* (MGM)
4. Guy Kibbee, Judy Garland and Mickey Rooney in *Girl Crazy* (MGM)
5. Elaine Shepard, Amelita Ward, Tom Conway and Richard Davies in *The Falcon in Danger* (RKO)
6. Gene Reynolds
7. Jack Buetel
8. Charles Smith, Mike Mazurki, Jimmy Lydon, Joan Mortimer and Vaughan Glaser in *Henry Aldrich Haunts a House* (Par)
9. Margaret Wycherly, John Emery (c), Sarah Padden and Jean-Pierre Aumont in *Assignment in Brittany* (MGM)

161

1

2

3

1. Bill Boyd and Andy Clyde in *Lost Canyon* (UA)
2. Roy Barcroft and Johnny Mack Brown in *The Stranger from Pecos* (MoP)
3. Dave O'Brien (l) and Jim Newill (r) in *The Rangers Take Over* (PRC)
4. Charles Starrett, Dick Curtis, Jimmy Wakely, Julie Duncan and Dub Taylor in *Cowboy in the Clouds* (Col)
5. I Stanford Jolley, Glenn Strange, Charles King and Larry 'Buster' Crabbe in *The Kid Rides Again* (PRC)
6. Kenneth MacDonald, Charles Starrett and Kay Harris in *Robin Hood of the Range* (Col)
7. Andy Clyde (c) and William Boyd in *The Leather Burners* (UA)
8. George 'Gabby' Hayes, William 'Wild Bill' Elliott and Harry Woods in *Bordertown Gun Fighters* (Rep)
9. Whip Wilson
10. Roy Barcroft, Edmund Cobb, Kenneth MacDonald and Johnny Mack Brown in *Six Gun Gospel* (MoP)

4

5

6

7

8 ◁
9 ◁

10 ▷

1

2

3

4

1. Dorothy Morris
2. Jean-Pierre Aumont, Gene Kelly, Wallace Ford, Jack Lambert, Cedric Hardwicke and Joseph Calleia in *The Cross of Lorraine* (MGM)
3. Binnie Barnes
4. Raymond Walburn, Barbara Pepper and Phyllis Ruth in *Let's Face It* (Par)
5. Betty Rhodes in *Salute for Three* (Par)
6. Arthur Lake, Larry Simms, Danny Mummert and Penny Singleton in *It's a Great Life* (Col)
7. Lupe Velez and Michael Duane (r) in *Redhead From Manhattan* (Col)
8. Kathryn Grayson
9. Mary Beth Hughes (c) in *Melody Parade* (MoP)

5

6

8

▽ 9

7

1. Tina Thayer
2. Eddie Bracken, Susan Hayward, William Holden and Barbara Britton in *Young and Willing* (UA)
3. Sara Haden
4. Raymond Hatton
5. Margaret Lockwood
6. Frank Sully, Jess Barker and Claire Trevor in *Good Luck, Mr Yates* (Col)
7. Ruth Terry and Roy Rogers in *Hands Across the Border* (Rep)
8. Dick Powell and Mary Martin in *True to Life* (Par)
9. Frances Langford
10. Raymond Hatton and Johnny Mack Brown in *Outlaws of Stampede Pass* (MoP)
11. Wally Brown

9 ▷

▽ 10   ▽ 11

1. Frances Rafferty
2. Joan Barclay, Jack Briggs, Iris Adrian, Russ Clark, Patsy Kelly and Max Baer in *Ladies Day* (RKO)
3. Brian Aherne
4. Arthur Treacher
5. Brenda Marshall in *Paris After Dark (GB The Night Is Ending)* (Fox)
6. Richard Fraser in *Thumbs Up* (Rep)
7. Geraldine Fitzgerald
8. John Sutton, Marcel Dalio and Ann Codee (all stdg) in *Tonight We Raid Calais* (Fox)
9. Ann Miller (c) in *Reveille With Beverly* (Col)

1. Leon Ames
2. Cliff Clark, Oliver Hardy and Stan Laurel in *The Dancing Masters* (Fox)
3. Donald Woods
4. Wendy Barrie, Richard Arlen and Abner Biberman in *Submarine Alert* (Par)
5. Marta Linden, Scotty Beckett and Edward Arnold in *The Youngest Profession* (MGM)
6. Richard Webb
7. Don Ameche
8. Morris Ankrum
9. Richard Travis, Virginia Christine and Ruth Ford in *Truck Busters* (WB)
10. Richard Lane
11. Dick Purcell, Richard Arlen, Chester Morris and Billy Benedict in *Aerial Gunner* (Par)

1. Michele Morgan and Alan Curtis in *Two Tickets to London* (Univ)
2. Evelyn Ankers and Neil Hamilton (std l) and Rosemary Lane in *All By Myself* (Univ)
3. Cheta, Johnny Weissmuller, Frances Gifford and Johnny Sheffield in *Tarzan Triumphs* (RKO)
4. Chester Clute, Red Skelton, Eleanor Powell, Thurston Hall, Richard Ainley and Patricia Dane in *I Dood It* (MGM)

5. Walter Woolf King, Joe Sawyer, Marjorie Woodworth, William Tracy and Robert Kent in *Fall In* (UA)
6. Walter Sande, Richard Lane, Lloyd Corrigan, Jan Buckingham, George E Stone, Chester Morris Ann Savage and Dick Elliott in *After Midnight With Boston Blackie* (Col)
7. Paulette Goddard, Ray Milland, Nestor Paiva and Sig Arno in *The Crystal Ball* (UA)

1. Chic Johnson and Ole Olsen in *Crazy House* (Univ)
2. Priscilla Lane and Jack Benny in *The Meanest Man in the World* (Fox)
3. Jean Parker and Russell Hayden in *Minesweeper* (Par)
4. Don Barry and Wally Vernon in *Man From Rio Grande* (Rep)
5. Leon Errol, Mary Beth Hughes and Eddie Quillan in *Follow the Band* (Univ)
6. Dorothy Lamour, Billy De Wolfe and Bing Crosby in *Dixie* (Par)
7. Linda Darnell and Michael Duane in *City Without Men* (Col)
8. Marilyn Maxwell, Fay Bainter and Wallace Beery in *Salute to the Marines* (MGM)
9. Lionel Barrymore, Arthur Loft, Henry O'Neil, Van Johnson and John Craven in *Dr Gillespie's Criminal Case* (GB *Crazy to Kill*) (MGM)

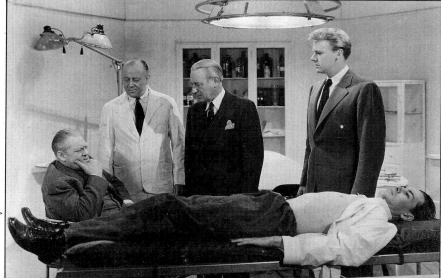

1. Sheila Ryan, Arline Judge and Roy Rogers in *Song of Texas* (Rep)
2. Louise Allbritton and Dennis O'Keefe in *Good Morning, Judge* (Univ)
3. Spring Byington and William Powell in *The Heavenly Body* (MGM)
4. Joe Sawyer (c) and Johnny Weissmuller in *Tarzan's Desert Mystery* (RKO)
5. Charles Boyer and Barbara Stanwyck in *Flesh and Fantasy* (Univ)
6. Philip Reed, Bette Davis and Dolores Moran in *Old Acquaintance* (WB)
7. Lana Turner and Robert Young in *Slightly Dangerous* (MGM)
8. David Bruce in *The Mad Ghoul* (Univ)
9. Humphrey Bogart in *Sahara* (Col)

169

1. Georgia Carroll
2. Guy Middleton
3. Veda Ann Borg
4. Virginia Field
5. John Shelton

6. Victor Jory
7. Billy De Wolfe
8. Donald O'Connor
9. Joyce Compton

6
◁
◁ 8

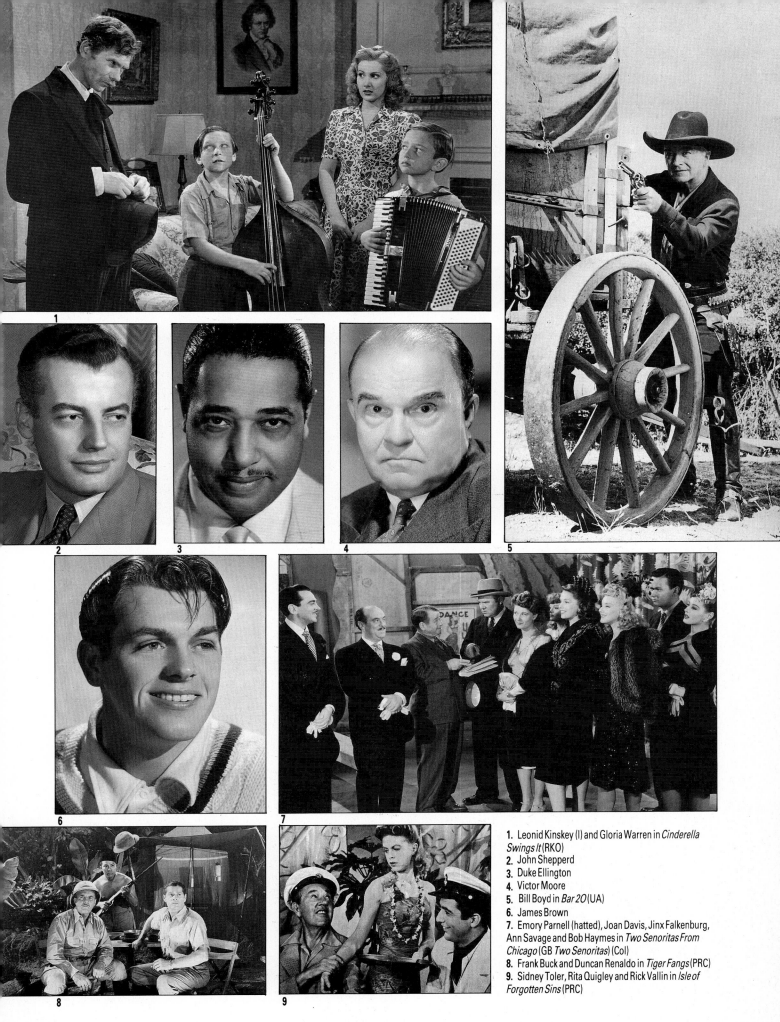

1. Leonid Kinskey (l) and Gloria Warren in *Cinderella Swings It* (RKO)
2. John Shepperd
3. Duke Ellington
4. Victor Moore
5. Bill Boyd in *Bar 20* (UA)
6. James Brown
7. Emory Parnell (hatted), Joan Davis, Jinx Falkenburg, Ann Savage and Bob Haymes in *Two Senoritas From Chicago* (GB *Two Senoritas*) (Col)
8. Frank Buck and Duncan Renaldo in *Tiger Fangs* (PRC)
9. Sidney Toler, Rita Quigley and Rick Vallin in *Isle of Forgotten Sins* (PRC)

1. James Mason
2. William Haade
3. John Litel
4. Donald MacBride
5. Dennis O'Keefe
6. George Macready
7. Hugh Herbert
8. Eddie Albert
9. Dan Tobin
10. Cecil Parker
11. Rossano Brazzi
12. Lon Chaney Jr
13. Douglas Fowley
14. Milburn Stone

1. Francis Pierlot
2. Joyce Reynolds
3. Louise Beavers
4. George Raft
5. Edwin Maxwell
6. Stewart Granger and Phyllis Calvert in *The Man In Grey* (G'boro)
7. Eric Blore and Alan Baxter in *Submarine Base* (PRC)
8. Richard Le Grand, Freddie Mercer, Margaret Landry and Michael Road in *Gildersleeve On Broadway* (RKO)
9. Bela Lugosi and Arnold Van Damm (The Ape) in *The Ape Man* (GB *Lock Your Doors*) (MoP)

9

◁ 8

173

1. Donald Crisp, Roddy McDowall and Elsa Lanchester in *Lassie Come Home* (MGM)
2. Jean Brooks
3. Michele Morgan
4. Adolphe Menjou and Pola Negri in *Hi Diddle Diddle* (UA)
5. David Bruce and Harriet Hilliard in *Honeymoon Lodge* (Univ)
6. Marc Lawrence, Patric Knowles, Joe Sawyer, Elyse Knox, Sheldon Leonard and Ginny Simms in *Hit the Ice* (Univ)
7. Michael O'Shea in *Jack London* (UA)
8. Glenn Strange (l) and Eugene Pallette (r) in *The Kansan* (UA)
9. Margie Stewart in *Gildersleeve's Bad Day* (RKO)
10. Olivia de Havilland
11. Frank Craven (l) and Bobby Readick (r) in *Harrigan's Kid* (MGM)
12. Robert Young

Tender Comrade (RKO) was a wartime weepie in which Ginger Rogers' soldier husband, Robert Ryan is killed on the battlefield before news of the birth of his son can reach him. This tear-jerker certainly resulted in dry eyes for the producers for, despite its unhappy story, the film netted well over $800,000 in profits.

1. Robert Ryan and Ginger Rogers
2. Richard Gaines and Ruth Hussey
3. Mady Christians
4. Patricia Collinge
5. Kim Hunter
6. Ginger Rogers
7. Robert Ryan and Ginger Rogers
8. Richard Martin, Ruth Hussey and Kim Hunter
9. Richard Martin

7 ▷
8 ▷

175

1. Johnny Mack Brown, Raymond Hatton (c) and Karl Hackett in *The Texas Kid* (MoP)

2. Roy Barcroft, Buzzy Henry and Bill Elliott in *Calling Wild Bill Elliott* (Rep)

3. Raymond Hatton, Tom Seidel and Johnny Mack Brown in *The Ghost Rider* (MoP)

4. Max Terhune, Evelyn Finley, Ray Corrigan and Dennis Moore in *Cowboy Commandos* (MoP)

5. Don Barry (c) and Ariel Heath in *The Black Hills Express* (Rep)

6. John King and Gwen Gaze in *Two Fisted Justice* (MoP)

7. John Merton, Ray Corrigan, George Chesebro and Frank Ellis in *Black Market Rustlers* (MoP)

8. Martha Wentworth, Lita Ward and Noah Beery Snr in *Clancy Street Boys* (MoP)

William 'Wild Bill' Elliott

Clark Gable

1. Ralph Sanford
2. Fritz Leiber
3. Alan Marshal
4. Bernard Nedell
5. Phil Silvers
6. Hugo Haas
7. Jackie Gleason
8. Michael Shepley
9. Eddie Foy Jr
10. Jennifer Holt
11. Harriet Hilliard
12. Elena Verdugo
13. Irene Rich
14. Ethel Barrymore
15. George Zucco

Hattie McDaniel, Shirley Temple, Joseph Cotten and Claudette Colbert in *Since You Went Away* (UA)

Irene Dunne

Roddy McDowall in *The White Cliffs of Dover* (MGM)

VICTORY IN SIGHT

From 1944 onwards the number of war films made in Hollywood declined. The expense and complication of location shooting discouraged the studios. They preferred to devote big budgets to more popular genres, particularly the musical. The outcome of the war was no longer in doubt and there was less need of strident propaganda.

In *Since You Went Away*, David O Selznick turned to 'the story of that unconquerable fortress – the American Home Front, 1943'. Written by Selznick and directed with smooth skill by John Cromwell, *Since You Went Away* is a masterpiece of lush sentimentality, starring Claudette Colbert as a fashion plate Mrs Average American steering her family (Shirley Temple, Jennifer Jones) through the heartaches of the war while Father is away at the front. This is the war in glowing soft focus, but there are some skilfully mounted set pieces, notably a dance in an aircraft hangar, which tug at the most unyielding heart strings. Like its 'English' counterpart *Mrs Miniver* (1942), *Since You Went Away* was a huge hit.

Two of *Mrs Miniver's* (1942) screenwriters, Claudine West and George Froeschel, were involved in MGM's *The White Cliffs of Dover,* another tearjerking fantasy of England in which American Irene Dunne married baronet Alan Marshal who was killed in the First World War; their son, Peter Lawford, was killed in the Second. Rooted in more tragic reality was Twentieth Century-Fox's *The Sullivans,* the unrelentingly sad story of five Iowa brothers who were lost in the sinking of the cruiser *Juneau* off Guadalcanal.

The upheavals that war brought to small-town America were caricatured by Preston Sturges in *The Miracle of Morgan's Creek* in which good-time girl Betty Hutton's wild night of fun ends with a fake marriage and nine months later, sextuplets and a shotgun wedding to gormless Eddie Bracken.

In *Hail the Conquering Hero*, Sturges set up Marine reject Bracken as a fake warrior who finds the red carpet rolled out by the inhabitants of his home town. Sturges was out of step with the wartime Hollywood mainstream, a quality he shared with Britain's Michael Powell. His vision of a merry, corrupt and absurd America was unique and shortlived. By now he had left Paramount and embarked on a disastrous association with Howard Hughes.

The Japanese had long since joined the Germans as targets of the US propaganda machine. However, Hollywood's grasp of Japanese life and culture was tenuous. The enemy in the Pacific War were usually portrayed as sadistic grinning monkeys, hysterical in both victory and defeat. At Twentieth Century-Fox, Lewis Milestone's *The Purple Heart* was based on a real-life series of events in which a US bomber crew shot down over Japan, underwent a military trial accused of bombing civilian targets. The chief Japanese interrogator, Richard Loo, seems to have wandered in from a Republic 'Yellow Peril' serial. His failure to break the US airmen – a careful cross-section of ethnic types – drives him to commit suicide in court.

The first blow in the bombing campaign against Japan was commemorated in MGM's *Thirty Seconds Over Tokyo*. Directed by Mervyn LeRoy, it is a painstaking account of the Doolittle Raid, with Spencer Tracy as Lieutenant-Colonel Doolittle. The operational leader of the raid, Major Ted Lewis (played by Van Johnson), supervised the making of the film, which followed the operation from the planning stages to the final escape of a downed crew aided by Chinese patriots.

MGM paid tribute to America's Chinese allies in *Dragon Seed,* from Pearl S Buck's novel, starring Katharine Hepburn with strapped-up eyes and at her most infuriatingly coltish as a Chinese peasant who accounts for almost the entire Japanese High Command by slipping arsenic into their duck soup.

Gregory Peck made his debut in RKO's *Days of Glory*, playing a Russian partisan leader in love with ballerina Tamara Toumanova. They made a handsome couple, enthusiastically lobbing grenades at German tanks. Peck was immediately snapped up by Twentieth Century-Fox and rushed into *The Keys of the Kingdom* as a Scottish missionary in China.

Meanwhile MGM continued its brief love affair with the Soviet Union in *Song of Russia,* directed by Gregory Ratoff. Robert Taylor played an American conductor experiencing the joys of the Collective Way of Life and falling for Russian musician Susan Peters. Later, he claimed that he had made the film under protest.

MGM atoned for this aberration with *The Seventh Cross,* directed by Fred Zinnemann and starring Spencer Tracy as a fugitive from a pre-war German concentration camp. Tracy's gritty performance and Zinnemann's restrained direction, brilliantly evoking a totalitarian Germany, make this a film of great integrity and a far cry from the movies of 1940 in which Hollywood studios squeamishly eschewed the use of the words 'Nazi' and 'Jew'. Among the film's qualities

Richard Loo in *The Purple Heart* (Fox)

Tamara Toumanova in *Days of Glory* (RKO)

Gregory Peck and Rose Stradner in *The Keys of the Kingdom* (Fox)

Robert Taylor

Fredric March

Dan Seymour, Humphrey Bogart and Lauren Bacall in *To Have and Have Not* (WB)

Lauren Bacall

Brian Donlevy

was its readiness to recognize that not all Germans were bullet-headed Nazi beasts.

A small, ferocious Nazi beast, in the form of an orphaned German child, Skippy Homeier, invaded an American household in United Artists' *Tomorrow the World*. Fredric March played harassed host to this intractable fragment of the Hitler Youth, eventually converting him to more democratic ways.

'Anyone got a match?' In Howard Hawks' *To Have and Have Not* (Warner) this languid enquiry was made by 19-year-old Lauren Bacall, making one of the most remarkable debuts of the decade. *To Have and Have Not* was a free adaptation by William Faulkner of Hemingway's novel, set in Martinique under the Vichy French, whose chief representative is the marvellous Dan Seymour, a lisping heavy, oozing corruption. Bogart is an American running deep-sea fishing trips for wealthy tourists, who finds himself caught up with the Free French. But Hawks' efficient handling of the storyline takes second place to the crackling rapport he encouraged between Bogart and Bacall's glamorous drifter Slim. Her look is timeless, the lowered eyelids, tawny tumbling hair and smart little houndstooth two-piece still imitated today. Her cool sexiness is the mirror image of Bogart's sardonic masculinity. The charged atmosphere on the screen spilled over into an off-screen romance, and Bogart and Bacall were married in the following year.

Money alone cannot create such magic. At Twentieth Century-Fox Darryl F Zanuck sank $5.2 million into *Wilson*, an earnest, idealized portrait of the frosty President who had reluctantly led the United States into the First World War and played a big part in the formation of the ill-fated League of Nations. The English actor Alexander Knox gave a disciplined performance in the title role, but the film never catches fire and it was a commercial failure. Thereafter Zanuck abandoned Presidents and stuck to Betty Grable.

A more zesty slice of Americana was provided by MGM's *An American Romance,* directed by King Vidor, with Brian Donlevy excellent as the Polish immigrant who becomes a steel tycoon, a performance which captures the rough-edged vigour of the American Dream.

However, there was another America: a land of night and shadow, in which flickering neon bounced off rain-slicked city streets. An urban landscape populated by compromised men and predatory women who move through a twilight zone of pessimism, doomed obsessions, corruption and betrayal – the world of the *film noir*.

Central to the *film noir* was the *femme fatale*, and there was no more Fatal Lady than Barbara Stanwyck in Billy Wilder's *Double Indemnity* (Paramount), adapted from the novel by James M Cain, in which Stanwyck's Medusa-like Phyllis Dietrichson draws Fred MacMurray, an idly philandering insurance salesman, into a plot to kill her husband.

Double Indemnity's Dance of Death is played out in an oppressively observed South California. In contrast, Otto Preminger's *Laura* is set in a New York milieu of sumptuous affluence where custom-made sunlight is laid on for the rich. The characters cast their own shadows: Clifton Webb's feline dilettante Waldo Lydecker, suspected of murdering the girl of the title (Gene Tierney); Vincent Price's Shelby Carpenter, a suave parasite whose nourishment is provided by rich women; and his mistress Judith Anderson, who has to pay for her satisfaction. Negotiating this corrupt world is Dana Andrews, in the best role of his career, as the police detective who by degrees becomes obsessed with Laura's portrait.

Both Wilder and Preminger were exiled Germans, and many of the *film noir's* visual and thematic features were filtered through an Expressionist glass darkly. In Fritz Lang's *The Woman in the Window,* ineffectual clubman Edward G Robinson becomes the victim of ruthless seductress Joan Bennett. At Universal another exile, Robert Siodmak, coaxed tense performances from Ella Raines and Franchot Tone in *The Phantom Lady,* an intriguing thriller based on a novel by hard-boiled writer Cornell Woolrich.

Universal had given Siodmak a seven-year contract after his lugubriously inventive handling of *Son of Dracula* (1943), starring Lon Chaney Jr. Thereafter the studio kept Siodmak busy. *Christmas Holiday* was a forlorn attempt to nudge Deanna Durbin into adulthood, as a New Orleans nightclub singer who unwisely weds petty hoodlum Gene Kelly. *Cobra Woman* was the most uninhibitedly idiotic of Maria Montez' Technicolor 'Easterns', in which La Montez' minimal acting talents were stretched to the limit playing twin sisters. Naturally one is good and the other is evil. Eventually the evil one obliges us all by toppling off a high cliff backwards.

Rudolph Maté's camera caressed Rita Hayworth in Columbia's *Cover Girl,* directed by Charles Vidor and choreographed by Stanley Donen. She was teamed with Gene Kelly, who marked his transition from talented hoofer to genuinely inventive dancer with the 'alter ego' sequence, in which he capered with his reflection in a shop window.

Carmen Miranda was top-billed for the first time in *Greenwich Village,* while Eddie Cantor celebrated 35 years of eye-popping entertainment in RKO's *Show Business.* Goldwyn discovery Danny Kaye made a sensational debut in RKO's *Up in Arms,* a freewheeling version of Eddie Cantor's *Whoopee!* (1930), in which he played a hypochondriac soldier let loose in the Pacific and racing through scat songs like 'Melody in F' and 'Manic-Depressive Pictures Presents'.

The camera coyly followed Esther Williams underwater in MGM's *Bathing Beauty,* a ripe slice of escapism which climaxed with a gloriously kitsch water ballet to the strains of Strauss' 'Blue Danube Waltz'.

Warners hit the jackpot with the star-studded *Hollywood Canteen,* written and directed by Delmer Daves, in which

Barbara Stanwyck

Gene Kelly and Deanna Durbin in *Christmas Holiday* (Univ)

Rita Hayworth in *Cover Girl* (Col)

Carmen Miranda, Don Ameche, Vivian Blaine and William Bendix in *Greenwich Village* (Fox)

Robert Hutton, Dane Clark and S Z Sakall in *Hollywood Canteen* (WB)

Judy Garland and Margaret O'Brien in *Meet Me in St Louis* (MGM)

James Brown, Jean Heather and Bing Crosby in *Going My Way* (Par)

Ludwig Stossel and John Carradine in *Bluebeard*

soldier Robert Hutton was the lucky millionth guest at the famous Canteen and won a date with dream girl Joan Leslie.

Margaret O'Brien was the winning little 'Tootie' Smith, dancing a front parlour cakewalk in MGM's *Meet Me in St Louis,* directed by Vincente Minnelli, a beguiling family story illustrated with songs and set at the time of the 1904 World's Fair. This remains a magical film, its charm undimmed by the years. The cast includes a glowing Judy Garland as Esther Smith, singing 'The Boy Next Door' and 'The Trolley Song'.

Meet Me in St Louis was MGM's biggest grossing musical up to that date and second only to *Gone With the Wind* (1939) at the box-office.

However, another musical cleaned up at the Academy Awards ceremony. Paramount's *Going My Way,* directed by Leo McCarey, starred Bing Crosby as warm-hearted, warbling Catholic priest Father Charles O'Malley, despatched to help crotchety Father Barry Fitzgerald with his insolvent city parish. Two hours later Bing has hauled St Dominics out of debt, charmed the local Street Arabs into a choir, persuaded *diva* Rise Stevens to sing one of his songs at the Met, married off Jean Heather and James Brown, taught Fitzgerald to play golf and reunited him with his incredibly ancient Irish mother. Crosby's Best Actor Oscar was a foregone conclusion. *Going My Way* was voted Best Film and McCarey and Fitzgerald, respectively Best Director and Best Supporting Actor.

Peter Lorre and Sydney Greenstreet chased Zachary Scott (making his debut) halfway across the world in Warners' *The Mask of Dimitrios,* fluidly translated to the screen from Eric Ambler's novel by Jean Negulesco. Bette Davis sailed imperiously through the grand soap opera of *Mr Skeffington* as a society flirt who discovers the Meaning of Marriage after she has lost her looks and husband Claude Rains has lost his sight.

Dick Powell shrugged off his song-and-dance-man image to emerge as Raymond Chandler's laconic private eye Philip Marlowe, in RKO's *Murder My Sweet,* (GB *Farewell, My Lovely*) directed by Edward Dmytryk.

Murder was also on Laird Cregar's mind as he stalked the fog-shrouded streets of a Hollywood Whitechapel in Twentieth Century-Fox's *The Lodger* as a thinly veiled version of 'Jack the Ripper'. At PRC – a celebrated 'Poverty Row' studio – John Carradine gave a creepily effective performance as another haunted murderer, terrorizing *fin-de-siècle* Paris in Edgar G Ulmer's *Bluebeard,* a small B masterpiece.

Bluebeard's entire budget would hardly have paid for Ingrid Bergman's costume changes in MGM's *Gaslight,* (GB *The Murder in Thornton Square*) a plush period chiller in which her svelte husband Charles Boyer did his best to drive her mad in order to pick up her fortune. Bergman looked altogether too self-possessed to succumb to Boyer's sadistic manipulation, but her performance nevertheless won her the

Cary Grant

year's Best Actress Oscar. The Best Supporting Actress award went to Ethel Barrymore, who played the mother of Cockney crook Cary Grant in RKO's *None But the Lonely Heart.*

Charles Laughton enjoyed himself hugely in MGM's *The Canterville Ghost,* haunting a castle and locking horns with Margaret O'Brien in a keenly fought upstaging battle. At Twentieth Century-Fox, Orson Welles was a darkly romantic Mr Rochester in *Jane Eyre,* a brooding adaptation of Charlotte Bronte's novel directed with a gothic flourish by Robert Stevenson.

At MGM, Elizabeth Taylor made the best-remembered film of her childhood, *National Velvet,* training her steeplechaser to win the Grand National.

Silent star Harry Langdon died of a cerebral haemmorrhage, having spent his last years poverty-ridden and forgotten.

An even greater silent comedian, Buster Keaton, had also fallen on hard times. But he contributed a delightful cameo to a charming low-budget Universal comedy *San Diego I Love You,* directed by Reginald LeBorg, as a mournful bus driver persuaded by sparky Louise Allbritton to take a joyride along a moonlit beach.

In Britain, Laurence Olivier's *Henry V* struck a note appropriate for the victory which now lay ahead. The film was a personal tour de force for Olivier, who starred and directed, imaginatively blending stylised design and dramatic location shooting (in Ireland).

The outstanding British war film of the year was Carol Reed's *The Way Ahead,* which followed a mixed bunch of Army recruits through training and the torpedoing of their troopship to their baptism of fire in North Africa.

This Happy Breed, directed in low-key Technicolor by David Lean, was Noel Coward's tribute to the 'ordinary people' of Britain as personified by the Gibbons family of 17 Sycamore Road, Clapham.

Bernard Miles' *Tawny Pipit* was a whimsical rural celebration of 'Englishness', a notion which received a more complex, romantic treatment in Powell and Pressburger's *A Canterbury Tale,* the story of wartime 'pilgrims' to the ancient cathedral city.

In contrast Sidney Gilliat's *Waterloo Road* foreshadowed the 'realism' of the 1960s, capturing the seedy, teeming bustle of wartime London as Private John Mills went AWOL to rescue his young wife Joy Shelton from the clutches of slimy black marketeer Stewart Granger. In *Fanny by Gaslight* (US *Man of Evil*) Granger was on hand to save Phyllis Calvert from the savage embrace of James Mason.

In the hugely popular *Love Story* (US *A Lady Surrenders*) Granger romanced Margaret Lockwood to the strains of 'The Cornish Rhapsody'.

Like their American counterparts, British audiences now preferred escapism to wartime heroics.

Margaret O'Brien and Charles Laughton in *The Canterville Ghost* (MGM)

Laurence Olivier in *Henry V* (TC)

Stewart Granger

Ann Gillis

Robert Ryan in *Marine Raiders* (RKO)

Film Favourites 1944

The tide of war was now beginning to turn in the Allies' favour and the movie world was at its peak. Costume films of the *Ali Baba and the Forty Thieves* (Univ) and *The Princess and the Pirate* (RKO) variety were proving very popular. War Films were more realistic than romantic.

Charles Winninger, Anne Baxter and John Hodiak in *Sunday Dinner for a Soldier* (Fox)

◁ Wally Brown, Virginia Mayo, Amelita Ward and Alan Carney in *Seven Days Ashore* (RKO)

Sheila Ryan, Glenn Langan and Michael O'Shea in *Something for the Boys* (Fox)

▽ Anne Revere and Donald Crisp in *National Velvet* (MGM)

Patricia Roc, Stewart Granger and Margaret Lockwood in *Love Story* (US *A Lady Surrenders*) (G'boro)

▽ Irene Dunne in *Together Again* (Col)

▽ Constance Dowling in *Up in Arms* (RKO)

Nancy Gates, and George Coulouris in *The Master Race* (RKO)

Florence Rice ▷

Lewis Stone in *Andy Hardy's Blonde Trouble* (MGM)

Barbara Hale and Gordon Oliver in *Heavenly Days* (RKO)

George Brent and Albert Dekker in ▷
Experiment Perilous (RKO)

David Bruce, Anne Gwynne and Addison Richards in *Moon Over Las Vegas* (Univ)

Jeanne Bates, Art Smith and Larry Parks in *The Black Parachute* (Col)

▽ Maria Montez and Turhan Bey in *Ali Baba and the Forty Thieves* (Univ)

George E Stone (on car), Victor McLaglen and Preston Foster in *Roger Touhy, Gangster* (GB *The Last Gangster*) (Fox)

187

Bernie Sell, Jayne Hazard and John Hamilton in *Crazy Knights* (MoP)

Nelson Eddy (3rd l) and Constance Dowling (c) in *Knickerbocker Holiday* (UA)

Rochelle Hudson

Fred Kohler Jr, Dennis O'Keefe, Charlotte Greenwood and Janet Lambert in *Up in Mabel's Room* (UA) ▷

Charles 'Buddy' Rogers

Van Johnson and Gloria De Haven in *Between Two Women* (MGM)

▽ Three Pretty Maids in *The Princess and the Pirate* (SG)

Basil Rathbone, Joan Fontaine and Denis Green in *Frenchman's Creek* (Par)

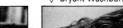

▽ Deanna Durbin in *Can't Help Singing* (Univ)

▽ Bryant Washburn

1

2

3

Picture Gallery for 1944

4

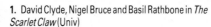

6

1. David Clyde, Nigel Bruce and Basil Rathbone in *The Scarlet Claw* (Univ)
2. Eddie Bracken and Betty Hutton in *The Miracle of Morgan's Creek* (Par)
3. Nils Asther and Helen Walker in *The Man In Half Moon Street* (Par)
4. Alan Curtis and Ella Raines in *Phantom Lady* (Univ)
5. Susan Peters and Robert Taylor in *Song of Russia* (MGM)
6. Joan Bennett and Edward G Robinson in *The Woman in the Window* (RKO)
7. Allan Jones, Dicky Love and June Vincent in *Sing a Jingle* (Univ)
8. Harriet Hilliard and Kirby Grant in *Hi Good-Lookin'* (Univ)

7

8

1

2

3

Lifeboat (Fox) showed to a remarkable degree just how much Alfred Hitchcock could get out of a good story, nine first-class actors and one small boat. Although the entire film is devoted to the efforts of nine shipwreck survivors (one of them, Walter Slezak, is a fanatical Nazi) to reach safety, not for a moment does the action of the film flag. A Hitchcock tour-de-force.

6

7

5

8

1. Mary Anderson and Hume Cronyn
2. John Hodiak, Tallulah Bankhead and Henry Hull
3. Mary Anderson and Hume Cronyn
4. John Hodiak and Tallulah Bankhead
5. Tallulah Bankhead, John Hodiak, Hume Cronyn (bckgd), Henry Hull and William Bendix
6. John Hodiak and Tallulah Bankhead
7. Canada Lee, Tallulah Bankhead, John Hodiak and William Bendix
8. John Hodiak, Walter Slezak, Tallulah Bankhead and Hume Cronyn
9. Hume Cronyn, Mary Anderson, John Hodiak and William Bendix
10. Walter Slezak, John Hodiak, Tallulah Bankhead, Henry Hull, William Bendix, Heather Angel, Mary Anderson, Canada Lee and Hume Cronyn
11. John Hodiak, Hume Cronyn, William Bendix, Mary Anderson and Tallulah Bankhead
12. Tallulah Bankhead, Mary Anderson and Hume Cronyn

10

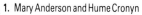

11 ◁
◁
▷ 12

9

1

2

3

4

1. Bernard Nedell, Lyle Talbot, Bela Lugosi, Douglas Fowley, Jean Parker and Jack Haley in *One Body Too Many* (Par)

2. Kay Marvis, Huntz Hall, Leo Gorcey, Roberta Smith and Fred Pressel in *Block Busters* (MoP)

3. Barbara Britton and Ray Milland in *Till We Meet Again* (Par)

4. Benny Fields in *Minstrel Man* (PRC)

5. Gl enn Strange, Julie Gibson, Arline Judge, Larry 'Buster' Crabbe and Milton Kibbee in *The Contender* (PRC)

6. Tom Conway, Joseph Vitale and Mona Maris in *The Falcon in Mexico* (RKO)

7. William Terry, Simone Simon and James Ellison in *Johnny Doesn't Live Here Any More* (MoP)

8. Claire Dubrey, Marjorie Rambeau and Jean Parker in *Oh, What A Night!* (MoP)

9. Tala Birell and J Carrol Naish in *The Monster Maker* (PRC)

5

6

7

8
◁
▷
9

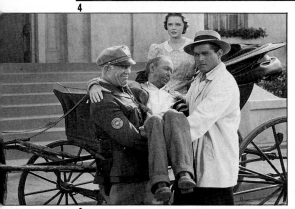

1. Barry Sullivan
2. Jimmy Lydon and Barbara Belden in *When The Lights Go On Again* (PRC)
3. Stanley Ridges
4. Frank Jenks, Douglas Fowley and Iris Adrian in *Shake Hands With Murder* (PRC)
5. Lynn Bari and Edward G Robinson in *Tampico* (Fox)
6. Edgar Dearing, Frank Craven, Gloria Jean and Alan Curtis in *Destiny* (Univ)
7. Phillip Terry and Loretta Young in *Ladies Courageous* (Univ)
8. Betty Hutton, Bing Crosby and Yvonne De Carlo in *Here Come the Waves* (Par)
9. Arthur Lake, Jeff Donnell and Marjorie Reynolds in *Three is a Family* (UA)

1. Eddie Quillan, Frances Langford and Lyle Talbot in *Dixie Jamboree* (PRC)
2. Ole Olsen and Chic Johnson
3. Charles Laughton
4. Joe Besser and Ann Miller in *Hey, Rookie* (Col)
5. David Bruce and Anne Gwynne in *South of Dixie* (Univ)
6. Ivan Lebedeff and Helen Vinson in *Are These Our Parents?* (MoP)
7. Bonita Granville and Lawrence Tierney in *Youth Runs Wild* (RKO)
8. Jack Carson and Jane Wyman in *Make Your Own Bed* (WB)
9. Edward Norris (I) and Mary Beth Hughes in *Men On Her Mind* (PRC)
10. Veda Ann Borg, Frank Jenks, Chester Clute, Emory Parnell and Tom Conway in *The Falcon In Hollywood* (RKO)
11. John Loder, Helen Walker, Dennis O'Keefe and William Bendix in *Abroad With Two Yanks* (UA)

10 ▷
▷
11

1. Cary Grant, Raymond Massey and Peter Lorre in *Arsenic and Old Lace* (WB)

2. Akim Tamiroff, Lynn Bari and Francis Lederer in *The Bridge of San Luis Rey* (UA)

3. Fredric March in *The Adventures of Mark Twain* (WB)

4. Betty Hutton and Fred MacMurray in *And the Angels Sing* (Par)

5. Phil Tead, Isabel la Mal, Gary Cooper, Teresa Wright and Robert Dudley in *Casanova Brown* (RKO)

6. Nat Pendleton

7. Dennis Morgan, Dane Clark and Faye Emerson in *The Very Thought of You* (WB)

8. Barry Sullivan, Dorothy Lamour, Eddie Bracken, Gil Lamb and Forrest Orr in *Rainbow Island* (Par)

9. Loretta Young, Alan Ladd and Cecil Kellaway in *And Now Tomorrow* (Par)

Rita Hayworth

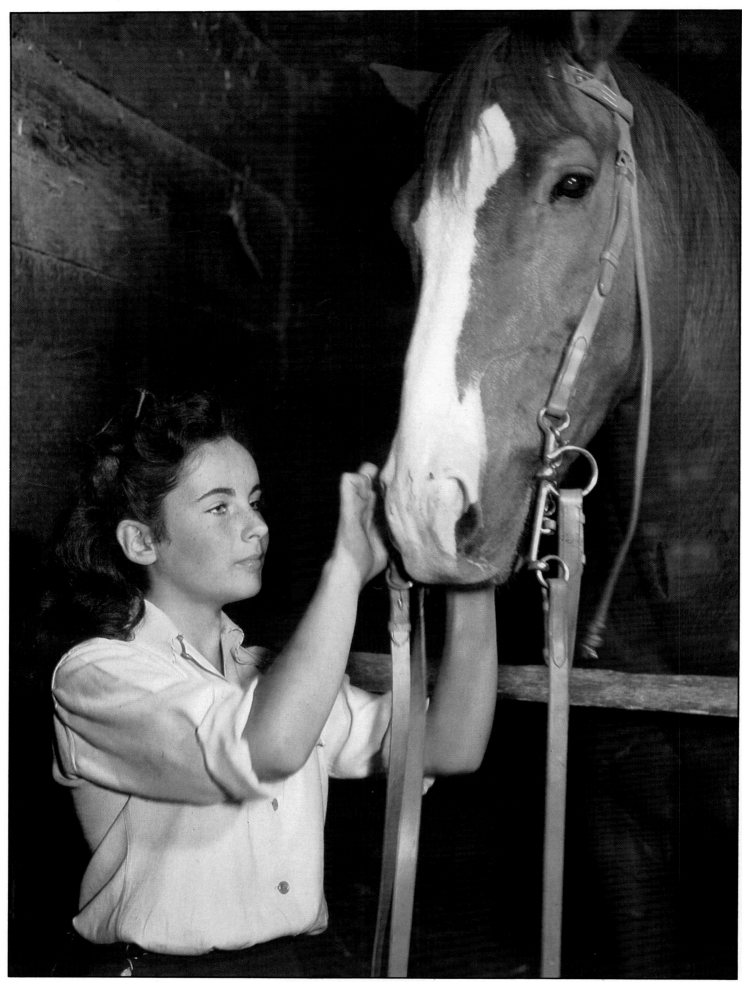

Elizabeth Taylor in *National Velvet* (MGM)

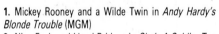

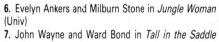

1. Mickey Rooney and a Wilde Twin in *Andy Hardy's Blonde Trouble* (MGM)

2. Nina Foch and Lloyd Bridges in *She's A Soldier Too* (Col)

3. William Boyd, Louise Currie, Jimmy Rogers and Robert Frazer in *Forty Thieves* (UA)

4. Jimmy Lydon and Joan Mortimer in *Henry Aldrich, Boy Scout* (Par)

5. Irene Ryan and Tim Ryan in *Hot Rhythm* (MoP)

6. Evelyn Ankers and Milburn Stone in *Jungle Woman* (Univ)

7. John Wayne and Ward Bond in *Tall in the Saddle* (RKO)

8. Elyse Knox (std), Rick Vallin, Oscar O'Shea and Sam Flint in *Army Wives* (MoP)

9. Nina Foch and Stephen Crane in *Cry of the Werewolf* (Col)

197

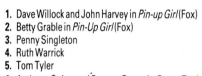

1. Dave Willock and John Harvey in *Pin-up Girl* (Fox)
2. Betty Grable in *Pin-Up Girl* (Fox)
3. Penny Singleton
4. Ruth Warrick
5. Tom Tyler
6. Anthony Quinn and Preston Foster in *Roger Touhy, Gangster* (GB *The Last Gangster*) (Fox)
7. Victor McLaglen, Horace MacMahon, Henry Morgan, George E Stone, Frank Jenks and Preston Foster in *Roger Touhy, Gangster* (GB *The Last Gangster*) (Fox)
8. Akim Tamiroff
9. Jeanne Bates and Tom Neal in *The Racket Man* (Col)
10. Rod Cameron and Dick Alexander in *Boss of Boom Town* (Univ)

1

2

1. Peter Glenville and Stewart Granger in *Madonna of the Seven Moons* (G'boro)
2. Peter Glenville in *Madonna of the Seven Moons* (G'boro)
3. Peter Glenville and Patricia Roc in *Madonna of the Seven Moons* (G'boro)
4. Peter Murray Hill and Phyllis Calvert in *Madonna of the Seven Moons* (G'boro)
5. Peter Murray Hill in *Madonna of the Seven Moons* (G'boro)
6. Jinx Falkenburg, Leslie Brooks and Marcia Mae Jones in *Nine Girls* (Col)
7. Peter Glenville, Phyllis Calvert, Stewart Granger and Nancy Price in *Madonna of the Seven Moons* (G'boro)
8. John Wengraf, Eric Rolf, Bruce Bennett and Arno Frey in *U Boat Prisoner* (Col)
9. Bob Haymes and Arthur Lake in *Sailor's Holiday* (Col)
10. Jack Haley and Fritz Feld in *Take It Big* (Par)

3

4

6

7

8

10

◁ 9

199

1

2

5

3

4

8

6

7

9

1. Janis Paige
2. Sonny Tufts
3. Charles Korvin in *Enter Arsene Lupin* (Univ)
4. Adele Mara in *Thoroughbreds* (Rep)
5. Wallace Beery
6. Huntz Hall, J Farrell Macdonald, Leo Gorcey and the East Side Kids in *Follow the Leader* (MoP)
7. Wallace Beery and Binnie Barnes in *Barbary Coast Gent* (MGM)
8. Turhan Bey and Maria Montez in *Ali Baba and the Forty Thieves* (Univ)
9. Paul Lukas in *Address Unknown* (Col)
10. Lowell Gilmore, Toumanova, Dena Penn, Glenn Vernon, Gregory Peck, Edward Durst, Igor Dolgoruki and Hugo Haas in *Days of Glory* (RKO)
11. Penelope Ward in *English Without Tears* (US *Her Man Gilbey*) (TC)
12. Lowell Gilmore and Maria Palmer in *Days of Glory* (RKO)

10

11

12

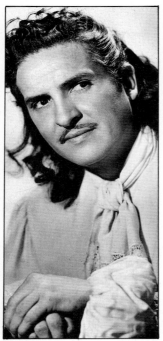

1. Basil Rathbone in *Frenchman's Creek* (Par)
2. Arturo de Cordova in *Frenchman's Creek* (Par)
3. Monte Hale
4. Joel McCrea in *Buffalo Bill* (Fox)
5. Ben Blue
6. Chic Johnson, Ole Olsen, Martha O'Driscoll, Walter Catlett and Gloria Jean in *Ghost Catchers* (Univ)

7. Howard Freeman, Ann Miller, Victor Moore, Kay Kyser and Georgia Carroll in *Carolina Blues* (Col)
8. Carmen Miranda in *Four Jills in a Jeep* (Fox)
9. Alice Faye in *Four Jills in a Jeep* (Fox)
10. Charles Winninger and Florence Bates in *Belle of the Yukon* (RKO)
11. Laraine Day in *Bride by Mistake* (RKO)

◁ 11

201

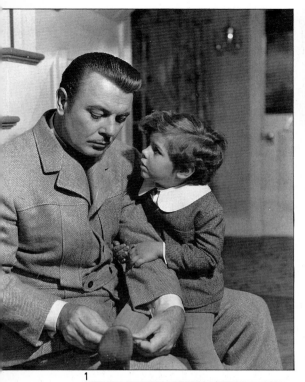

1

2

3

1. George Brent and Billy Ward in *Experiment Perilous* (RKO)
2. Paul Lukas, Albert Dekker and George Brent in *Experiment Perilous* (RKO)
3. Stephanie Bachelor and George Brent in *Experiment Perilous* (RKO)
4. Don Defore
5. Robert Lowery
6. Ann Blyth and Arthur Treacher in *Chip Off The Old Block* (Univ)
7. Marguerite Chapman
8. Marian Jordan and Jim Jordan (c) in *Heavenly Days* (RKO)
9. Clarence Kolb, Dick Haymes, Monty Woolley, Beverly Whitney and Anthony Quinn in *Irish Eyes Are Smiling* (Fox)
10. Richard Greene
11. Allan Lane (l) in *Call of the South Seas* (Rep)
12. Jonathan Hale (c) in *The Black Parachute* (Col)
13. Scott McKay and Anne Baxter in *Guest in the House* (UA)

4

5

6

7

8

9

10

11

13

◁12

1

2

3

4

5

8

6

7

9

10

1. Joyce Reynolds in *Janie* (WB)
2. Angela Lansbury
3. Judy Canova, Matt Willis and Minerva Urecal in
Louisiana Hayride (Col)
4. Constance Moore
5. Carol Raye and William Hartnell in *Strawberry Roan*
(BN)
6. Tom Tully, Spring Byington, Joseph Cotten and
Ginger Rogers in *I'll Be Seeing You* (UA)
7. Edward Ryan and Anne Baxter in *The Sullivans* (Fox)
8. Anne Gwynne, Vera Vague and Alan Dinehart in
Moon Over Las Vegas (Univ)
9. Barton MacLane and Robert Ryan in *Marine Raiders*
(RKO)
10. Anne Baxter and John Hodiak in *Sunday Dinner For
a Soldier* (Fox)
11. The English archers in *Henry V* (TC)
12. Laurence Olivier in *Henry V* (TC)

11
▷
▷
12

1

2

3

4

5

6

7

8

1. Don Barry and Emma Dunn in *My Buddy* (Rep)
2. Jane Wyatt in *None But The Lonely Heart* (RKO)
3. Geraldine Fitzgerald and Alexander Knox in *Wilson* (Fox)
4. Gracie Allen
5. Douglas Fowley, Robert Walker and Donald Curtis in *See Here, Private Hargrove* (MGM)
6. George Tobias
7. Peter Cookson and Marjorie Weaver in *Shadow of Suspicion* (MoP)
8. Allyn Joslyn and Evelyn Keyes in *Strange Affair* (Col)
9. John Wayne in *Tall in the Saddle* (RKO)
10. Percy Waram, Hillary Brooke, Ray Milland and Marjorie Reynolds in *Ministry of Fear* (Par)
11. Ella Raines in *Tall in the Saddle* (RKO)
12. John Wayne and Ward Bond in *Tall in the Saddle* (RKO)

9

10

11

◁ 12

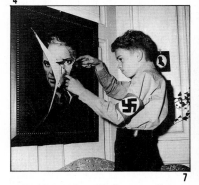

1. Dennis O'Keefe and Mischa Auer in *Up in Mabel's Room* (UA)

2. Gordon Oliver and Elaine Shepard in *Seven Days Ashore* (RKO)

3. William Powell, Myrna Loy, Lucile Watson and Harry Davenport in *The Thin Man Goes Home* (MGM)

4. Mischa Auer, John Hubbard, Binnie Barnes, Charlotte Greenwood with Dennis O'Keefe and Marjorie Reynolds (on floor) in *Up in Mabel's Room* (UA)

5. Alan Dinehart and Marjorie Gateson in *Seven Days Ashore* (RKO)

6. Myrna Loy and William Powell in *The Thin Man Goes Home* (MGM)

7. Skip Homeier in *Tomorrow the World* (UA)

8. Alexander Knox (r) in *None Shall Escape* (Col)

9. Adele Jergens

10. Shelley Winters and Constance Dowling in *Knickerbocker Holiday* (UA)

11. Billy Gilbert and Shemp Howard in *Three of a Kind* (MoP)

◁11

1. Stanley Ridges, Gigi Perreau and Osa Massen in *The Master Race* (RKO)
2. Nancy Gates and Lloyd Bridges in *The Master Race* (RKO)
3. Griffith Jones
4. George Coulouris and Nancy Gates in *The Master Race* (RKO)
5. Sheila Ryan and Michael O'Shea in *Something for the Boys* (Fox)
6. Glenn Langan and Sheila Ryan in *Something for the Boys* (Fox)
7. Arline Judge
8. Margaret Lockwood and Stewart Granger in *Love Story* (US *A Lady Surrenders*) (G'boro)
9. Michael O'Shea and Anne Shirley in *Man From Frisco* (Rep)
10. John Laurie and Stanley Holloway in *The Way Ahead* (TC)
11. Margaret O'Brien, Judy Garland and Henry Daniels Jr in *Meet Me in St. Louis* (MGM)
12. Hugh Burden, James Donald, Raymond Huntley, John Laurie, Stanley Holloway and Jimmy Hanley in *The Way Ahead* (TC)

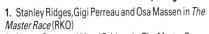

1. James Brown and Gail Russell in *Our Hearts Were Young and Gay* (Par)
2. Bill Edwards, Gail Russell, James Brown and Diana Lynn in *Our Hearts Were Young and Gay* (Par)
3. George Murphy and Constance Moore in *Show Business* (RKO)
4. Nancy Kelly in *Show Business* (RKO)
5. Don Douglas and Constance Moore in *Show Business* (RKO)
6. Gloria Jean in *Reckless Age* (Univ)
7. James Cardwell and Lynn Bari in *Sweet and Low-Down* (Fox)
8. Leon Belasco and Maxie Rosenbloom in *Night Club Girl* (Univ)
9. Leon Belasco, Vivian Austin and Billy Dunn in *Night Club Girl* (Univ)

1

2

3

4

1. Barbara Stanwyck in *Double Indemnity* (Par)
2. Ann Richards and Brian Donlevy in *An American Romance* (MGM)
3. Peggy Ryan in *Bowery to Broadway* (Univ)
4. Donald O'Connor in *Bowery to Broadway* (Univ)
5. John Qualen and Brian Donlevy in *An American Romance* (MGM)
6. Stan Laurel, Harry Hayden, Oliver Hardy, Arthur Space, Doris Merrick and Veda Ann Borg in *The Big Noise* (Fox)
7. Googie Withers, Clive Brook, Beatrice Lillie and Roland Culver in *On Approval* (IP)
8. Roland Culver, O B Clarence and Beatrice Lillie in *On Approval* (IP)
9. Googie Withers and Roland Culver in *On Approval* (IP)
10. Beatrice Lillie and Clive Brook in *On Approval* (IP)

5

6

7

8

9

10

1

4

1. Lon Chaney Jr in *Dead Man's Eyes* (Univ)
2. James Mason and Virginia Keiley in *Fanny By Gaslight* (US *Man of Evil*) (G'boro)
3. Peter Jones in *Fanny By Gaslight* (US *Man of Evil*) (G'boro)
4. Jane Withers
5. Don Douglas
6. Philip Friend
7. Minerva Urecal
8. Art Miles (Gorilla), and Maxie Rosenbloom in *Crazy Knights* (MoP)
9. Jeanne Crain and Walter Brennan in *Home in Indiana* (Fox)
10. Charlotte Greenwood and Lon McCallister in *Home in Indiana* (Fox)
11. June Haver and Ward Bond in *Home in Indiana* (Fox)

2

3

5

6

7

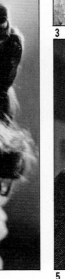

8

9
▷

10

11
▷

1

2

3

4

5

6

1. June Duprez
2. Jerome Courtland
3. Donald Cook
4. Judy Holliday
5. Maris Wrixon
6. Fredric March
7. Natalie Schafer
8. Andrea King
9. Elisha Cook Jr

7
8

9

1

2

1. Turhan Bey and Katharine Hepburn in *Dragon Seed* (MGM)
2. Walter Huston and Aline MacMahon in *Dragon Seed* (MGM)
3. Leslie Brooks
4. June Vincent
5. June Lockhart
6. Victor McLaglen and Bob Hope in *The Princess and the Pirate* (SG)
7. Richard Greene in *Don't Take It To Heart* (TC)
8. Three Piratical Starlets in *The Princess and the Pirate* (SG)
9. Bob Hope and Virginia Mayo in *The Princess and the Pirate* (SG)

5

6

7

8

9

1. Stanley Prager, Henry Morgan, Michael O'Shea, Vincent Price, William Eythe and Murray Alper in *The Eve of St Mark* (Fox)
2. Dennis O'Keefe and John Wayne in *The Fighting Seabees* (Rep)
3. Franchot Tone and Nils Asther in *The Hour Before the Dawn* (Par)
4. Gypsy Rose Lee
5. Jerome Cowan, Stuart Crawford and Jane Wyman in *Crime by Night* (WB)
6. Robert Lowery, Phyllis Brooks and Charles Arnt in *Dangerous Passage* (Par)
7. Marlene Dietrich and Orson Welles in *Follow the Boys* (Univ)
8. Charles La Torre, John Loder, William Bendix, Tom Fadden and Roman Bohnen in *The Hairy Ape* (UA)

The Three Caballeros © 1944 Walt Disney Company

James Stewart

1

2

3

4

1. Anthony Quinn, Robin Raymond and Sheila Ryan (all std l to r) in *Ladies of Washington* (Fox)
2. Dana Andrews, and Gene Tierney in *Laura* (Fox)
3. Ida Lupino, Nazimova and Paul Henreid in *In Our Time* (WB)
4. Ronald Colman and Marlene Dietrich in *Kismet* (MGM)
5. Phillip Terry and Anne Shirley in *Music in Manhattan* (RKO)
6. Barry Kelly
7. Claude Rains, Bette Davis and Robert Shayne in *Mr Skeffington* (WB)
8. Jane Frazee, star of *Kansas City Kitty* (Col)
9. Bill Henry, Jean Parker and Robert Lowery in *The Navy Way* (Par)

5

7

8
◁
◁
9

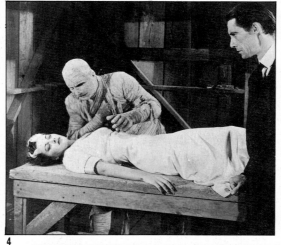

1. Stan Laurel, David Leland, Oliver Hardy and Mary Boland in *Nothing but Trouble* (MGM)

2. Walter Sande, Paulette Goddard and Mary Treen in *I Love a Soldier* (Par)

3. Vivian Blaine

4. Ramsey Ames, Lon Chaney Jr and John Carradine in *The Mummy's Ghost* (Univ)

5. Allyn Joslyn in *Strange Affair* (Col)

6. Betty Field and Joel McCrea in *The Great Moment* (Par)

7. Tamara Toumanova

8. Anne Gwynne, Nella Walker and John Litel (all std), and Andrew Toombes, Ian Wolfe, Frank Marlow, June Preisser, Betty Kean, Grace McDonald and Regis Toomey in *Murder in the Blue Room* (Univ)

9. Linda Darnell in *It Happened Tomorrow* (UA)

8 ◁
9 ▷

1. Mervyn Johns
2. Paul Dupuis
3. Margaret O'Brien and June Allyson in *Music for Millions* (MGM)
4. Eve Amber, Dean Harens, Charles Laughton, Maude Eburne and Clifford Brooke in *The Suspect* (Univ)
5. Ann Miller and Jess Barker (std) in *Jam Session* (Col)
6. Kirby Grant
7. Jean Parker (r) in *Lady in the Death House* (PRC)
8. George Dolenz, Margaret Irving, Steven Geray, Lou Costello and Arthur Treacher in *In Society* (Univ)
9. Lauren Bacall and Humphrey Bogart in *To Have and Have Not* (WB)

217

1

2

1. Craig Stevens, Alexis Smith, John Ridgley, Ann Sheridan, Jack Carson, Jane Wyman and Eve Arden in *The Doughgirls* (WB)
2. Hedy Lamarr and Paul Henreid in *The Conspirators* (WB)
3. Belita in *Lady, Let's Dance* (MoP)
4. The Wilde Twins
5. Gloria DeHaven, George Murphy, Eddie 'Rochester' Anderson and Charles Winninger in *Broadway Rhythm* (MGM)
6. Ross Hunter, Ann Savage and Fritz Feld in *Ever Since Venus* (Col)
7. Tom Tully, Jill Browning, Jimmy Lydon, Minna Gombell and Freddie Bartholomew in *The Town Went Wild* (PRC)
8. Jane Ball in *Winged Victory* (Fox)
9. Bela Lugosi and Matt Willis in *Return of the Vampire* (Col)

3

4

5

6

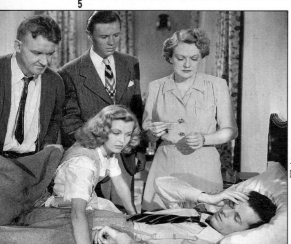

7

8

9

1. Jerry Colonna (in pram), Constance Moore (kneeling) and Paul Whiteman in *Atlantic City* (Rep)
2. John Hubbard, Byron Foulger, Joan Davis, Jane Frazee, Judy Clark and Bob Haymes in *Beautiful But Broke* (Col)
3. Peter Coe, Lon Chaney Jr and Martin Kosleck in *The Mummy's Curse* (Univ)
4. Carl 'Alfalfa' Switzer, Robert 'Buzzy' Henry, Edythe Elliott and Stuart Erwin in *The Great Mike* (PRC)
5. Dennis Hoey, Victor Kilian, Lucile Watson and Wallis Clark (std) in *Uncertain Glory* (WB)
6. Greer Garson in *Mrs Parkington* (MGM)
7. Constance Dowling (c) and the Goldwyn Girls in *Up In Arms* (RKO)
8. Audrey Totter in *Main Street After Dark* (MGM)
9. Jean Howard in *Bermuda Mystery* (Fox)

219

1. Peggy Stewart and Allan Lane in *Silver City Kid* (Rep)
2. Tex Ritter in *Oklahoma Raiders* (Univ)
3. Marjorie Main, Donna Reed and James Craig in *Gentle Annie* (MGM)
4. Christine McIntyre, Raymond Hatton and Johnny Mack Brown in *West of the Rio Grande* (MoP)
5. Dennis Moore, Kay Forrester and Jimmy Wakely in *Song of the Range* (MoP)
6. Smiley Burnette and Sunset Carson (c) in *Border Town Trail* (Rep)
7. Tex Ritter (l), Dan White and Herbert Rawlinson (r) in *The Marshal of Gunsmoke* (Univ)
8. Kent Taylor and Nils Asther in *Alaska* (MoP)

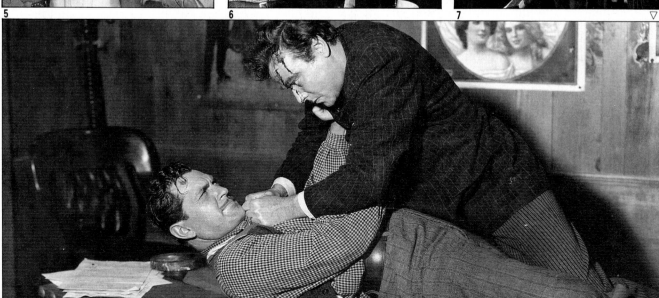

1

2

3

4

1. Al 'Fuzzy' St John, Kermit Maynard and Larry 'Buster' Crabbe in *Frontier Outlaws* (PRC)

2. Johnny Bond and his Red River Valley Boys with Fuzzy Knight and Tex Ritter (r) in *Arizona Trail* (Univ)

3. Jack Ingram and Johnny Mack Brown in *Range Law* (MoP)

4. Raymond Hatton and Johnny Mack Brown in *Partners of the Trail* (MoP)

5. Henry Hall, Marjorie Clements, Bud Osborne, Guy Wilkerson, Tex Ritter and Dave O'Brien in *Dead or Alive* (PRC)

6. Ben Johnson, Jack Overman and Robert Mitchum in *Nevada* (RKO)

7. Roy Rogers and Dale Evans in *San Fernando Valley* (Rep)

8. Ray Bennett and Johnny Mack Brown in *Raiders of the Border* (MoP)

9. Andrew Tombes, Bob Crosby and Fay McKenzie in *The Singing Sheriff* (Univ)

10. Budd Buster, Fuzzy Knight, and Rod Cameron in *Riders of the Santa Fe* (Univ)

5

6

7

8

9
▷
◁
10

1

2

3

4

5

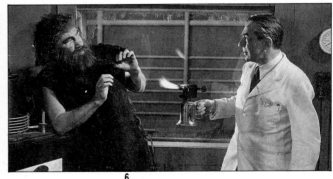

6

7

8

1. Dick Powell and Anne Shirley in *Murder My Sweet* (GB *Farewell My Lovely*) (RKO)

2. Jimmy Lydon, Charles Smith and Barbara Pepper in *Henry Aldrich Plays Cupid* (GB *Henry Plays Cupid*) (Par)

3. Edmund Lowe in *Girl in the Case* (Col)

4. Andrew Tombes (l) and Robert Paige (r) in *Can't Help Singing* (Univ)

5. W C Fields, Charlie McCarthy and Edgar Bergen in *Sensations of 1945* (UA)

6. George Zucco and Bela Lugosi in *Return of the Ape Man* (MoP)

7. Lionel Barrymore

8. Lesley Brook

9. Byron Foulger and J Carrol Naish in *The Whistler* (Col)

10. Sigrid Gurie and J Edward Bromberg in *Voice in the Wind* (UA)

9
▷◁
10

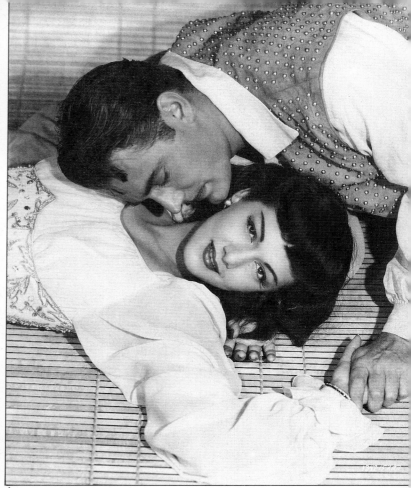

1. Spencer Tracy and Agnes Moorehead in *The Seventh Cross* (MGM)

2. Jon Hall and Louise Allbritton in *San Diego, I Love You* (Univ)

3. Elizabeth Patterson, Eddie Bracken, Ella Raines, Georgia Caine and William Demarest in *Hail the Conquering Hero* (Par)

4. Maria Montez and Jon Hall in *Gypsy Wildcat* (Univ)

5. Ann Savage, Abner Biberman, J Alex Havier and Tom Neal in *Two-Man Submarine* (Col)

6. Pat O'Brien and Ruth Warrick in *Secret Command* (Col)

7. Sam Jaffe

8. Lynne Roberts and Arthur Lake in *The Ghost That Walks Alone* (Col)

9. Ralph Richardson

10. Bernadene Hayes, Richard Lane and Edward G Robinson in *Mr Winkle Goes to War* (Col)

1

2

3

4

5

7

6

8

1. Phyllis Stanley
2. George Dolenz
3. Marilyn Maxwell
4. Robert Kent
5. Mary Boland
6. Glenn Langan
7. Jean Kent
8. Porter Hall
9. Phil Regan
10. Isabel Jewell
11. Russell Hicks

9
10

11

1. Lee Bowman and Jean Arthur in *The Impatient Years* (Col)

2. Robert Paige and Louise Allbritton in *Her Primitive Man* (Univ)

3. George Macready, Jeanne Bates and Erik Rolf in *The Soul of a Monster* (Col)

4. Tom Powers, Isabel Randolph, Fred MacMurray, Claudette Colbert and Cecil Kellaway in *Practically Yours* (Par)

5. Linda Darnell, Hugo Haas and George Sanders in *Summer Storm* (UA)

6. John Hodiak, Natalie Schafer and Lana Turner in *Marriage Is a Private Affair* (MGM)

7. Olga Fabian, Maris Wrix on and John Carradine in *Waterfront* (PRC)

8. Marie Wilson and Johnnie 'Scat' Davis (on floor) in *You Can't Ration Love* (Par)

9. Richard Arlen and Vera Hruba Ralston in *Storm Over Lisbon* (Rep)

10. John Craven, Lucille Ball, Howard Freeman and Dick Powell in *Meet the People* (MGM)

9
▷
10

1. Bob Murphy, Jack Carson, Ann Sheridan and Dennis Morgan in *Shine on Harvest Moon* (WB)
2. Mona Freeman
3. Ozzie Nelson and Harriet Hilliard in *Take It Big* (Par)
4. Simone Simon and Ann Carter in *The Curse of the Cat People* (RKO)
5. Paul Langton
6. Edgar Barrier
7. Orson Welles, Joan Fontaine and Hillary Brooke in *Jane Eyre* (Fox)
8. Charles Starrett, Shirley Patterson and Steve Clark in *Riding West* (Col)
9. Frank Albertson, Jane Frazee, Vera Vague and Frank Jenks in *Rosie the Riveter* (Rep)

226

1. Fuzzy Knight
2. Bob Crosby, Gloria Jean, Patsy O'Connor, Marjorie Weaver and Mel Torme in *Pardon My Rhythm* (Univ)
3. Pat Parrish and Clifford Severn in *They Live in Fear* (Col)
4. Otto Kruger in *They Live in Fear* (Col)
5. John Beal
6. Alan Curtis
7. June Carlson
8. Don Ameche in *Wing and a Prayer* (Fox)
9. Lina Romay, Ben Blue and Xavier Cugat in *Two Girls and a Sailor* (MGM)

9 ▷

1

2

3

4

5

6

1. Grace McDonald, Bob Crosby, Betty Kean and Walter Catlett in *My Gal Loves Music* (Univ)
2. Bela Lugosi in *Voodoo Man* (MoP)
3. Martha O'Driscoll and Noah Beery Jr in *Weekend Pass* (Univ)
4. Lon Chaney Jr, Sabu and Maria Montez in *Cobra Woman* (Univ)
5. Barbara Everest, Ray Milland and Ruth Hussey in *The Uninvited* (Par)
6. Rose Hobart
7. Joss Ambler
8. Fay Holden
9. Nancy Kelly
10. Tom D'Andrea

7

8 ▷

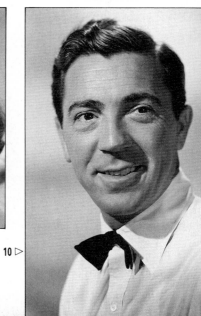

9

10 ▷

1. Bonita Granville, Jackie Moran (c) and Jill Browning in *Song of the Open Road* (UA)

2. Eddie Quillan and Anne Rooney in *Slightly Terrific* (Univ)

3. Paul Langton (c) and Jacqueline White in *Thirty Seconds Over Tokyo* (MGM)

4. Ben Weldon, Warner Baxter, Edward Norris, Nina Foch and Charles Halton (at piano) in *Shadows in the Night* (Col)

5. Gale Sondergaard and Deanna Durbin in *Christmas Holiday* (Univ)

6. Gwen Littlefield and Guy Madison in *Since You Went Away* (UA)

7. H B Warner (3rd l) and Lenore Aubert in *Action in Arabia* (RKO)

8. Benson Fong and Sidney Toler in *The Chinese Cat* (MoP)

9. William 'Wild Bill' Elliott in *Vigilantes of Dodge City* (Rep)

10. Bert Lahr

11. Bruce Kellogg as he appeared in *Barbary Coast Gent* (MGM)

◁ **10**

1

2

3

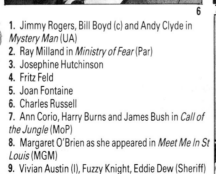

5 ◁

6

1. Jimmy Rogers, Bill Boyd (c) and Andy Clyde in
Mystery Man (UA)
2. Ray Milland in *Ministry of Fear* (Par)
3. Josephine Hutchinson
4. Fritz Feld
5. Joan Fontaine
6. Charles Russell
7. Ann Corio, Harry Burns and James Bush in *Call of
the Jungle* (MoP)
8. Margaret O'Brien as she appeared in *Meet Me In St
Louis* (MGM)
9. Vivian Austin (l), Fuzzy Knight, Eddie Dew (Sheriff)
and Rod Cameron in *Trigger Trail* (Univ)

◁ 8

9 ▷

ERROL **FLYNN**

"OBJECTIVE BURMA"

WILLIAM PRINCE · JAMES BROWN · GEORGE TOBIAS · HENRY HULL · WARNER ANDERSON Directed by RAOUL WALSH

PRESENTED BY **WARNER BROS.**

Laurence Olivier's PRESENTATION IN TECHNICOLOR

of **HENRY V**

by WILLIAM SHAKESPEARE

A TWO CITIES FILM · EAGLE-LION DISTRIBUTION

Ingrid Bergman

CHAPTER SIX

1945

ADJUSTING TO PEACETIME

In Europe the war came to an end with VE Day on 8 May. In the Far East, VJ Day arrived on 15 August. Ironically, now that the struggle was over, Hollywood produced three of the finest films of the war. As if in atonement for the mindless heroics with which the studios had entered the conflict, these films distilled the accumulated experience of over three years of fighting into acutely observed depictions of the ordinary fighting man.

For United Artists, William Wellman directed *The Story of GI Joe* (aka *War Correspondent*), based on the writing of the war correspondent Ernie Pyle, played in the film by Burgess Meredith. Its subjects were the infantrymen of C Company, slogging through North Africa and up the road to Rome, their horizons bounded by mud, muddle and fatigue. As Pyle observes to the men's captain (Robert Mitchum): 'But the GI lives so miserably and dies so miserably'. At the climax of the film there is a desperate assault on a German-held monastery. As the survivors of C Company slump exhausted by the road they have cleared to Rome, Mitchum's body is brought down from the hilltop by mule. Out of the disordered impressions of war Pyle fashions a picture in which different campaigns inexorably blur into one, mitigated only by the small rituals of comradeship, the arrival of mail from home, or the treat of whisky and turkey at Christmas.

Lewis Milestone's *A Walk in the Sun* Twentieth Century-Fox, based closely on the novel by Harry Brown, was a measured, lyrical account of a platoon's progress from the beach-head at Salerno to their capture of a heavily defended farmhouse six miles inland. This was the war in microcosm, rhythmically scripted by Robert Rossen to catch the cadences of the men's tense conversation as they snatch uneasy bouts of rest between bursts of action.

John Ford's *They were Expendable* (MGM) was his first war feature and his first film after Navy service during which he had been wounded while making the Award-winning documentary *The Battle of Midway* (1942). *They Were Expendable* was an elegiac tribute to the role played by PT

Robert Montgomery in *They Were Expendable* (MGM)

Robert Montgomery, Marshall Thompson and John Wayne in *They Were Expendable* (MGM)

Dane Clark

Charles Kempson, Percy Kilbride and Zachary Scott in
The Southerner (UA)

Zachary Scott, Jack Carson and Joan Crawford in *Mildred
Pierce* (WB)

boats in the withdrawal from the Philippines. It starred Robert Montgomery, also returning from Navy service, who played a character closely modelled on Commander John D Bulkeley, the pioneer of the PT boat in combat. John Wayne co-starred in more conventionally heroic mode, although he gave an admirably restrained performance. Joseph August's photography, in the last of his 14 films with Ford, was immaculate.

Warner Brothers tackled the theme of postwar readjustment in *Pride of the Marines,* (GB *Forever In Love*) in which John Garfield played a Marine blinded at Guadalcanal and now facing a harrowing new battle back in the United States. This was a brave film, but the studio feebly hedged its bets by producing posters which showed Garfield and his co-stars Eleanor Parker and Dane Clark grinning broadly and walking arm-in-arm in best musical comedy fashion. The studio displayed a similarly uncertain touch in *Objective Burma!,* directed by Raoul Walsh, a relatively realistic combat film which nevertheless gave the unfortunate impression that Errol Flynn had liberated Burma singlehanded.

The movie of the year was Paramount's *The Lost Weekend,* directed by Billy Wilder, which won the Academy Award for Best Picture and a Best Actor Award for Ray Milland as the alcoholic failed writer Don Birnam. In the same film Frank Faylen gave one of the most telling cameos of the decade as a sadistic nurse in the alcoholic ward where Milland is briefly and traumatically confined. The film, and Milland's persuasive performance – showing all the chinks in his suave armour – have stood the test of time, marred only by a trite 'happy ending' in which Milland is saved by the love of his fiancee Jane Wyman. Don Birnam seems a man too hazily trapped in the terrible romance of booze to be so glibly hauled back from the brink.

The drab New York streets through which Don Birnam trudged desperately trying to hock his typewriter on Yom Kippur – when both the Jewish and Catholic pawnbrokers are shut – was a cityscape stripped of all glamour. A film of studio gloss clings stubbornly to Twentieth Century-Fox's *A Tree Grows in Brooklyn,* directed by Elia Kazan, which chronicled the struggles of a working-class family in turn-of-the-century New York. James Dunn won the Best Supporting Actor Oscar for his performance as the kindly alcoholic father, and Joan Blondell stole the show as the indomitable Aunt Cissy.

Jean Renoir's *The Southerner* (United Artists) brought a gentle poetry to the drama of a young sharecropping couple's fight against man and the elements. Too gentle, perhaps, for a portrait of grinding rural poverty. Renoir's warm humanity washes all over the carefully deglamourised actors, Zachary Scott and Betty Field, who nevertheless look absurdly sleek when compared with Walker Evans' harrowing photographs of the gaunt Dust Bowl family which stare awkwardly out from the pages of *Let Us Now Praise Famous Men*.

Joan Crawford had left MGM in 1943. She had made no film for two years (save for a brief appearance in *Hollywood Canteen* (1944) but came back with a bang in Warners' *Mildred Pierce,* directed by Michael Curtiz. Doomed in romance and the victim of predatory men, Crawford's movie heroines were paradigms of her own unhappy life and manic success drive. In *Mildred Pierce* she achieved the complete fusion of life and art as the relentlessly over-achieving Mildred, suffering mightily at the hands of Zachary Scott and poisonous brat of a daughter Ann Blyth. It was a signal triumph, winning Crawford the year's Best Actress Oscar and launching her on a string of roles in which she played driven women hovering on the edge of middle age.

John Kelly, Eddie Acuff and Danny Kaye in *Wonder Man* (SG)

The film musical was at its peak, but MGM's brilliant producer Arthur Freed overreached himself when he tried to push back the boundaries of the genre in the ambitious *Yolanda and the Thief.* A flimsy fairy tale set in South America, it starred Fred Astaire as a conman who sets out to fleece gullible young heiress Lucille Bremer but finds his plans going awry when love takes a hand. *Yolanda and the Thief's* stylised blend of song, dance and colour proved too whimsical for contemporary audiences and it lost over $1.6 million at the box office.

At Paramount Betty Hutton tore hell for leather into the part of the legendary nightclub hostess Texas Guinan in *Incendiary Blonde.* Audiences got two Danny Kayes for the price of one in RKO's *Wonder Man,* a zippy musical fantasy in which he played two brothers, the serious one taking the place of his devil-may-care nightclub singer sibling when the latter is bumped off by the Mob. As well as being one of the year's top earners, *Wonder Man* also introduced Vera-Ellen, third-billed as the murdered brother's dancing partner.

Merle Oberon and Cornel Wilde in *A Song to Remember* (Col)

Columbia pulled out all the stops on *A Song to Remember,* starring strapping Cornel Wilde as the tubercular Chopin and glacial Merle Oberon as a nattily besuited George Sand, puffing a cigar and telling him, 'You could make miracles of music in Majorca'. Later she advises Wilde to 'Discontinue that so-called Polonaise jumble you've been playing for days'. But Wilde soldiers gamely on until he expires over a keyboard splattered with Technicolor blood. The news is broken to Oberon as she is posing for a Famous French Painter. Unruffled, she barks, 'Continue, Monsieur Delacroix!'.

The posters for MGM's *Adventure* proclaimed, 'Gable's Back and Garson's Got Him!', but the King's return after the war service was a limp affair. Some of the old magic seemed to have flaked away. In contrast Bing Crosby's career sailed serenely on, floating 'straight down the middle' with the lazy effortless parabola of one of his golf drives. In *The Bells of St Mary's,* Leo McCarey's artful sequel to *Going My Way* (1944) – made for contractual reasons at RKO – Bing told Sister Superior Ingrid Bergman, 'If you're ever in trouble, dial O for O'Malley'.

MGM's *The Clock* (GB *Under the Clock*), directed by

Matt McHugh, Ingrid Bergman and Ruth Donnelly in *The Bells of St. Mary's* (RKO)

Joan Bennett and Dan Duryea in *Scarlet Street* (Univ)

Rhonda Fleming in *Spellbound* (UA)

Lowell Gilmore, Hurd Hatfield and George Sanders in *The Picture of Dorian Gray* (MGM)

Vincente Minnelli, was one of the most charming wartime romances, in which Judy Garland married soldier Robert Walker on his 24-hour leave. Garland blossomed under Minnelli's direction (they were married that year), establishing her credentials as a dramatic actress and ensuring that at the end of the year she was one of the top ten moneymakers. Fritz Lang, Edward G Robinson, Joan Bennett and Dan Duryea joined forces in another masterly film noir, Universal's *Scarlet Street,* a remake of *La Chienne* (1931). Bennett was the vulgar streetwalker Lazy Legs and Dan Duryea her giggling stripe-suited pimp, casually destroying hen-pecked Sunday painter Edward G Robinson. They pay with their lives; Robinson with his identity.

Hollywood was beginning to flirt with psychoanalysis. In Alfred Hitchcock's *Spellbound,* Ingrid Bergman scraped her hair back and donned spectacles to play a psychiatrist delving into anguished Gregory Peck's subconscious, in the process revealing some Salvador Dali-designed dream sequences of startling beauty. At MGM, Phyllis Thaxter was *Bewitched,* playing a homicidal schizophrenic in an intriguing B-movie which anticipated *The Three Faces of Eve* (1957).

Laird Cregar was the unhinged composer George Harvey Bone in Twentieth Century-Fox's *Hangover Square.* An immensely handsome adaptation of Patrick Hamilton's novel, transplanted to Victorian London, it gave Cregar a final chance to display his genius for the portrayal of highly strung menace and mad genius. He died the same year, from a heart attack brought on by strenuous dieting.

At the beginning of his career Cregar had enjoyed considerable success playing Oscar Wilde on stage. And it was to Wilde that MGM turned in their lush version of *The Picture of Dorian Gray,* written and directed by Albert Lewin and introducing the coldly handsome Hurd Hatfield as the joylessly decadent swell who lets the portrait in the attic do the aging for him. Skilfully juxtaposing huge, luxurious interior spaces with striking close-ups, and tactfully hinting at the story's strong homosexual undertow, *The Picture of Dorian Gray* remains one of the most elegantly realised films of the period. The baleful portrait, putrescing from within, is shown in shocking colour. Equally colourful were the Wildean epigrams scattered like confetti by George Sanders' louche Lord Henry Wotton, the rake who inadvertently sets Hatfield on the path to eternal youth.

On Poverty Row, Monogram Pictures attempted to revive the gangster cycle, which had been dormant since the beginning of the decade, with *Dillinger,* a hard-hitting melodrama padded out with generous chunks of footage from *You Only Live Once* (1937) and starring newcomer Lawrence Tierney as the hard-faced Public Enemy Number One. Another B-factory, PRC, had their own cut-rate equivalent of partnerships like Ladd and Lake or Bogart and Bacall. Ann Savage and Tom Neal achieved a modest immortality as the doomed couple in Edgar G Ulmer's

Detour, a minimalist masterpiece made for only $20,000 and one of the best films to emerge from Hollywood's lower depths.

Bob Hope, Bing Crosby and Dorothy Lamour set out on the *Road to Utopia,* prospecting for Alaskan gold. Arguably the most inventive of the 'Road' series, *Road to Utopia* is packed with sight-gags and sly jokes about Hollywood and the stars themselves. As they trudge past an Alaskan peak, which bears a striking resemblance to the Paramount trademark, Hope exlaims, 'Look at all that bread and butter!' 'You're losing your grip, that's a mountain', Bing observes – at which point the summit is ringed with stars. 'It may be a mountain to you, but it's bread and butter to me', replies Hope.

An RKO quickie, *First Yank Into Tokyo,* released a month after the destruction of Hiroshima and Nagasaki, was the first movie to make a topical reference to the A-bomb. Atom secrets were at the centre of Twentieth Century-Fox's *The House on 92nd Street,* directed by Henry Hathaway. William Eythe played the federal undercover man infiltrating Signe Hasso's spy ring and Lloyd Nolan the head of the FBI unit involved. The film was produced by *The March of Time's* Louis de Rochemont, who brought his documentary approach to Hollywood, and made with the full co-operation of the FBI. Hathaway underlined its authenticity with much location shooting, a feature which looked forward to the strident 'realism' of films like *The Naked City* (1948).

Republic celebrated its tenth anniversary with *Flame of the Barbary Coast,* starring John Wayne and Ann Dvorak and a spectacular recreation of the San Francisco earthquake. Seismic tremors of a different kind were now running through Hollywood. Now that the war was over, and the pressure on wage restraint relaxed, the majority of studio employees demanded better pay and conditions. An eight-month union strike at the studios followed.

In Britain the film industry was riding on the crest of a wave. Annual cinema admissions crept towards 1,600 million. Olivier's *Henry V* had scored an immense prestige success in the United States, and films like *The Seventh Veil,* starring James Mason and Ann Todd, were making inroads into the American market.

James Mason was a dominating figure, a silky-voiced matinée idol whose characters were frequently mad, bad and dangerous to know. In *They Were Sisters* he was a snarling domestic tyrant, driving Dulcie Gray to suicide. In *The Seventh Veil* he was concert pianist Ann Todd's sardonic, crippled guardian, bringing his cane crashing down on her hands in a frenzy of impotent rage. In *The Wicked Lady* – the finest example of 'Gainsborough Gothic' – he was Captain Terry Jackson, a seventeenth-century highwayman who acquires a stimulating partner in crime in the shape of adventuress Margaret Lockwood.

The melancholy norms of suburbia triumphed over passion in David Lean's *Brief Encounter,* developed from a pre-war one-act play by Noel Coward. Celia Johnson and Trevor

William Eythe in *The House on 92nd Street* (Fox)

Ann Dvorak

Peter Murray Hill and Phyllis Calvert in *They Were Sisters* (G'boro)

Celia Johnson and Trevor Howard in *Brief Encounter* (Cine)

Michael Allan, Mervyn Johns and Sally Ann Howes in *Dead of Night* (Univ)

Jean-Louis Barrault (r) in *Les Enfants du Paradis* (GB *Children of Paradise*) (Tricolore Films Inc)

Howard gave immaculate performances as the middle-class housewife and doctor – both of whom are happily married – who drift into a barren affair amid the Virol advertisements and rock-hard Banbury cakes of the steam-shrouded station buffet at Milford Junction. Restraint was also the keynote of Anthony Asquith's *The Way to the Stars* (US *Johnny in the Clouds*) which caught the underlying rhythms of war as they affected the British and American aircrew on a Midlands bomber base and the local people who enter their lives.

With its emphasis on Anglo-US relations, *The Way to the Stars* was aimed equally at the American and British markets. But a more significant pointer to the future of British films in the second half of the decade was the modest, parochial and highly efficient output of Ealing Studios. Among the films Ealing released in 1945 were the classic portmanteau collection of supernatural tales, *Dead of Night; Painted Boats,* (US *The Girl on the Canal*) a charming semi-documentary film of canal life; and *Pink String and Sealing Wax,* a superbly designed period melodrama.

A world away from the exquisitely designed sets of *Pink String and Sealing Wax* were the dangerous streets of Rome in *Roma, Citta Aperta* (GB *Rome, Open City*), (US *Open City*), a study of the last chaotic days of the German occupation before the liberation of the Italian capital by the allies. Its director, Roberto Rossellini, had made a number of films for the Fascists, notably *La Nave Bianca* (*The White Ship*, 1941), a semi-documentary about a hospital ship supervised by the Naval Ministry, but was now in Rome as the representative of the Christian Democrats in the film branch of the Committee of National Liberation. The filming of *Roma, Città Aperta* began in conditions of great secrecy and technical difficulty before the liberation in June 1944. Much of its improvised feel stemmed from shortage of equipment but its formlessness made a powerful impact at the time and was hailed as a great breakthrough. It also introduced the earthy Anna Magnani to an international audience.

In France Marcel Carné completed *Les Enfants du Paradis* (US *Children of Paradise*), a picaresque panorama of Parisian life in the 1830s, scripted by Jacques Prévert, on which work had begun in 1942. Starring Jean-Louis Barrault as the great mime artist Baptiste Deburau and Arletty as the beautiful demi-mondaine Garance, *Les Enfants du Paradis* was both an artistic and logistical triumph. Not the least of Carné's achievements was the reconstruction, at a time of acute shortages, of a quarter of a mile of the Boulevard du Temple, teeming with 25,000 extras who vividly convey the vibrant, extravagant street life of the time. For the French, emerging from the humiliation of defeat and occupation, the romantic brilliance of *Les Enfants du Paradis* bore witness to the survival of the French film artistry and of France herself.

For Germany there was only defeat. The death rattle of Nazi cinema was Veit Harlan's *Kolberg,* two years in the making and based with grim symbolism on the siege of the town during the Napoleonic Wars.

Harry Hayden and Fred Allen in *It's in the Bag* (UA)

Fred Allen and Jack Benny in *It's in the Bag* (UA)

Ann Rutherford in *Bedside Manner* (UA)

Film Favourites 1945

In spite of all the travail of the war years, films were buoyant and prolific in subject and quantity. Musicals, sophisticated comedies, costume extravaganzas and war films abounded. The Second World War was drawing to a close and it seemed as though the movie world had nothing more to fear.

Evelyn Keyes, Cornel Wilde and Adele Jergens in *A Thousand and One Nights* (Col)

Dean Stockwell, Frank Sinatra and Gene Kelly in *Anchors Aweigh* (MGM)

Yvonne de Carlo in *Salome Where She Danced* (Univ)

Turhan Bey and Susanna Foster in *Frisco Sal* (Univ)

Arturo de Cordova in *A Medal for Benny*

Larry Parks, John Tyrell and Eddie Acuff in *Sergeant Mike* (Col)

Pat O'Brien and Adolphe Menjou in *Man Alive* (RKO)

Paul Langton and Frances Rafferty in *The Hidden Eye* (MGM)

Lawrence Tierney (c) and Lee 'Lasses' White in *Dillinger* (MoP)

Gloria Jean

Mike Mazurki, Paul Henreid, J M Kerrigan and Curt Bois in *The Spanish Main* (RKO)

Ingrid Bergman, Joan Carroll and Bing Crosby in *The Bells of St Mary's* (RKO)

Charles Korvin and Merle Oberon in *This Love of Ours* (Univ)

Paulette Goddard, the star of *Kitty* (Par)

Richard Attenborough (c) in *Journey Together* (RAF Film Unit)

Paulette Goddard in *Kitty* (Par) ▷

Mary Gordon (l), Olin Howlin and Mary Philips in *Captain Eddie* (Fox)

Lee Tracy and Nancy Kelly in *Betrayal from the East* (RKO)

Jayne Hazard, Warren William and Sally Eilers in *Strange Illusion* (PRC)

Marie Lohr, Godfrey Tearle and Margaret Johnson in *The Rake's Progress* (US *Notorious Gentleman*) (l)

Errol Flynn, S Z Sakall, Alexis Smith and Florence Bates in *San Antonio* (WB)

Gene Tierney ▷

Chester Morris in *Boston Blackie's Rendezvous* (Col)

Jean Sullivan, Bill Kennedy, Samuel S Hinds, Kurt Kreuger, Philip Dorn (on floor), Helmut Dantine (kneeling), Rudolph Anders and Hans Schumm in *Escape in the Desert* (WB)

George Raft and Signe Hasso in *Johnny Angel* (RKO)

Turhan Bey and Susanna Foster in *Frisco Sal* (Univ)

Irene Dunne and Charles Coburn in *Over 21* (Col)

Joan Fontaine and George Brent in *The Affairs of Susan* (Par)

Adele Jergens in *Tonight and Every Night* (Col) △

Tito Guizar in *Mexicana* (Rep)

Lon Chaney Jr, Milburn Stone and Elena Verdugo in *The Frozen Ghost* (Univ)

Richard Arlen and Lynne Roberts in *The Phantom Speaks* (Rep)

1

3

4

1. Fred MacMurray and Helen Walker in *Murder He Says* (Par)
2. Jane Powell and Constance Moore in *Delightfully Dangerous* (UA)
3. Signe Hasso and James Craig in *Dangerous Partners* (MGM)
4. Joan Blondell, William Bendix and Phil Silvers in *Don Juan Quilligan* (Fox)
5. Vivien Leigh and Claude Rains in *Caesar and Cleopatra* (IP)
6. Basil Sydney, Vivien Leigh and Claude Rains in *Caesar and Cleopatra* (IP)
7. Vera Hruba Ralston and John Wayne in *Dakota* (Rep)
8. Zachary Scott and Faye Emerson in *Danger Signal* (WB)
9. Porter Hall and James Cagney in *Blood on the Sun* (UA)

5

6

ABERCROMBIE LANDING

8

7
▷

9
▷

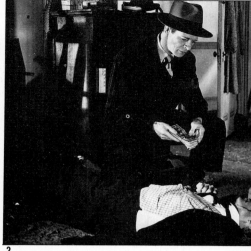

1. Yvonne De Carlo, Beverly Sue Simmons and Rod Cameron in *Frontier Gal* (GB *The Bride Wasn't Willing*) (Univ)
2. Morgan Conway in *Dick Tracy* (GB *Splitface*) (RKO)
3. Nancy Brinckman and Leo Gorcey in *Mr Muggs Rides Again* (MoP)
4. Billy Benedict (I), Leo Gorcey and Huntz Hall and the East Side Kids in *Docks of New York* (MoP)
5. Betty Grable and Dick Haymes in *Diamond Horseshoe* (Fox)
6. Lon Chaney Jr, Tala Birell, Milburn Stone and Elena Verdugo in *The Frozen Ghost* (Univ)
7. Lynne Carver, Raymond Hatton and Johnny Mack Brown in *Flame of the West* (MoP)
8. The Chorus Line in *George White's Scandals* (RKO)

1. Carmen Miranda in *Doll Face* (Fox)
2. Dennis O'Keefe and Constance Moore in *Earl Carroll Vanities* (Rep)
3. Vivian Blaine, Dennis O'Keefe and Michael Dunne in *Doll Face* (Fox)
4. Ingrid Bergman and Bing Crosby in *The Bells of St Mary's* (RKO)
5. Ruth Donnelly, Ingrid Bergman and Bing Crosby in *The Bells of St Mary's* (RKO)
6. Bing Crosby and Ingrid Bergman in *The Bells of St Mary's* (RKO)
7. Martha Sleeper, William Gargan and Bing Crosby in *The Bells of St Mary's* (RKO)
8. Pierre Brasseur in *Les Enfants du Paradis* (GB *Children of Paradise*) (TFI)
9. Charles Bickford, Dana Andrews and Percy Kilbride in *Fallen Angel* (Fox)
10. Benson Fong and Sidney Toler in *The Red Dragon* (MoP)
11. Rod Cameron (I) in *Beyond the Pecos* (Univ)

11 ▷

1. Philip Ahn in *China Sky* (RKO)
2. Janis Carter
3. Dan Duryea and Joan Bennett in *Scarlet Street* (Univ)
4. Irene Dunne in *Over 21* (Col)
5. Martha O'Driscoll and Alan Curtis in *The Daltons Ride Again* (Univ)
6. Robert Clarke
7. Marie Lohr, Godfrey Tearle and Margaret Johnston in *The Rake's Progress* (US *Notorious Gentleman*) (IP)
8. Constance Cummings, Rex Harrison and Margaret Rutherford in *Blithe Spirit* (TC)
9. Jess Barker, Douglas Dumbrille and Milburn Stone in *The Daltons Ride Again* (Univ)
10. Audrey Long and Phillip Terry in *Pan Americana* (RKO)

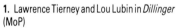

1. Lawrence Tierney and Lou Lubin in *Dillinger* (MoP)

2. Vivian Blaine in *Nob Hill* (Fox)

3. Lee 'Lasses' White and Lawrence Tierney in *Dillinger* (MoP)

4. Lawrence Tierney, Elsa Janssen and Ludwig Stossel in *Dillinger* (MoP)

5. Elisha Cook Jr, Marc Lawrence, Edmund Lowe (s), Lawrence Tierney and Eduardo Ciannelli in *Dillinger* (MoP)

6. Paul Langton, Friday and Frances Rafferty in *The Hidden Eye* (MGM)

7. Dusty Anderson

8. Ethel Smith

9. David Thursby, Dennis Hoey and Basil Rathbone in *The House of Fear* (Univ)

10. Nina Foch and Moy Wing in *Prison Ship* (Col)

246

The main appeal of *A Thousand and One Nights* (Col) was pulchritude and spectacle. It was a lavish production, another variation of the Aladdin story with Evelyn Keyes as a surprising genie of the lamp. Cornel Wilde was, of course, Aladdin with Adele Jergens as the beauteous Princess Armina.

1. Phil Silvers
2. Evelyn Keyes, Cornel Wilde and Adele Jergens
3. Dusty Anderson
4. Evelyn Keyes
5. Adele Jergens
6. Rex Ingram and Cornel Wilde
7. Cornel Wilde
8. Phil Silvers

1. Micheline Cheirel and Dick Powell in *Cornered* (RKO)
2. Walter Slezak in *Cornered* (RKO)
3. Susanna Foster and Alan Curtis in *Frisco Sal* (Univ)
4. Turhan Bey, Susanna Foster, Alan Curtis and Samuel S Hinds in *Frisco Sal* (Univ)
5. Alan Curtis, Susanna Foster and Fuzzy Knight in *Frisco Sal* (Univ)
6. Andy Devine and Turhan Bey in *Frisco Sal* (Univ)
7. Robert Lowery in *High Powered* (Par)
8. Monty Woolley and Gracie Fields in *Molly and Me* (Fox)
9. Ginny Simms and Charles Coburn in *Shady Lady* (Univ)
10. Joan Lorring and John Dall in *The Corn is Green* (WB)
11. Sunset Carson and Linda Stirling in *Sheriff of Cimarron* (Rep)

1

2

3

4

5

6

7

8

9

10

11

248

1. Ann Richards and Alec Craig in *Love Letters* (Par)
2. Reginald Owen in *Captain Kidd* (UA)
3. Keenan Wynn and Walter Pidgeon in *Weekend at the Waldorf* (MGM)
4. Marie McDonald in *It's a Pleasure* (RKO)
5. Sonja Henie and Bill Johnson in *It's a Pleasure* (RKO)
6. Ellen Drew in *Man Alive* (RKO)
7. Adolphe Menjou and Pat O'Brien in *Man Alive* (RKO)
8. Rudy Vallee, Ellen Drew and Pat O'Brien in *Man Alive* (RKO)

◁ **8**

1. Robert Walker (c) in *The Clock* (GB *Under the Clock*) (MGM)
2. Betty Hutton in *Incendiary Blonde* (Par)
3. Evelyn Ankers
4. Tom Neal and Barbara Hale in *The First Yank into Tokyo* (RKO)
5. Smiley Burnette
6. Geraldine Fitzgerald and George Sanders in *The Strange Affair of Uncle Harry* (Univ)
7. Patricia Roc
8. Dennis Morgan and Barbara Stanwyck in *Christmas in Connecticut* (WB)
9. Danny Kaye
10. Nina Foch

10 ▷

1
2
3
4
5
6
7
8
9

1. Paul Lucas
2. Arthur Walsh
3. Warren Mills
4. Ann Todd in *The Seventh Veil* (Theatrecraft/Ortus)
5. John Mills, Clement McCallin and Basil Radford in *The Way to the Stars* (US *Johnny in the Clouds*) (TC)
6. Fred Astaire, Leon Ames, Frank Morgan and Remo Bufano in *Yolande and the Thief* (MGM)
7. Pat O'Brien and Adolphe Menjou in *Man Alive* (RKO)
8. Rudy Vallee, Ellen Drew and Pat O'Brien in *Man Alive* (RKO)
9. Laurence Tierney

2

1

3

4

1. Arturo de Cordova in *A Medal for Benny* (Par)
2. Yvonne De Carlo in *Salome Where She Danced* (Univ)
3. Yvonne De Carlo and David Bruce in *Salome Where She Danced* (Univ)
4. Chris-Pin Martin, J Carroll Naish, Arturo de Cordova and Dorothy Lamour in *A Medal for Benny* (Par)
5. Phillip Terry, Jane Wyman and Ray Milland in *The Lost Weekend* (Par)
6. Roy Rogers and Estelita Rodriguez in *Along the Navajo Trail* (Rep)
7. Ray Milland in *The Lost Weekend* (Par)
8. Nestor Paiva and Estelita Rodriguez in *Along the Navajo Trail* (Rep)
9. Jean Sullivan, Bill Kennedy, Rudolph Anders, Helmut Dantine and Philip Dorn in *Escape in the Desert* (WB)

5

▽ 7

6

8

▽ 9

1. Robert Alda in *Rhapsody in Blue* (WB)
2. Herbert Rudley and Robert Alda in *Rhapsody in Blue* (WB)
3. Paul Whiteman in *Rhapsody in Blue* (WB)
4. Oscar Levant and Robert Alda in *Rhapsody in Blue* (WB)
5. Paul Whiteman, Charles Coburn, Robert Alda and Albert Basserman in *Rhapsody in Blue* (WB)
6. Douglas Montgomery, Bonar Colleano and John Mills in *The Way to the Stars* (US *Johnny in the Clouds*) (TC)
7. Ian Keith and Dorothy Granger in *Under Western Skies* (Univ)
8. Alexis Smith, Errol Flynn and John Litel in *San Antonio* (WB)
9. Errol Flynn in *San Antonio* (WB)
10. Errol Flynn and Tom Tyler in *San Antonio* (WB)

ND JOHN . MICHAEL REDGRAVE

1

2

3

4

5

6

7

1. Peter Graves in *I'll Be Your Sweetheart* (G'boro)
2. Walter Abel in *The Affairs of Susan* (Par)
3. Linda Darnell in *Hangover Square* (Fox)
4. Jack Watling in *Journey Together* (RAF Film Unit)
5. Jeanne Bates and Larry Parks in *Sergeant Mike* (Col)
6. Anne Jeffreys and Jack Haley in *Sing Your Way Home* (RKO)
7. Jack Watling and Richard Attenborough in *Journey Together* (RAF Film Unit)
8. Rex Harrison, Anna Neagle and Dean Jagger in *I Live in Grosvenor Square* (US *A Yank in London*) (ABPC)
9. Ray Milland, Reginald Owen and Cecil Kellaway in *Kitty* (Par)

8

9 ▷

256

Gene Kelly danced while Kathryn Grayson sang. Frank Sinatra crooned and Jose Iturbi played the piano in the Technicolor extravaganza *Anchors Aweigh* (MGM). Gene dancing with a cartoon mouse was one of the highlights of this merry musical.

1. Frank Sinatra and Gene Kelly
2. Frank Sinatra, Kathryn Grayson and Gene Kelly
3. Dean Stockwell, Gene Kelly and Frank Sinatra
4. Kathryn Grayson and Gene Kelly
5. Henry O'Neill, Gene Kelly and Frank Sinatra
6. Frank Sinatra, Kathryn Grayson and Gene Kelly
7. Pamela Britton and Frank Sinatra
8. Frank Sinatra, Kathryn Grayson, Billy Gilbert and Gene Kelly

◁ 8

257

1

2

3

5

6

7

1. Gary Cooper in *Saratoga Trunk* (WB)
2. Ingrid Bergman and Gary Cooper in *Saratoga Trunk* (WB)
3. Gary Cooper, Glenn Strange, Jerry Austin (c) and Hank Bell (r) in *Saratoga Trunk* (WB)
4. Flora Robson and Ingrid Bergman in *Saratoga Trunk* (WB)
5. Thurston Hall in *West of the Pecos* (RKO)
6. Richard Martin in *West of the Pecos* (RKO)
7. Thurston Hall and Barbara Hale in *West of the Pecos* (RKO)
8. June Havoc
9. Carl Esmond and Merle Oberon in *This Love of Ours* (Univ)
10. Charles Korvin in *This Love of Ours* (Univ)
11. Charles Korvin and Merle Oberon in *This Love of Ours* (Univ)
12. Edward Norris in *Penthouse Rhythm* (Univ)

4

8

◁9

10

12

◁11

1. Regis Toomey and Jimmy Lydon in *Strange Illusion* (PRC)

2. Peggy Ann Garner, Joan Blondell, Ted Donaldson and Ferike Boros in *A Tree Grows in Brooklyn* (Fox)

3. Peggy Ann Garner, Ferike Boros and Ted Donaldson in *A Tree Grows in Brooklyn* (Fox)

4. Chic Johnson and Ole Olsen (in wigs) in *See My Lawyer* (Univ)

5. Maria Montez, George Zucco and Jon Hall in *Sudan* (Univ)

6. Maria Montez in *Sudan* (Univ)

7. Turhan Bey and Maria Montez in *Sudan* (Univ)

8. Rita Hayworth and Lee Bowman in *Tonight and Every Night* (Col)

1

If in *The Spanish Main* (RKO) Binnie Barnes and Paul Henreid seemed at first sight to have been miscast in the swashbuckling roles that they played (actually they were both very good), there was no mistaking the apt casting of Walter Slezak as the cunning, silk-tongued villain of the piece. The film was a good rousing actioner of the genre.

1. Maureen O'Hara and Paul Henreid
2. Walter Slezak, Maureen O'Hara and Fritz Leiber
3. Binnie Barnes and Walter Slezak
4. Maureen O'Hara, Binnie Barnes and Paul Henreid
5. Binnie Barnes, Maureen O'Hara and Paul Henreid
6. Paul Henreid and Maureen O'Hara
7. Maureen O'Hara, Walter Slezak, Fritz Leiber and Antonio Moreno
8. Maureen O'Hara
9. John Emery, Maureen O'Hara and Paul Henreid

2

3
4

5

6

7

8

9

261

1. Linda Darnell, Wallace Ford, Greg McClure (std) and George Matthews in *The Great John L* (GB *A Man Called Sullivan*)(UA)

2. Raymond Walburn, David Holt, Joseph Schildkraut, Eugene Pallette and Ruth Terry in *The Cheaters* (Rep)

3. June Allyson and Robert Walker in *Her Highness and the Bell Boy* (MGM)

4. Tom Powers and Don Barry in *The Chicago Kid* (Rep)

5. Allyn Joslyn, Peggy Ann Garner and Sylvia Field in *Junior Miss* (Fox)

6. Buster Crabbe, Al 'Fuzzy' St John and Lorraine Miller in *Border Badmen* (PRC)

7. Celia Johnson (r) and Trevor Howard in *Brief Encounter* (Cine)

8. Patricia Burke

9. Kane Richmond and Ralph Morgan in *Black Market Babies* (MoP)

10. Richard Lane, Lynn Merrick, Chester Morris and Frank Sully in *Boston Blackie Booked on Suspicion* (Col)

1. Rose Hobart in *Conflict* (WB)

2. Louise Allbritton, Jon Hall and Peggy Ryan in *Men In Her Diary* (Univ)

3. Robert Homans, Sidney Toler and Benson Fong in *The Scarlet Clue* (MoP)

4. Ann Savage and William Gargan in *Midnight Manhunt* (Par)

5. Lauritz Melchior and Tommy Dorsey in *Thrill of a Romance* (MGM)

6. Lloyd Nolan and Michael O'Shea in *Circumstantial Evidence* (Fox)

7. Andrea King, Helmut Dantine and George Coulouris in *Hotel Berlin* (WB)

8. Pamela Blake, Virginia Brissac and Charles Gordon in *Three's A Crowd* (Rep)

9. Susanna Foster and Franchot Tone in *That Night With You* (Univ)

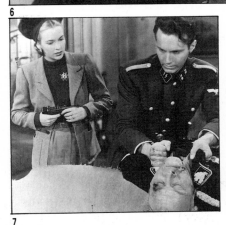

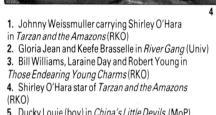

1. Johnny Weissmuller carrying Shirley O'Hara in *Tarzan and the Amazons* (RKO)
2. Gloria Jean and Keefe Brasselle in *River Gang* (Univ)
3. Bill Williams, Laraine Day and Robert Young in *Those Endearing Young Charms* (RKO)
4. Shirley O'Hara star of *Tarzan and the Amazons* (RKO)
5. Ducky Louie (boy) in *China's Little Devils* (MoP)
6. Charles Coburn and William Eythe in *Colonel Effingham's Raid* (GB *Man of the Hour*) (Fox)
7. Janis Carter, Jim Bannon, Jean Stevens and George Macready in *The Missing Juror* (Col)
8. George E Stone, Richard Lane, Chester Morris, Nina Foch and Steve Cochran in *Boston Blackie's Rendezvous* (Col)
9. Iris Adrian in *Boston Blackie's Rendezvous* (Col)
10. Elaine Riley, Veda Ann Borg and Michael St Angel in *What a Blonde* (RKO)

9 ◁
▷
10

264

1. Sidney Toler and Hardie Albright in *The Jade Mask* (MoP)
2. Mary Beth Hughes in *The Great Flamarion* (Rep)
3. Gloria Jean and Kirby Grant (r) in *I'll Remember April* (Univ)
4. June Allyson and Robert Walker in *The Sailor Takes a Wife* (MGM)
5. Charles Dingle, Claudette Colbert and Don Ameche in *Guest Wife* (UA)
6. Eddie Acuff, Grace McDonald and Allan Jones in *Honeymoon Ahead* (Univ)
7. Sonja Henie and Michael O'Shea in *It's a Pleasure* (RKO)
8. Edmund MacDonald, Frank Fenton, Eddie Bracken and Veronica Lake in *Hold That Blonde* (Par)
9. Marjorie Riordan, Leslie Vincent, Nigel Bruce, Rosalind Ivan and Basil Rathbone in *Pursuit to Algiers* (Univ)

9 ▷

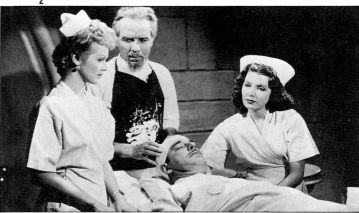

1

2

3

4

5

1. Lynn Bari, Clem Bevans and Fred MacMurray in *Captain Eddie* (Fox)
2. Laraine Day and Bill Johnson in *Keep Your Powder Dry* (MGM)
3. George Raft, Signe Hasso and Hoagy Carmichael in *Johnny Angel* (RKO)
4. Martha O'Driscoll, Onslow Stevens and Jane Adams in *House of Dracula* (Univ)
5. Tito Guizar, Estelita Rodriguez and Leo Carrillo in *Mexicana* (Rep)
6. Alan Ladd, Gail Russell and Spring Byington in *Salty O'Rourke* (Par)
7. Warner Baxter, Lupita Tovar and Anthony Caruso in *The Crime Doctor's Courage* (Col)
8. Dorothy McGuire and Mildred Natwick in *The Enchanted Cottage* (RKO)
9. Mildred Natwick
10. Danny Mummert, Bonita Granville and Allan Jones in *Senorita From the West* (Univ)

6

7

8

9

10 ▷

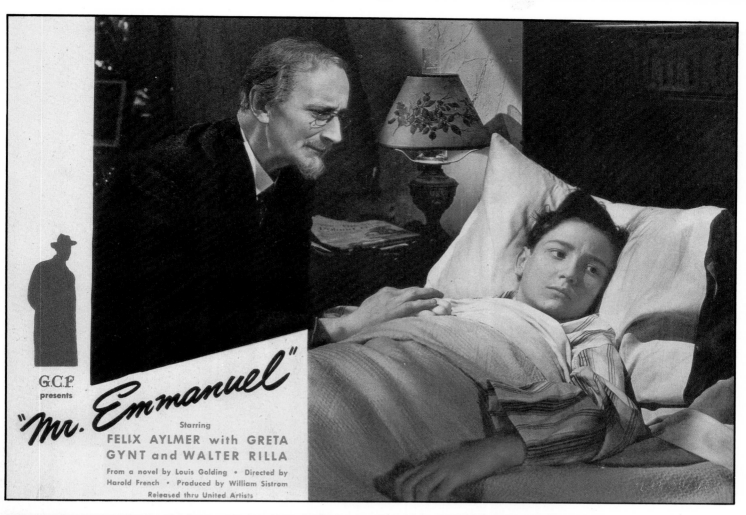

G.C.F. presents

"Mr. Emmanuel"

Starring

FELIX AYLMER with GRETA GYNT and WALTER RILLA

From a novel by Louis Golding • Directed by Harold French • Produced by William Sistrom
Released thru United Artists

A REPUBLIC PICTURE

WOMAN WHO CAME BACK

Lauren Bacall

1. Bud Osborne, Al 'Fuzzy' St John, Buster Crabbe and I Stanford Jolley in *Fighting Bill Carson* (PRC)

2. Natalie Schafer, Arturo de Cordova and Dorothy Lamour in *Masquerade In Mexico* (Par)

3. Edward Ashley, Virginia Bruce and Victor McLaglen in *Love, Honor and Goodbye* (Rep)

4. Brenda Joyce, Billy Severn and Edmund Lowe in *The Enchanted Forest* (PRC)

5. Veronica Lake and Bill Edwards in *Miss Susie Slagle's* (Par)

6. Kay Aldridge and David O'Brien in *The Man Who Walked Alone* (PRC)

7. Peter Cookson, Gale Storm and Jerome Cowan in *G I Honeymoon* (MoP)

8. Joy Harrington and Nina Foch in *My Name is Julia Ross* (Col)

9. Sonny Tufts, Joan Caulfield and Bill Edwards in *Miss Susie Slagle's* (Par)

10. Rita Corday, Sharyn Moffett and Tom Conway in *The Falcon in San Francisco* (RKO)

◁ 7

10 ▷

1

4

5

7

9

6

8

1. Jackie Moran, Sidney Miller and Wanda McKay in *There Goes Kelly* (MoP)
2. John Loder and Karen Morley in *Jealousy* (Rep)
3. James Dunn and Sheila Ryan in *The Caribbean Mystery* (Fox)
4. June Havoc in *Brewster's Millions* (UA)
5. Nana Bryant, Herbert Rudley, Helen Walker, Dennis O'Keefe, Eddie 'Rochester' Anderson and Joe Sawyer in *Brewster's Millions* (UA)
6. Gene Tierney, Cornel Wilde and Darryl Hickman in *Leave Her to Heaven* (Fox)
7. Marie McDonald and Barry Sullivan in *Getting Gerties Garter* (UA)
8. Loretta Young, Gary Cooper and William Demarest in *Along Came Jones* (RKO)
9. Paul Kelly and Kay Francis in *Allotment Wives* (MoP)

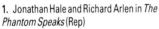

1. Jonathan Hale and Richard Arlen in *The Phantom Speaks* (Rep)
2. Larry Parks and Paul Muni in *Counter Attack* (GB *One Against Seven*) (Col)
3. Lee Tracy and Nancy Kelly in *Betrayal From the East* (RKO)
4. Russell Hayden
5. Bud Abbott and Lou Costello in *Here Come the Co-Eds* (Univ)
6. Martha O'Driscoll in *Her Lucky Night* (Univ)
7. Penny Singleton, Larry Simms, Daisy (the dog) and Arthur Lake in *Leave It To Blondie* (Col)
8. Michael Dunne
9. Ann Dvorak in *Flame of the Barbary Coast* (Rep)
10. Ann Dvorak, John Wayne, Virginia Grey and William Frawley in *Flame Of The Barbary Coast* (Rep)
11. June Duprez, Louis Hayward, Richard Haydn, Mischa Auer and C Aubrey Smith in *And Then There Were None* (GB *Ten Little Niggers*) (Fox)
12. Claudia Drake, John Carroll, Bert Roach and Ruth Hussey in *Bedside Manner* (UA)

◁ 11

271

1. Jimmy Dodd (l) and Steven Geray (r) in *Crimson Canary* (Univ)
2. Betty Hutton, Victor Moore, Marjorie Reynolds, James Flavin and Ed Gardner in *Duffy's Tavern* (Par)
3. Darryl Hickman in *Kiss and Tell* (Col)
4. Katherine Alexander, Walter Abel, Porter Hall, Edna Holland, Jerome Courtland and Shirley Temple in *Kiss and Tell* (Col)
5. Virginia Welles in *Kiss and Tell* (Col)
6. Charles Coburn, William Eythe and Tallulah Bankhead in *A Royal Scandal* (GB *Czarina*) (Fox)
7. Cass Daley, Diana Lynn, Eddie Bracken and Veronica Lake in *Out of this World* (Par)
8. Sonny Tufts, Veronica Lake and Eddie Bracken in *Bring on the Girls* (Par)
9. Marjorie Weaver
10. Joe Sawyer

7 ◁

9 ◁
10

1. Charles Halton, Sig Rumann, Ava Gardner, Reginald Owen, James Craig, Edmund Gwenn and Frances Gifford in *She Went to the Races* (MGM)
2. Leyland Hodgson, J Carrol Naish, Lon Chaney Jr and Brenda Joyce in *Strange Confession* (Univ)
3. Deborah Kerr and Robert Donat in *Perfect Strangers* (US *Vacation from Marriage*) (MGM/LF)
4. Janis Carter and Richard Dix in *The Power of the Whistler* (Col)
5. Leon Errol, George Lynn, Joan Davis, Donald MacBride and William Gargan in *She Gets Her Man* (Univ)
6. Manton Moreland, Walter Fenner, Sidney Toler, Benson Fong and James Cardwell in *The Shanghai Cobra* (MoP)
7. Paul Langton, Chill Wills and Robert Walker in *What Next, Corporal Hargrove?* (MGM)
8. Richard Gaines, Gail Patrick and Preston Foster in *Twice Blessed* (MGM)

1

2

3

4

5

6

7

8

273

1. Pat Parrish, Jackie Moran, Arnold Stang, June Preisser, Mel Torme and Jimmy Lloyd in *Let's Go Steady* (Col)
2. Mary Anderson, Edward Ryan and Thomas Mitchell in *Within These Walls* (Fox)
3. John Loder and Nancy Kelly in *The Woman Who Came Back* (Rep)
4. James Gleason (l) and Wallace Beery (r) in *This Man's Navy* (MGM)
5. Bobby Blake, Wild Bill Elliott and Emmett Lynn in *Wagon Wheels Westward* (Rep)
6. Jack Oakie (l), Peggy Ryan and Otto Kruger in *On Stage Everybody* (Univ)
7. Henry Daniell, Hillary Brooke, Basil Rathbone and Percival Vivian in *The Woman in Green* (Univ)
8. Bela Lugosi
9. Gene Sheldon and Fred MacMurray in *Where Do We Go From Here?* (Fox)

1. Cheryl Walker in *Identity Unknown* (Rep)
2. Richard Arlen, Cheryl Walker, Charles Jordan and Nelson Leigh in *Identity Unknown* (Rep)
3. Rosemary De Camp, Robert Hutton and Arthur Shields in *Too Young to Know* (WB)
4. Joan Leslie, Robert Lowell and Robert Hutton in *Too Young to Know* (WB)
5. Arthur Shields, Preston Foster, Donald Crisp and Gregory Peck in *The Valley of Decision* (MGM)
6. Lee Bowman and Rosalind Russell in *She Wouldn't Say Yes* (Col)
7. George 'Gabby' Hayes, Dale Evans and Roy Rogers in *Utah* (Rep)
8. Chester Morris and Victor McLaglen in *Rough, Tough and Ready* (Col)
9. Edward Everett Horton (r) and Deanna Durbin in *Lady on a Train* (Univ)
10. Sunset Carson (l) and Peggy Stewart in *Oregon Trail* (Rep)

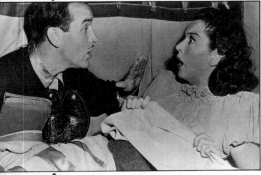

◁ 9

10 ▷

1. Fortunio Bonanova, Judy Canova, Doris Merrick and Ross Hunter in *Hit the Hay* (Col)
2. Gail Russell (l) in *The Unseen* (Par)
3. Edward Gargan and Jane Randolph (c) in *A Sporting Chance* (Rep)
4. Janis Carter in *One Way to Love* (Col)
5. Lynn Merrick, Ted Donaldson, Mary McLeod, Sam Flint and Ross Hunter in *A Guy, a Gal and a Pal* (Col)
6. *The True Glory* (Col)
7. Frank Jenks, Kay Aldridge, Dave O'Brien and Jack Mulhall in *The Phantom of 42nd Street* (PRC)
8. Marjorie Manners and Dale Evans in *The Big Show-Off* (Rep)
9. Sunset Carson and John Merton in *The Cherokee Flash* (Rep)
10. Paulette Goddard

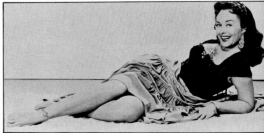

1. Jean Porter
2. Lola Lane, Pamela Blake and Elisha Cook Jr in *Why Girls Leave Home* (PRC)
3. William Gaxton
4. Phyllis Calvert, Pamela Kellino and James Mason in *They Were Sisters* (G'boro)
5. Karl Hackett, Al 'Fuzzy' St John, Mady Lawrence, Stanford Jolley, Buster Crabbe and Ray Brent in *Lightning Raiders* (PRC)
6. Diana Lewis
7. Frank Jenks, Russell Hopton, Wally Brown, Alan Carney and Sheldon Leonard in *Zombies on Broadway* (RKO)
8. Grant Withers, Charles Gordon and Peggy Stewart in *The Vampire's Ghost* (Rep)

◁ 6

277

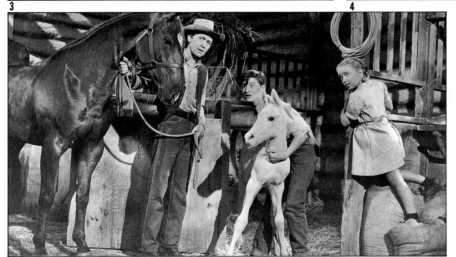

1. Bob Cason, Al 'Fuzzy' St John and Charles King in *Shadows of Death* (PRC)
2. Phyllis Adair, Jimmy Wakely and John James in *Riders of the Dawn* (MoP)
3. Sunset Carson (l) and Frank Jacquet (r) in *Santa Fe Saddlemates* (Rep)
4. Johnny Mack Brown, Raymond Hatton and Riley Hill in *The Navajo Trail* (MoP)
5. James Bell, Roddy McDowall and Diana Hale in *Thunderhead - Son of Flicka* (Fox)
6. James Warren, Audrey Long and Richard Martin in *Wanderer of the Wasteland* (RKO)
7. Roy Butler, Ray Bennett, Steve Clark and Johnny Mack Brown in *Gunsmoke* (MoP)
8. Raymond Hatton, Eddie Parker and Johnny Mack Brown in *Frontier Feud* (MoP)
9. Johnny Mack Brown and Raymond Hatton in *Law of the Valley* (MoP)

8
◁
▷
9

1

2

3

4

1. Audrey Long
2. Vivian Austin
3. Eva Gabor
4. John Slater in *Murder in Reverse* (US *Query*) (BN)
5. Carole Landis and George Murphy in *Having Wonderful Crime* (RKO)
6. George Murphy and Pat O'Brien in *Having Wonderful Crime* (RKO)
7. John Laurie, Roger Livesey and Wendy Hiller in *I Know Where I'm Going* (IP)
8. Howard da Silva
9. Charles Bickford in *Fallen Angel* (Fox)
10. Robert Stanton, Lynne Merrick and Thurston Hall in *Blonde from Brooklyn* (RKO)

5

6

7

8

9
◁
▷
10

Two Famous Threesomes   **Top** Roy Rogers, Dale Evans and Gabby Hayes   **Bottom** Bob Hope, Dorothy Lamour and Bing Crosby

1. Michael Kirby
2. Alexis Smith, Jack Benny and Dolores Moran in *The Horn Blows at Midnight* (WB)
3. Barbara Read
4. Warner Anderson
5. Maxie Rosenbloom
6. Marie McDonald
7. George 'Gabby' Hayes, Richard Arlen and Lynne Roberts in *The Big Bonanza* (Rep)
8. Phyllis Thaxter and Horace McNally in *Bewitched* (MGM)
9. Glenn Strange and Boris Karloff in *House of Frankenstein* (Univ)

1

2

3

4

5

6▷

Based on Magdalen King-Hall's best selling novel *The Wicked Lady* the film of *The Wicked Lady* (G'boro) was, despite the critics contemptuous notices, one of the British studios' great successes. Perhaps the near-naked bosoms of the leading ladies had something to do with the queues that formed outside cinemas everywhere, although in retrospect the movie was good all-round entertainment.

1. Margaret Lockwood and Michael Rennie
2. Patricia Roc and Griffith Jones
3. Patricia Roc and Michael Rennie
4. Margaret Lockwood and Patricia Roc
5. Patricia Roc and Michael Rennie
6. Griffith Jones and Patricia Roc
7. Margaret Lockwood and James Mason (both masked)
8. Margaret Lockwood and James Mason
9. Margaret Lockwood and Michael Rennie
10. Patricia Roc and Griffith Jones

1. J Edward Bromberg, Eddy Waller and Frank Jenks in *The Missing Corpse* (PRC)
2. June Lang
3. Joan Barclay
4. John Hodiak and Gene Tierney in *A Bell for Adano* (Fox)
5. Gale Storm, Johnny Downs, Frank Craven and C Aubrey Smith in *Forever Yours* (MoP)
6. Byron Barr in *Love Letters* (Par)
7. Frances Rafferty
8. Karen Morley
9. Colleen Townsend
10. Charles Korvin
11. Albert Basserman
12. Ned Sparks
13. Spring Byington
14. Fernando Lamas
15. Norma Varden and Richard Powers in *Girls of the Big House* (Rep)

1. Dick Haymes, Fay Bainter, Jeanne Crain and Charles Winninger in *State Fair* (Fox)
2. Victoria Horne
3. A E Matthews
4. Rex Harrison
5. Hal K Dawson
6. Byron Barr in *Follow That Woman* (Par)
7. Richard Haydn
8. Jody Gilbert
9. S Z Sakall (in white jacket) in *The Dolly Sisters* (Fox)
10. Jinx Falkenburg and Jim Bannon in *The Gay Senorita* (Col)

◁ 9

1

2

3

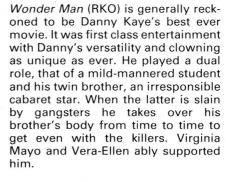

4

6

5

Wonder Man (RKO) is generally reckoned to be Danny Kaye's best ever movie. It was first class entertainment with Danny's versatility and clowning as unique as ever. He played a dual role, that of a mild-mannered student and his twin brother, an irresponsible cabaret star. When the latter is slain by gangsters he takes over his brother's body from time to time to get even with the killers. Virginia Mayo and Vera-Ellen ably supported him.

1. Virginia Mayo
2. Danny Kaye
3. Danny Kaye and Virginia Mayo
4. Bertha Belmore and Danny Kaye
5. Danny Kaye and Maxie Rosenbloom
6. Danny Kaye and Donald Woods
7. Danny Kaye
8. Danny Kaye
9. Danny Kaye
10. Vera-Ellen
11. Gisela Werbiseck and S Z Sakall
12. Virginia Mayo and Grant Mitchell
13. Vera-Ellen, Danny Kaye and Roseanne Murray
14. Danny Kaye and Vera-Ellen
15. Richard Lane (l) and Danny Kaye

7 ▷

8

9

10

11

12

13

14

15 ▷

Guy Madison, star of *Till the End of Time* (RKO)

Harold Russell, Dana Andrews and Fredric March in *The Best Years of our Lives* (SG)

Virginia Mayo

CHAPTER SEVEN
1946
POST-WAR RECOVERY

Hollywood entered the postwar period in a mood of buoyant optimism. Cinema was unchallenged as the most important medium of mass entertainment. Television was merely a small cloud on the horizon. Cinema audiences reached their peak. Every week 90 million Americans went to the movies. In Britain the figure was 30 million, and in France eight million.

The dominating theme of the year was postwar readjustment. RKO's *Till the End of Time,* directed by Edward Dmytryk, focused on the postwar fortunes of three ex-Marines, Guy Madison, Robert Mitchum and Bill Williams, the last playing an ex-boxer who had lost both his legs.

RKO also distributed Goldwyn's *The Best Years of Our Lives,* directed by William Wyler, which showed in microcosm the experiences of millions of American servicemen returning to a world which had moved on since they went away to war. In perhaps the best sequence three veterans huddle together in relaxed intimacy in the plexiglass nose of the bomber flying them home. Back in the Mid-Western town of Boone City, former bank employee Fredric March, ex-soda jerk Dana Andrews and maimed sailor Harold Russell (an actual veteran who had lost both his arms in the war) attempt to pick up the threads of their former lives. March discovers that he has grown away from his wife Myrna Loy and is a stranger to his daughter Teresa Wright. Andrews, humiliatingly reduced from officer to soda jerk, is disillusioned with the wife (Virginia Mayo) he had known for only 20 days. And Russell, giving a poignant performance in his only film, rejects his fiancée Cathy O'Donnell because he fears her pity.

The Best Years of Our Lives was rewarded with many Academy Awards, including Best Picture, Director, Actor (March), Supporting Actor (Russell), Screenplay (Robert Sherwood), Editing (Daniel Mandell) and Scoring (Hugo Friedhofer).

Hard on its heels came Frank Capra's *It's a Wonderful Life,* (RKO) the director's personal favourite in which guardian Angel Henry Travers persuades suicidal James Stewart not to kill himself by showing him a vision of his home town as it

Alan Ladd and Veronica Lake in *The Blue Dahlia* (Par)

might have been had he never been born. In a sly pastiche of *film noir* imagery, a peaceful, prosperous community is transformed into a blaring hell-hole of sleazy joints and dingy bars. Stewart dispenses bags of gangling charm, and there is a remarkably candid performance from Gloria Grahame as a good-time girl gone to the bad, but Capra's sunny view of the over-riding values of a folksy, conformist America seemed out of step with the public's wish for 'realism', however contrived. *It's A Wonderful Life* lost $525,000 at the box-office. It failed where *The Best Years of Our Lives* succeeded although at the time the similarities between the two films were not appreciated.

In Paramount's *The Blue Dahlia,* – Raymond Chandler's only original screenplay – Alan Ladd returns from war service in the Pacific, stumbles over the corpse of his tramp of a wife (Doris Dowling) and finds himself the prime suspect in the murder hunt.

At Warner Brothers, Humphrey Bogart provided the perfect incarnation of Raymond Chandler's private eye Philip Marlowe in *The Big Sleep,* directed by Howard Hawks. This was pure essence of Chandler, evoking the worlds of suffocating luxury and exquisitely observed squalor between which Bogart's Marlowe must pick his way: a millionaire (Charles Waldron) preserved in the stifling heat of an orchid house; his predatory daughters, the thumb-sucking nymphomaniac (Martha Vickers) and the insolently blasé divorcée (Lauren Bacall); the furtive, cringing bodyguard (inevitably Elisha Cook Jr); and, in a startlingly original touch, Dorothy Malone's bookshop assistant, rolling down the blinds on a rainy afternoon and casually offering Bogart the quickest of lays.

At MGM Robert Montgomery made his debut as a director with another Chandler adaptation, *The Lady in the Lake.* The story was told in the first person throughout, with Montgomery's Philip Marlowe glimpsed only in the occasional mirror. This intriguing gimmick soon becomes rather obtrusive, but the film is nudged along by an impressive supporting cast, including the viperish Audrey Totter, and in blistering form, Lloyd Nolan as a rogue cop.

Sydney Greenstreet and Peter Lorre were teamed again in Jean Negulesco's *Three Strangers,* forming a doomed trio with Geraldine Fitzgerald as three desperate characters who hold winning sweepstake tickets in weird circumstances. Greenstreet was particularly fine as the crooked lawyer Jerome K Arbutny, fastidiously arranging a buttonhole before setting about an elaborate suicide attempt.

Robert Siodmak provided a Gothic flourish to *The Spiral Staircase,* the first co-production venture between RKO and David O Selznick's Vanguard Films. Siodmak extracted every last drop of tension from the plight of Dorothy McGuire, the deaf-mute servant of bedridden Ethel Barrymore menaced by a deranged murderer of maimed women. In Universal's *The Killers,* based on a Hemingway story, Siodmak collaborated with producer Mark Hellinger

Lauren Bacall and Humphrey Bogart in *The Big Sleep* (WB)

Alan Napier, Peter Lorre and Sydney Greenstreet in *Three Strangers* (WB)

Dorothy McGuire and Kent Smith in *The Spiral Staircase* (RKO)

Charles McGraw and William Conrad in *The Killers* (Univ)

Thomas Mitchell and Olivia de Havilland in *The Dark Mirror* (Univ)

Rita Hayworth in *Gilda* (Col)

Lana Turner

to exploit the postwar fashion for realism and also to introduce Burt Lancaster to cinema audiencies, striking sparks off sultry Ava Gardner.

Siodmak had less to work with in *The Dark Mirror,* where the action was confined to an apartment and the consulting room of psychiatrist Lew Ayres, who is confronted with the knotty problem of discovering which one of identical twins – one nice, one nasty – has committed a murder.

Bette Davis applied her formidable technique to a similar challenge in Warner's *A Stolen Life,* in which she put her pulsing eyes and angular mannerisms to work as sisterly rivals for Glenn Ford.

Warners always brought tremendous panache and conviction to these preposterous melodramas, and never more so than in *Humoresque,* directed by Jean Negulesco. Its star, Joan Crawford, was at her best in such high-class trash. Here she was a bored, alcoholic socialite smothering working-class violin virtuoso John Garfield. *Humoresque* is a monument to the studio's endearing weakness for absurd cultural overtones. Advancing purposefully on Garfield for the first time, Crawford utters the immortal line, 'Bad manners, Mr Boray. The infallible sign of talent'. Later Crawford observes that Martinis – in the consumption of which she is in the W C Fields class – 'are an acquired taste, like Ravel'. Eventually Garfield decides that his music is more important to him than Crawford and her Ravel-like Martinis. To the strains of his rendering of Wagner's Liebestod, and wearing a shimmering evening gown, she stalks imperiously into the sea, leaving behind a trail of bubbles and a shoal of startled fish.

Posters for Columbia's *Gilda* proclaimed 'There Never Was a Woman Like Gilda!' prompting British critic C A Lejeune to observe 'Blimey! There Never Was!' As incarnated by Rita Hayworth, Gilda Mundsen represented the height of Hollywood eroticism, sheathed in black, lustrous hair tumbling over one eye and glistening lips slightly parted as she taunts Glenn Ford, singing (in Anita Ellis' dubbed voice) 'Put the Blame on Mame' in her husband George Macready's Buenos Aires casino. *Gilda* established Hayworth as the sleekest of sexual animals, the dream mistress of men the world over.

In MGM's *The Postman Always Rings Twice,* directed by Tay Garnett, carnality of a harder more vulgar kind was embodied in Lana Turner's murderous adulteress, clad in burning white and letting her lipstick roll slowly across the floor of a greasy diner to rest at the feet of doomed drifter John Garfield.

In RKO's *Notorious,* a scintillating espionage thriller, Alfred Hitchcock poked impish fun at the Production Code, manoeuvring Cary Grant and Ingrid Bergman through the longest embrace in screen history, a small masterpiece of calculated eroticism.

Bergman broke into the Top Ten, joining Bing Crosby, Van Johnson, Gary Cooper, Bob Hope, Humphrey Bogart,

Greer Garson, Margaret O'Brien, Betty Grable and Roy Rogers. At Republic, Rogers made his favourite film, *My Pal Trigger,* which reveals the origins of his faithful equine companion. A Western mounted on a more ambitious scale was David O Selznick's *Duel in the Sun,* a kind of Texan *Gone With the Wind* (1939), – quickly dubbed 'Lust in the Dust' – in which lecherous Gregory Peck and decent Joseph Cotten played Cain and Abel brothers locked in battle over voluptuous half-caste Jennifer Jones.

Villainy was never Peck's strongest suit. In Clarence Brown's *The Yearling* (MGM), he was his usual noble, uncomplicated and slightly wooden self, playing Claude Jarman Jr's homesteading father like a young backwoods Lincoln. The yearling in question was a deer, raised by Jarman, and the film one of the most ravishing examples of Technicolor. It won Oscars for Cinematography, Art Direction and a special Oscar for newcomer Jarman.

John Ford's *My Darling Clementine* (Twentieth Century-Fox) was a classically formal Western and the best of all the films about Wyatt Earp, here played with gauche dignity by Henry Fonda. *My Darling Clementine* is located squarely in Ford's own legendary West, Monument Valley, Arizona. The film is suffused with the lyrical quality of American myth, particularly the sequence in which Tombstone's church is dedicated, with a spruced-up Fonda dancing a clumsily beautiful measure with Cathy Downs.

Jean Renoir had always been uneasy in Hollywood but found a subject to his liking in United Artists' *The Diary of a Chambermaid,* adapted from Octave Mirbeau's novel, which exploited Paulette Goddard's gaiety and beauty as the pert Paris-born servant of the title who bestows her favours above and below stairs.

Mark Robson explored a similar milieu in RKO's *Bedlam,* a Val Lewton chiller set in the infamous London insane asylum and inspired by the eighth painting in Hogarth's 'The Rake's Progress'.

Hal B Wallis discovery Kirk Douglas was introduced as Barbara Stanwyck's callow, alcoholic husband in Paramount's *The Strange Love of Martha Ivers,* directed by Lewis Milestone, a high-octane psychological melodrama, redolent of the period, in which Stanwyck gave a definitive performance as a ruthlessly ambitious woman in thrall to her past. Tyrone Power's comeback film after war service was Twentieth Century-Fox's *The Razor's Edge,* adapted from Somerset Maugham's novel. Anne Baxter won the Best Supporting Actress Oscar as the alcoholic whom Power romances, on the rebound from Gene Tierney. Mickey Rooney's first after war service was MGM's unsuccessful *Love Laughs at Andy Hardy,* a watershed film in his career.

Rex Harrison made his Hollywood debut in Twentieth Century-Fox's *Anna and the King of Siam,* as the Eastern monarch at cultural cross-purposes with the indomitable governess Irene Dunne. Lilli Palmer's first American film was Warners' *Cloak and Dagger,* directed by Fritz Lang, a

Roy Rogers

Gregory Peck (c) and Forrest Tucker in *The Yearling* (MGM)

Henry Fonda (l) and Linda Darnell in *My Darling Clementine* (Fox)

Barbara Stanwyck and Van Heflin in *The Strange Love of Martha Ivers* (Par)

Larry Parks in *The Jolson Story* (Col)

Cary Grant and Alexis Smith in *Night and Day* (WB)

Virginia Hunter in *The Ziegfeld Follies* (MGM)

Ivor Barnard and John Mills in *Great Expectations*
(Cine/IP)

wartime espionage thriller, much mangled by the studio, in which she played an Italian partisan helping nuclear scientist Gary Cooper.

Death took one of the great cowboy stars of the silent era, poker-faced William S Hart; Florence Turner, the original 'Vitagraph Girl'; and George Arliss the veteran British thespian who had been an unlikely top box-office draw in the early 1930s. With an immaculate sense of timing, W C Fields died on Christmas Day. He had always professed to loathe the Yuletide season.

Musical smash of the year was Columbia's *The Jolson Story,* starring Larry Parks as the legendary vaudevillian Al Jolson, whose voice – now rather scratchy – dubbed most of the songs. An artful assembly of almost every showbiz cliché, *The Jolson Story* took $8 million and was the studio's biggest money-earner up to that time.

Warners' *Night and Day* was a tribute to Cole Porter, uneasily impersonated by Cary Grant, which bore little or no relation to the facts of the composer's life (his homosexuality was, naturally enough, swept under the carpet). Paramount reunited Fred Astaire and Bing Crosby in *Blue Skies,* scored by Irving Berlin and brought electrifyingly to life by Fred's interpretation of 'Puttin' on the Ritz', choreographed by Hermes Pan.

In MGM's *Ziegfeld Follies* we find the great showman Flo Ziegfeld (quizzical William Powell) translated to Heaven, where he amuses himself by dreaming up his show of shows. Lending a helping hand were Fred Astaire and Gene Kelly (making their only appearance together in a film musical), Cyd Charisse, Lucille Bremer and Judy Garland – giving a wicked impersonation of the stately Greer Garson.

Olivia de Havilland won the year's Best Actress Oscar for her performance in Paramount's *To Each His Own,* an unashamed tearjerker in which she played an unwed mother who must remain 'aunt' to her son John Lund (making his debut), who also played the father. The characters which Lund played were both aviators and the film soared into stratospheres of sentiment.

Cinema admissions in Britain reached an all-time high of 1,635 million, a remarkable figure considering that many cinemas were still closed by bomb damage. Gainsborough continued to pump out popular costume melodramas, scoring a big hit with *The Magic Bow,* in which Stewart Granger gave an athletic impersonation of the violin virtuoso Paganini (dubbed by Yehudi Menuhin). *Caravan* fitted snugly into the Gainsborough formula, with Dennis Price enjoying himself as an evil Regency baronet, rehearsing his villainy with juicy self-confidence; 'Serve the wine downwind or, so help me, I'll lay my cane across your back', he sneers at a malodorous Spanish waiter.

Sidney Gilliat's *Green for Danger* was a charming pastiche of the detective thriller, starring Alastair Sim as an eccentric detective unravelling a hospital murder at the height of the V-bomb Blitz. Frank Launder's *I See a Dark*

Stranger (US *The Adventuress*), was a well-crafted chase thriller, with Deborah Kerr in bewitching form as a gullible young Irish girl caught up in a spy ring and Trevor Howard as the young British officer who falls for her.

Powell and Pressburger's *A Matter of Life and Death* (US *Stairway to Heaven*), had been prompted by a suggestion from the British Ministry of Information that they make a film about Anglo-American relations. The Ministry got more than it bargained for, a remarkable fantasy – full of dazzling, hallucinatory effects – built around bomber pilot David Niven's miraculous escape from death.

Peter Ustinov's *School for Secrets* (US *Secret Flight*), was a sprightly, highly fictionalized account of wartime research into airborne radar. Ealing's *The Captive Heart,* directed by Basil Dearden, was a thoughtful war film, set in a prisoner-of-war camp in Germany, in which the stories of the inmates were interwoven with the lives of their families.

David Lean's *Great Expectations* remains the finest screen adaptation of Charles Dickens' works, an object lesson in compression, definition and narrative drive.

Carol Reed's *Odd Man Out* was a rhythmic, ornate tour de force following the long day's dying of wounded I R A gunman James Mason.

It was not a great popular success – the public was much more interested in escapism and costume melodrama. Nevertheless, it established many of the themes, and the clichés, which were to run through the cycle of war films which dominated British cinema in the following decade.

In France Jean Cocteau returned to film-making with *La Belle et la Bête* (*Beauty and the Beast*), a surreal fantasy based on the age-old fairy tale. Josette Day was an ethereal Beauty and Jean Marais a memorably disfigured Beast.The haunting score was by Georges Auric.

In Italy the neo-realist movement gathered pace. Cesare Zavattini, the writer of Vittorio De Sica's major films, believed that the task of cinema was no longer simply to 'entertain' but to confront audiences with the 'reality' of their lives, using non-professional actors and real locations. This begged many questions about the ambiguous nature of cinematic 'realism' – some of the locations in *Roma Città Aperta* (1945) had been studio sets – but it nevertheless produced some fine films.

Roberto Rossellini's *Paisà* was an anecdotal dramatization of the effects of war on Italy. Vittorio De Sica's *Sciuscià* (Shoeshine) was a bitter parable of childhood betrayed by a corrupt adult world, in which two small shoeshine boys' brush with the black market leads to crime, imprisonment and heart-rending tragedy.

This was life in a Europe still reeling from the effects of war. From the rubble-choked ruins of the Soviet-occupied zone of Berlin came Wolfgang Staudte's *Die Morder Sind Unter Uns* (GB *The Murderers Are Amongst Us,*) a melancholy study of war criminals melting back into society to escape the punishment they so richly deserved.

Alastair Sim in *Green for Danger* (IP)

James Harcourt and Deborah Kerr in *I See a Dark Stranger* (US *The Adventuress*) (I)

Betty Potter, Kim Hunter and Roger Livesey in *A Matter of Life and Death* (US *Stairway to Heaven*) (A/IP)

Jean Kent and Stewart Granger in *Caravan* (G'boro)

Thomas Mitchell (c) in *The Dark Mirror* (Univ)

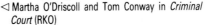

Ann Todd and Richard Greene in *Gaiety George* (US *Showtime*) (Emb)
◁ Martha O'Driscoll and Tom Conway in *Criminal Court* (RKO)
▽ Barton Yarborough, Ludwig Donath, Jim Bannon, Anita Louise and Michael Duane in *The Devil's Mask* (Col)

Film Favourites 1946

The confident supremacy of films in mass entertainment continued. Taut thrillers such as *The Big Sleep* (WB) were replacing war films and top-rate musicals such as *Till the Clouds Roll By* (MGM) were still prominent. All seemed well with Hollywood but a small cloud hovered on the horizon. Its name? Television.

George Brent; Merle Oberon and Paul Lukas in *Temptation* (Univ)
▽ Lloyd Bridges, Hoagy Carmichael, Ray Teal, Stanley Ridges, Dana Andrews and Brian Donlevy in *Canyon Passage* (Univ)

Willie Best, Victor Sen Yung, Sidney Toler, Gloria Warren, Joseph Crehan, Joe Allen Jr, Rick Vallin (pointing) and Dick Elliott in *Dangerous Money* (MoP)

Martha Hyer ▷

Ursula Jeans· △

Andrea King, Lisa Golm, John Alvin and Helmut Dantine in *Shadow of a Woman* (WB) ▷

Mark Stevens   Kim Hunter

Sharyn Moffett and Katherine Emery in *The Locket* (RKO)
▽ George Chandler, Deanna Durbin and Franchot Tone in *Because of Him* (Univ)

Ilona Massey and Leon Belasco in *Holiday in Mexico* (MGM)

Willard Robertson in *Renegades* (Col)

Humphrey Bogart and Lauren Bacall in *The Big Sleep* (WB)

Tony Martin in *Till the Clouds Roll By* (MGM) ▷

Lucille Bremer and Judy Garland in *Till the Clouds Roll By* (MGM)

Keenan Wynn and Evelyn Keyes in *The Thrill of Brazil* (Col)

Valerie Hobson and John Mills in *Great Expectations* (Cine/IP)

Ann Todd

Keenan Wynn in *The Thrill of Brazil* (Col)

▽ Barbara Lawrence and Conrad Janis in *Margie* (Fox)

Marlene Dietrich, star of *Martin Roumagnac* (FrF)

Picture Gallery for 1946

1. Raymond Walburn in *Breakfast in Hollywood* (GB *The Mad Hatter* (UA)
2. Lina Romay
3. Roger Livesey in *A Matter of Life and Death* (US *Stairway to Heaven*) (A/IP)
4. Viviane Romance in *Panique* (FrF)
5. John James and Rosemary La Planche in *Devil Bat's Daughter* (PRC)
6. Ann Gillis, Elyse Knox and Alan Hale Jr (r) in *Sweetheart of Sigma Chi* (MoP)
7. Pavel Kadochnikov and Nikolai Cherkasov in *Ivan the Terrible* (Part 2) (USSR)
8. Kim Hunter in *A Matter of Life and Death* (US *Stairway to Heaven*) (A/IP)
9. Bette Davis and Paul Henreid in *Deception* (WB)

9 ▷

1

2

3

4

5

6

7

8 ▷
▷ 9

1. Edward Cassidy, Al 'Fuzzy' St John, Patricia Knox and Larry 'Buster' Crabbe in *Prairie Badmen* (PRC)
2. Lee 'Lasses' White, Jimmy Wakely and Jonathan Black in *Song of the Sierras* (MoP)
3. Roscoe Ates, Louise Currie, Al 'Lash' LaRue, Jean Carlin, Eddie Dean, Sarah Padden, Chief Yowlachie and Robert 'Buzzy' Henry in *Wild West* (PRC)
4. David Sharpe and Eddie Dean in *Colorado Serenade* (PRC)
5. Steve Darrell, Larry 'Buster' Crabbe, George Chesebro, Al 'Fuzzy' St John and Budd Buster in *Terrors on Horseback* (PRC)
6. Lee 'Lasses' White, John Boxley, Budd Buster and Jimmy Wakely in *Rainbow Over the Rockies* (MoP)
7. Kirby Grant (c) and Louise Currie in *Gun Town* (Univ)
8. William Gould, Ramsay Ames and Gilbert Roland in *Beauty and the Bandit* (MoP)
9. Johnny Mack Brown and John Merton in *Shadows on the Range* (MoP)

1. Freddie Stewart and Isabelita in *High School Hero* (MoP)
2. Larry Simms, James Stewart and Donna Reed in *It's a Wonderful Life* (RKO)
3. Sheila Ryan
4. Pierre Watkin
5. Angela Greene
6. Betty Hutton
7. Carleton Young, Rose La Rose and Evelyn Ankers in *Queen of Burlesque* (PRC)
8. John Payne, William Bendix, Lillian Bronson, Connie Marshall and Maureen O'Hara in *Sentimental Journey* (Fox)
9. Lynn Bari, Randolph Scott, James Gleason, Peggy Ann Garner, Dean Stockwell and Connie Marshall in *Home Sweet Homicide* (Fox)

1

2

3

4

5

Over and over again, successful movies have been based on the novels of Charles Dickens and *Great Expectations* (Cine/I) was certainly no exception. It was superb from beginning to end and won two Oscars, one for Photography and the other for Art Direction.

1. Valerie Hobson and Torin Thatcher
2. Anthony Wager and Bernard Miles
3. Anthony Wager and Bernard Miles
4. John Mills and Ivor Barnard
5. Anthony Wager
6. Valerie Hobson and John Mills
7. John Mills
8. John Mills
9. Francis L Sullivan, Martita Hunt and John Mills

6

7

8
◁
▷
9

Lucille Bremer and Fred Astaire in *Ziegfeld Follies* (MGM)

Lucille Ball in *Ziegfeld Follies* (MGM)

1

2

3

4

Bella Donna, Robert Hichens' famous novel about a cold-blooded woman who took first to poisoning her husband and then her blackmailing lover, has been filmed at least three times – twice by Paramount – before Universal presented Merle Oberon in the role of the demon poisoner. The film is *Temptation* and Merle fairly revelled through the melodramatic sequences.

1. Merle Oberon
2. Merle Oberon and Arnold Moss
3. Merle Oberon and Suzanne Cloutier
4. Robert Capa, Lenore Ulric and Merle Oberon
5. Merle Oberon, Robert Capa and George Brent
6. Merle Oberon and Charles Korvin
7. Merle Oberon and Charles Korvin
8. John Eldredge, Merle Oberon, George Brent, Ilka Gruning, Ludwig Stossel and Gavin Muir
9. Andre Charlot, Merle Oberon and Ludwig Stossel
10. George Brent, Merle Oberon and Paul Lukas
11. Merle Oberon and Lenore Ulric

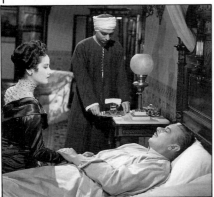

5

7

8

9

10
◁
▷
11

1

2

3

4 5

1. Fred Astaire and Gene Kelly in *Ziegfeld Follies*
(MGM)
2. Robertson Hare
3. Robert Benchley and Conrad Janis in *SNAFU*
(GB *Welcome Home*) (Col)
4. Kurt Katch, Bruce Lester, Osa Massen and
Paul Kelly in *Strange Journey* (Univ)
5. Thomas Mitchell
6. Kent Smith in *The Spiral Staircase* (RKO)
7. Adele Mara in *The Tiger Woman* (Rep)
8. Dorothy McGuire in *The Spiral Staircase*
(RKO)
9. Gordon Oliver in *The Spiral Staircase* (RKO)
10. Joe Sawyer (c) and Rod Cameron in *The
Runaround* (Univ)
11. Janet Beecher

7 ▷

6

8 ▽ 10

9 ▽ 11

1. Randolph Scott and Edgar Buchanan (r) in *Abilene Town* (JLP)

2. Ann Dvorak in *Abilene Town* (JLP)

3. George Macready, Ludwig Donath, Barbara Britton and Ray Collins in *The Return of Monte Cristo* (GB *Monte Cristo's Revenge* (Col)

4. Brian Aherne, Gene Raymond and Laraine Day in *The Locket* (RKO)

5. Louis Hayward and Barbara Britton in *The Return of Monte Cristo* (GB *Monte Cristo's Revenge* (Col)

6. Vincent Price in *Shock* (Fox)

7. Signe Hasso in *A Scandal in Paris* (AKA *Thieves' Holiday*) (UA)

8. George Sanders in *A Scandal in Paris* (AKA *Thieves' Holiday*) (UA)

9. Jack Carson and Janis Paige in *The Time, the Place and the Girl* (WB)

10. Dennis Morgan and Martha Vickers in *The Time, the Place and the Girl* (WB)

11. Jack Carson, Janis Paige and S Z Sakall in *The Time, the Place and the Girl* (WB)

△ 11

▽ 11

1. Harry Davenport in *Three Wise Fools* (MGM)
2. Dorothy Patrick and Cameron Mitchell in *The Mighty McGurk* (MGM)
3. Hazel Court and William Eythe in *Meet Me At Dawn* (Exc)
4. Janet Blair, Alfred Drake, Jeff Donnell, Sid Caesar and Marc Platt in *Tars and Spars* (Col)
5. Henry Morgan
6. Donald Barry
7. David Horne, Peter Graves and Carol Raye in *Spring Song* (US *Springtime*) (BN)
8. Charles Evans and George Macready in *The Man Who Dared* (Col)
9. Peter Graves in *Spring Song* (US *Springtime*) (BN)
10. Leslie Brooks and George Macready in *The Man Who Dared* (Col)

10 ▷

306

1. Gregory Peck and Claude Jarman Jr in *The Yearling* (MGM)
2. Claude Jarman Jr in *The Yearling* (MGM)
3. Claude Jarman Jr in *The Yearling* (MGM)
4. Gregory Peck and Jane Wyman in *The Yearling* (MGM)
5. Gregory Peck, Clem Bevans, Margaret Wycherly, Chill Wills and Forrest Tucker in *The Yearling* (MGM)
6. Gregory Peck, Claude Jarman Jr, Jane Wyman, Henry Travers and June Lockhart in *The Yearling* (MGM)
7. Hurd Hatfield
8. George Brent
9. Dennis Price, Marie Lohr and Phyllis Calvert in *The Magic Bow* (G'boro)
10. Jean Kent and Stewart Granger in *The Magic Bow* (G'boro)
11. Cecil Parker and Stewart Granger in *The Magic Bow* (G'boro)

1

2

3

1. Hedy Lamarr and Louis Hayward in *The Strange Woman* (HuS)
2. Marsha Hunt
3. Tyrone Power, Anne Baxter and Gene Tierney in *The Razor's Edge* (Fox)
4. Gilbert Roland in *South of Monterey* (MoP)
5. Frank Latimore as he appeared in *Three Little Girls in Blue* (Fox)
6. Walter Catlett
7. Peggy Knudsen, Tom D'Andrea and Errol Flynn in *Never Say Goodbye* (WB)
8. Barbara Lawrence and Conrad Janis in *Margie* (Fox)
9. Barbara Lawrence, Conrad Janis, Alan Young and Jeanne Crain in *Margie* (Fox)
10. Barbara Lawrence and Conrad Janis in *Margie* (Fox)
11. Conrad Janis, Barbara Lawrence and Hobart Cavanaugh in *Margie* (Fox)

5

4

6

7

8

9

10

11 ▷

1. John Laurenz in *Sunset Pass* (RKO)
2. Robert Clarke, Steve Brodie and Harry Woods in *Sunset Pass* (RKO)
3. Jane Greer and John Laurenz in *Sunset Pass* (RKO)
4. Robert Clarke in *Sunset Pass* (RKO)
5. Ben Carter
6. Johnny Weissmuller
7. William Marshall, Mona Freeman and James Dunn in *That Brennan Girl* (Rep)
8. Johnnie Schofield, Derek Farr and Garry Marsh in *The Shop at Sly Corner* (US *The Code of Scotland Yard*) (PP/LF)
9. Edmund Gwenn and Paul Henreid in *Of Human Bondage* (WB)
10. Rita Johnson
11. Robert Hutton, Jack Carson, John Loder, Alexis Smith and Dennis Morgan in *One More Tomorrow* (WB)

11 ▷

1

2

3

4

5

6

7

9

8

10

◁ 11

1. Guy Madison, Stan Johnson and Dorothy McGuire in *Till The End of Time* (RKO)
2. Ruth Nelson, Tom Tully and Guy Madison in *Till The End of Time* (RKO)
3. Mikhail Rasumny in *Anna and the King of Siam* (Fox)
4. Dorothy McGuire and Guy Madison in *Till The End of Time* (RKO)
5. Signe Hasso
6. William Gargan and Carole Landis in *Behind Green Lights* (Fox)
7. Sonny Tufts in *The Virginian* (Par)
8. Barbara Britton in *The Virginian* (Par)
9. Cornel Wilde in *The Bandit of Sherwood Forest* (Col)
10. Roscoe Karns, Bruce Cabot, Helen Mowery and John Good in *Avalanche* (PRC)
11. Alfred Drake

310

1. Sonny Tufts in *The Well-Groomed Bride* (Par)
2. Janet Blair in *Gallant Journey* (Col)
3. Bonita Granville in *Breakfast in Hollywood* (UA)
4. Alexander Knox in *Sister Kenny* (RKO)
5. Frank Sully, Fred Astaire and Frank Faylen in *Blue Skies* (Par)
6. Alistair Sim and Trevor Howard in *Green for Danger* (I/IP)
7. Penny Singleton and Arthur Lake in *Blondie Knows Best* (Col)
8. Jonathan Hale, Elizabeth Risdon and Lee Bowman in *The Walls Came Tumbling Down* (Col)
9. Eric Portman and Phyllis Calvert in *Men of Two Worlds* (US *Kisenga*) (TC)
10. Arnold Marle, Robert Adams and Eric Portman in *Men of Two Worlds* (US *Kisenga*) (TC)
11. William Bendix, Dan Duryea and Ella Raines in *White Tie and Tails* (Univ)

Hollywood producers were always happy to utilise the services of world-famous instrumentalists to provide music for film sound tracks. So it was with *I've Always Loved You* (GB *Concerto*) (Rep) which featured the irrational jealousy of a well-known pianist for his girl pupil Vanessa Brown with whom he professes to be in love. Arthur Rubinstein, the world-famous pianist, provided the musical soundtrack.

1. William Carter
2. Philip Dorn and Catherine McLeod
3. Maria Ouspenskaya and Philip Dorn
4. Catherine McLeod, Philip Dorn and Fritz Feld
5. Catherine McLeod and Philip Dorn
6. William Carter and Maria Ouspenskaya
7. William Carter and Catherine McLeod
8. Philip Dorn and Maria Ouspenskaya
9. Catherine McLeod, Vanessa Brown and Philip Dorn
10. Catherine McLeod, Philip Dorn and Maria Ouspenskaya

1. Mickey Rooney
2. Charles Laughton, Deanna Durbin and Stanley Ridges in *Because of Him* (Univ)
3. Lilli Palmer in *Cloak and Dagger* (WB)
4. Franchot Tone, Deanna Durbin and Stanley Ridges in *Because of Him* (Univ)
5. Gino Corrado (I), J Carrol Naish and Pedro de Cordoba in *The Beast With Five Fingers* (WB)
6. George Tobias and Marshall Thompson in *Gallant Bess* (MGM)
7. Marshall Thompson and Clem Bevans in *Gallant Bess* (MGM)
8. Clem Bevans, George Tobias and Marshall Thompson in *Gallant Bess* (MGM)
9. Frances Rafferty and Marshall Thompson in *Bad Bascomb* (MGM)
10. William Henry in *The Mysterious Mr Valentine* (Rep)
11. Richard Denning and Mona Freeman in *Black Beauty* (Fox)

9 ◁
10 ◁

11 ▷

1

2

3

4

5

6

7

8

9

10

11 ◁
▷
12

1. Joyce Howard
2. George Macready in *Gilda* (Col)
3. Rita Hayworth in *Gilda* (Col)
4. Rita Hayworth and Glenn Ford in *Gilda* (Col)
5. Olivia de Havilland, Ida Lupino, Arthur Kennedy and Paul Henreid in *Devotion* (WB)
6. Arthur Kennedy, Olivia de Havilland and Nancy Coleman in *Devotion* (WB)
7. Walter Huston, Joseph Cotten, Jennifer Jones, Gregory Peck and Lionel Barrymore in *Duel in the Sun* (DS)
8. Olivia de Havilland and Lew Ayres in *The Dark Mirror* (Univ)
9. Leon Ames, Marshall Thompson and Frank Morgan in *The Cockeyed Miracle* (GB *Mr Griggs Returns*) (MGM)
10. Dana Andrews and Susan Hayward in *Canyon Passage* (Univ)
11. Thomas Mitchell, Olivia de Havilland and Lew Ayres in *The Dark Mirror* (Univ)
12. Andy Devine in *Canyon Passage* (Univ)

1. Frank Morgan in *Lady Luck* (RKO)
2. Barbara Hale in *Lady Luck* (RKO)
3. Robert Young, Frank Morgan, Barbara Hale and James Gleason in *Lady Luck* (RKO)
4. Robert Young and Barbara Hale in *Lady Luck* (RKO)
5. Douglas Morrow, Robert Young and Barbara Hale in *Lady Luck* (RKO)
6. James Gleason, Robert Young, Harry Davenport, Teddy Hart and Joseph Vitale in *Lady Luck* (RKO)
7. Jean Kent and Stewart Granger in *Caravan* (G'boro)
8. Sharyn Moffett and Harry Cheshire in *Child of Divorce* (RKO)
9. Ian Keith and Adrian Booth in *Valley of the Zombies* (Rep)
10. Reginald Owen, Hurd Hatfield, Francis Lederer and Paulette Goddard in *Diary of a Chambermaid* (UA)

9
▷
◁
▷
10

1. Jane Withers and Gene Autry in *Shooting High* (Fox)
2. Bob Steele, Tom London, Sunset Carson and Kenne Duncan in *Rio Grande Raiders* (Rep)
3. Ian Keith, Ken Curtis, Matt Willis and Dusty Anderson in *Singing on the Trail* (Col)
4. Larry Parks and Evelyn Keyes in *Renegades* (Col)
5. Larry 'Buster' Crabbe (r) in *Ghost of Hidden Valley* (PRC)
6. Bill Elliott and Tom London in *Sun Valley Cyclone* (Rep)
7. Raymond Hatton (l), Pierce Lyden (stdg), and Johnny Mack Brown in *Trigger Fingers* (MoP)
8. Roy Rogers, George 'Gabby' Hayes, Edmund Cobb and Lyle Talbot in *Song of Arizona* (Rep)
9. Sunset Carson and Marie Harmon in *The El Paso Kid* (Rep)

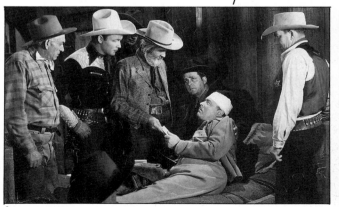

316

1. Alan Ladd and Geraldine Fitzgerald in *OSS* (Par)
2. Renie Riano and Joe Yule in *Bringing up Father* (MoP)
3. Mark Stevens and Lucille Ball in *The Dark Corner* (Fox)
4. Tom Conway and Martha O'Driscoll in *Criminal Court* (RKO)
5. Larry Simms, Arthur Lake, Penny Singleton and Marjorie Kent in *Life With Blondie* (Col)
6. Charles Boyer and Jennifer Jones in *Cluny Brown* (Fox)
7. Sidney Toler and Benson Fong in *Dark Alibi* (MoP)
8. June Clyde and James Cardwell in *Behind the Mask* (MoP)
9. Tom Conway and Edward S Brophy in *The Falcon's Adventure* (RKO)

1. Barbara Stanwyck in *My Reputation* (WB)
2. Rondo Hatton and Virginia Grey in *House of Horrors* (GB *Joan Medford is Missing*) (Univ)
3. Allen Jenkins, Phillip Terry and Ann Savage in *The Dark Horse* (Univ)
4. Douglas Fowley (r) in *The Glass Alibi* (Rep)
5. Joan Crawford, Paul Cavanagh and John Garfield in *Humoresque* (WB)
6. Gavin Muir (l), Barbara Stanwyck and Ray Milland in *California* (Par)
7. Sylvia Sidney in *Mr Ace* (UA)
8. Frances Langford in *The Bamboo Blonde* (RKO)
9. Jess Barker, Dewey Robinson and Julie Bishop in *Idea Girl* (Univ)

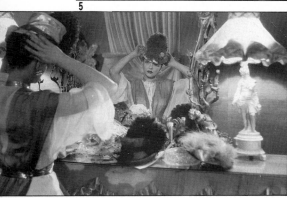

9 ▷

Randolph Scott

Corinne Calvet

1. Tom Drake (c) with Lassie in *Courage of Lassie* (MGM)
2. Virginia O'Brien in *'Til The Clouds Roll By* (MGM)
3. Chester Morris and Brian O'Hare in *Boston Blackie and the Law* (Col)
4. Ruth Warrick and Pat O'Brien in *Perilous Holiday* (Col)
5. George Dolenz and Jess Barker in *Girl on the Spot* (Univ)
6. Vera Ralston, Gail Patrick and William 'Wild Bill' Elliott in *The Plainsman and the Lady* (Rep)
7. Jane Frazee in *A Guy Could Change* (Rep)
8. Anna Lee and Boris Karloff in *Bedlam* (RKO)
9. Mark Stevens and Joan Fontaine in *From This Day Forward* (RKO)

1. Joan Caulfield in *Monsieur Beaucaire* (Par)
2. Micheline Cheirel and Steven Geray in *So Dark the Night* (Col)
3. Maria Palmer and William Gargan in *Rendezvous 24* (Fox)
4. James Craig and Frances Gifford in *Little Mr Jim* (MGM)
5. Vera Zorina, Lucille Ball and George Brent in *Lover Come Back* (Univ)
6. Jackie 'Butch' Jenkins and Frances Gifford in *Little Mr Jim* (MGM)
7. Anabel Shaw, John Shepperd, Preston Foster and Signe Hasso in *Strange Triangle* (Fox)
8. Ken Curtis and Guinn 'Big Boy' Williams in *That Texas Jamboree* (Col)
9. Buster Crabbe, Carol Thurston and Johnny Weissmuller in *Swamp Fire* (Par)

1. George Murphy and Ann Sothern in *Up Goes Maisie* (MGM)
2. Marjorie Reynolds in *The Time of Their Lives* (Univ)
3. Diana Lynn, Sara Haden, Gail Russell and James Brown in *Our Hearts Were Growing Up* (Par)
4. Martha Stewart in *Johnny Comes Flying Home* (Fox)
5. Dick Curtis and Allan Lane in *Santa Fe Uprising* (Rep)
6. Charles Arnt, William Powell and Angela Lansbury in *The Hoodlum Saint* (MGM)
7. Julie Bishop, Joan Leslie and Ruth Donnelly in *Cinderella Jones* (WB)
8. Phil Silvers, Carmen Miranda, Vivian Blaine and Harry James in *If I'm Lucky* (Fox)
9. Margaret Dumont and Lou Costello in *Little Giant* (GB *On the Carpet*) (Univ)
10. Jane Adams, Kirby Grant, Fuzzy Knight and Karl Hackett in *Lawless Breed* (Univ)

◁ 10

1

2

3

4

5

6

1. Peter Lorre, Michele Morgan, Lloyd Corrigan and Steve Cochran in *The Chase* (UA)
2. Audrey Long and John Loder in *A Game of Death* (RKO)
3. Diana Lynn and Robert Cummings in *The Bride Wore Boots* (Par)
4. Peggy Wood in *The Bride Wore Boots* (Par)
5. Richard Dix and Mike Mazurki in *Mysterious Intruder* (Col)
6. Pamela Blake, Bobby Jordan, Leo Gorcey, Billy Benedict and Huntz Hall in *Live Wires* (MoP)
7. Jack Haley, Ozzie Nelson, Helen Walker, Rudy Vallee and Philip Reed in *People Are Funny* (Par)
8. Rondo Hatton and Jane Adams in *The Brute Man* (PRC)
9. Janis Carter, Willard Parker, Anita Louise and Edgar Buchanan in *The Fighting Guardsman* (Col)
10. Janis Carter and Willard Parker in *The Fighting Guardsman* (Col)

7

▽ 9

8

▽ 10

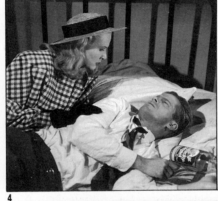

1. June Haver and George Montgomery in
Three Little Girls in Blue (Fox)
2. Celeste Holm in *Three Little Girls in Blue* (Fox)
3. Barbara Britton and Robert Lowery in *They
Made Me A Killer* (Par)
4. June Vincent and Dan Duryea in *The Black
Angel* (Univ)
5. Ann Richards in *Badman's Territory* (RKO)
6. Roland Culver, Eric Portman, Bonar Colleano,
Edna Wood and Stanley Holloway in *Wanted for
Murder* (Exc)
7. Tris Coffin and Roy Rogers in *Under Nevada
Skies* (Rep)
8. Albert Lieven and Lilli Palmer in *Beware of Pity* (TC)
9. Preston Foster, Robert Paige and Francis
McDonald in *Tangier* (Univ)

1

2

3

4

5

1. Harpo Marx, Groucho Marx and Chico Marx in *A Night in Casablanca* (UA)
2. Ginger Rogers and David Niven in *Magnificent Doll* (Univ)
3. Gloria Stuart in *She Wrote The Book* (Univ)
4. Joan Davis and Jack Oakie in *She Wrote The Book* (Univ)
5. Anne Baxter and Fred MacMurray in *Smoky* (Fox)
6. Anita Louise and Michael Duane in *Shadowed* (Col)
7. Doris Merrick, Constance Worth and Robert Lowery in *Sensation Hunters* (MoP)
8. Sunset Carson and Edmund Cobb in *Red River Renegades* (Rep)
9. Janis Carter and William Gargan in *Night Editor* (Col)

6

◁ 7

8

9

326

1. Ann Rutherford, Helen Walker, William Marshall, Vera Hruba Ralston and Julie Bishop in *Murder in the Music Hall* (Rep)

2. Virginia Huston, Lynn Bari and George Raft in *Nocturne* (RKO)

3. Whit Bissell, Margo Woode, Allyn Joslyn, Carole Landis and Ralph Sanford in *It Shouldn't Happen to a Dog* (Fox)

4. Martha O'Driscoll and Peter Whitney in *Blonde Alibi* (Univ)

5. Butch Jenkins and Edward Arnold in *My Brother Talks to Horses* (MGM)

6. William Eythe in *Centennial Summer* (Fox)

7. Joan Fulton, Desi Arnaz, Beverley Simmons and Pedro De Cordoba in *Cuban Pete* (Univ)

8. Jeanne Bates and Erich Von Stroheim in *The Mask of Dijon* (PRC)

1. Wally Brown and Alan Carney in *Genius at Work* (RKO)
2. Wally Brown and Anne Jeffreys in *Genius at Work* (RKO)
3. Adele Mara and Warren Douglas in *The Inner Circle* (Rep)
4. Gloria Warren in *Dangerous Money* (MoP)
5. Bill Shannon in *Step by Step* (RKO)
6. Bob Steele (l) in *Sheriff of Redwood Valley* (Rep)
7. Philip Reed and Jean Rogers in *Hot Cargo* (Par)
8. Charles Starrett and Smiley Burnette in *The Fighting Frontiersman* (Col)
9. Philip Reed and William Gargan in *Hot Cargo* (Par)

1

2

3

4

5

6

7

9 ▷
◁
8

4

In *The Jolson Story* (Col) Larry Parks' singing was dubbed by Al Jolson himself but apart from that, Parks was superb in the role. The film was such a success that a sequel was ensured. Three years later Columbia produced *Jolson Sings Again* with Larry Parks once again as Jolson.

1. William Demarest (l), Ludwig Donath, Larry Parks and Tamara Shayne

2. Larry Parks

3. Larry Parks and John Alexander

4. Evelyn Keyes

5. Ludwig Donath, Tamara Shayne, Evelyn Keyes and William Demarest

6. William Goodwin, Ludwig Donath, Tamara Shayne, Larry Parks, Evelyn Keyes and William Demarest

7. Larry Parks, William Goodwin and William Demarest

8. Ludwig Donath and Larry Parks

9. Evelyn Keyes, Ludwig Donath, Tamara Shayne, Eric Wilton, Larry Parks and William Demarest

1. Sam Levene, Albert Dekker (on floor),
Edmond O'Brien and Ava Gardner in *The Killers* (Univ)

2. Billy Halop (r) in *Gas House Kids* (PRC)

3. Edmond O'Brien and Ava Gardner in *The Killers* (Univ)

4. Ann Todd and Richard Greene in *Gaiety George* (US *Showtime*) (EMB)

5. Joan Greenwood in *A Girl in a Million* (Boc)

6. Maureen O'Hara and Harry James in *Do You Love Me?* (Fox)

7. Humphrey Bogart, Lauren Bacall and Louis Jean Heydt in *The Big Sleep* (WB)

8. Lauren Bacall and Humphrey Bogart in *The Big Sleep* (WB)

9. Humphrey Bogart and Lauren Bacall in *The Big Sleep* (WB)

8
▷
▷
9

1. Ilona Massey and Walter Pidgeon in *Holiday in Mexico* (MGM)

2. Roddy McDowall and Jane Powell in *Holiday in Mexico* (MGM)

3. Ann Dvorak in *The Bachelor's Daughters* (GB *Bachelor Girls*) (UA)

4. Jose Iturbi, Jane Powell and Walter Pidgeon in *Holiday in Mexico* (MGM)

5. Xavier Cugat and Walter Pidgeon in *Holiday in Mexico* (MGM)

6. Gail Russell, John Whitney, Billie Burke, Adolphe Menjou and Ann Dvorak in *The Bachelor's Daughters* (GB *Bachelor Girls*) (UA)

7. Eve Arden, Steve Cochran, Vera-Ellen, Danny Kaye and Walter Abel in *The Kid From Brooklyn* (RKO)

8. Vera-Ellen in *The Kid From Brooklyn* (RKO)

9. Chester Morris

10. Samuel S Hinds

11. Tom Conway, Rita Corday and Emory Parnell in *The Falcon's Alibi* (RKO)

12. Dermot Walsh and Margaret Lockwood in *Hungry Hill* (TC)

1. Harry Barris (piano) and Nita Hunter in *Susie Steps Out* (UA)
2. Edward Norris
3. Paul Kelly
4. Fred Brady, Frank McHugh, Beverley Simmons, Dorothy Morris and Fay Holden in *Little Miss Big* (GB *The Baxter Millions*) (Univ)
5. Warren Mills, June Preisser and Freddie Stewart in *Junior Prom* (MoP)
6. Anne Jeffreys and Glenn Vernon in *Ding Dong Williams* (GB *Melody Maker*) (RKO)
7. Sheldon Leonard and Charles Starrett in *Decoy* (MoP)
8. John Alvin, Helmut Dantine and Andrea King in *Shadow of a Woman* (WB)
9. Sheldon Leonard (with gun), Huntz Hall, Leo Gorcey and Teala Loring in *Bowery Bombshell* (MoP)
10. Erskine Sanford, Wallace Ford, Herbert Marshall, Claire Trevor, Ray Collins, Damian O'Flynn and Pat O'Brien in *Crack Up* (RKO)

◁ 8

9

10 ▷

1. Ann Rutherford, Joe Sawyer, Jimmie Moss and Alan Curtis in *Inside Job* (Univ)

2. June Preisser, Warren Mills and Freddie Stewart in *Freddie Steps Out* (MoP)

3. Catherine McLeod, Philip Dorn and Vanessa Brown in *I've Always Loved You* (Rep)

4. Johnny Sheffield, Tommy Cook, Brenda Joyce and Johnny Weissmuller in *Tarzan and the Leopard Woman* (RKO)

5. Tom Dugan, Barbara Reed and Kane Richmond in *The Shadow Returns* (MoP)

6. Romney Brent

7. Joan Greenwood

8. Rod Cameron

9. Harry Davenport, Dorothy McGuire, Robert Young, Anthony Sydes and Elsa Janssen in *Claudia and David* (Fox)

◁ **9**

333

1

2

Dragonwyck (Fox) was without doubt a Vincent Price 'Special'. He plays the part of an arrogant scion of an old Dutch family who still believes in collecting both tithes and rent from his down trodden farmer tenantry. Not the sort of tyrant to allow anything to stand in the way of anything he wants, he poisons his wife because she cannot present him with an heir. He selects Gene Tierney as the possible supplier of the son he has set his ruthless heart on having. It is no surprise then, to learn of the relief felt by Gene when along comes handsome Glenn Langan to rescue her from the fate that awaits her at the hands of haughty Vincent who has now decided that the time has arrived for him once again to enjoy life as a widower. Throw in an old spooky house and you have all the ingredients of a real old-type melodrama. Incidentally, the film was based on a best-selling novel by popular Anya Seton.

3

4 ▷

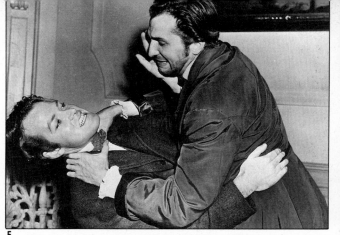

5

6

7

8

1. Gene Tierney
2. Vincent Price and Gene Tierney
3. Vincent Price, Gene Tierney and Glenn Langan
4. Walter Huston, Anne Revere, Vincent Price and Gene Tierney
5. Glenn Langan and Vincent Price
6. Gene Tierney, Walter Huston and Anne Revere
7. Gene Tierney and Vincent Price
8. Gene Tierney, Vincent Price and Glenn Langan
9. Glenn Langan and Gene Tierney
10. Reinhold Schunzel, Vincent Price, Glenn Langan and Henry Morgan

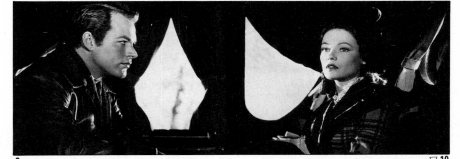

9

▽ 10

1. Claude Rains and Gloria Holden in *Strange Holiday* (PRC)
2. James Cagney in *13 Rue Madeleine* (Fox)
3. Olivia de Havilland and Phillip Terry in *To Each His Own* (Par)
4. Sonny Tufts and Ann Blyth in *Swell Guy* (Univ)
5. Jack Carson, Lex Barker, Joan Leslie and Dennis Morgan in *Two Guys from Milwaukee* (WB)
6. John Eldredge, Phil Regan and Gale Storm in *Swing Parade of 1946* (MoP)
7. Peter Lorre and Sydney Greenstreet in *The Verdict* (WB)
8. Tom Dugan (arms up) and Johnny Mack Brown in *Under Arizona Skies* (MoP)

7
◁
▷
8

Yvonne De Carlo

Lana Turner

338

1. Helen Walker, Charles Judels, Tom Powers and Dennis O'Keefe in *Her Adventurous Night* (Univ)

2. Brian Donlevy, Albert Dekker and Alan Ladd in *Two Years Before the Mast* (Par)

3. Alan Mowbray, Nigel Bruce and Basil Rathbone in *Terror by Night* (Univ)

4. Tommy Dorsey

5. Michael Redgrave and Valerie Hobson in *The Years Between* (Box)

6. Bette Davis and Dane Clark in *A Stolen Life* (WB)

7. Kathleen Ryan and James Mason in *Odd Man Out* (US *Gang War*) (TC)

8. Elyse Knox, Guy Kibbee, Leon Errol and Joe Kirkwood Jr in *Gentleman Joe Palooka* (MoP)

9. Richard Haydn, Charles Coburn and Tom Drake in *The Green Years* (MGM)

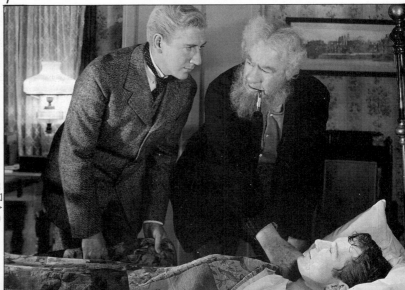

1

2

3

4

5

6

7

▽ 8

1. Peggy Stewart and Sunset Carson in *Alias Billy the Kid* (Rep)
2. Reno Browne, Steve Clark, Johnny Mack Brown and Raymond Hatton in *The Gentleman From Texas* (MoP)
3. Douglas Fowley, Lynne Carver, Ted Mapes, Steve Clark, Terry Frost, Johnny Mack Brown, Jack Rockwell and Raymond Hatton in *Drifting Along* (MoP)
4. Monte Hale, Adrian Booth, Tex Cooper, James Taggert and John Ince in *Last Frontier Uprising* (Rep)
5. Roy Rogers, Dale Evans, Bob Nolan, George Hayes and The Sons of the Pioneers in *My Pal Trigger* (Rep)
6. Tom London, Sunset Carson, Peggy Stewart and Eddie Parker in *Days of Buffalo Bill* (Rep)
7. George Morrell, Buster Crabbe, Al 'Fuzzy' St John and Patricia Knox in *Gentleman With Guns* (PRC)
8. Bob Nolan, Pat Brady, Tim Spencer, Dale Evans, Roy Rogers, Hugh Farr, Carl Farr and George 'Shug' Fisher in *Roll On, Texas Moon* (Rep)

1

2

3

It was 1946, the war was over and Hollywood lost no time in turning their attention to romantic comedies. *The Fabulous Suzanne* (Rep) was a good representative of that type of light-hearted fun. Backed by a cast of noted performers, the movie, without pretension, managed to amuse and entertain the cinema audiences.

1. Rudy Vallee, Otto Kruger and Richard Denning
2. Barbara Britton Otto Kruger and Veda Ann Borg
3. Barbara Britton and Bill Henry
4. Richard Denning, Rudy Vallee and Barbara Britton
5. Rudy Vallee, Richard Denning and Bill Henry
6. Bill Henry and Barbara Britton
7. Barbara Britton, Rudy Vallee, Herbert Evans and Richard Denning
8. Frank Darien and Barbara Britton
9. Rudy Vallee, Otto Kruger and Richard Denning
10. Otto Kruger (l)

4

5

6

7

6

9

8

◁ 10

341

Easy to Wed (MGM) was a remake of the same studio's 1936 movie *Libeled Lady* which starred William Powell, Myrna Loy, Jean Harlow and Spencer Tracy. This time MGM re-cast Van Johnson, Esther Williams, Lucille Ball and Keenan Wynn respectively and added a musical score just for good measure.

1. Esther Williams and Cecil Kellaway
2. Van Johnson and June Lockhart
3. Esther Williams and Ben Blue
4. Esther Williams, Van Johnson and Lucille Ball
5. Carlos Ramirez, Van Johnson and Esther Williams
6. Esther Williams, Van Johnson and Lucille Ball
7. Esther Williams and Van Johnson
8. Keenan Wynn, Lucille Ball, Cecil Kellaway, Van Johnson, and Esther Williams

8 ▷

CHAPTER EIGHT
1947
POLITICS IN FILMLAND

Edward G Robinson

The motion picture industry was poised on the brink of a prolonged period of crisis. The wartime boom, when almost anything on celluloid was guaranteed an audience, was now over. Foreign revenues fell by 30 per cent, at a time when box-office income in the United States had dropped by 20 per cent.

The shadow of Cold War paranoia also fell over Hollywood. J Parnell Thomas' House un-American Activities Committee (HUAC) began its investigation into alleged Communist infiltration of the film industry.

Eight writers, a producer and a director – who became known as 'The Hollywood Ten' – declined to testify before the Committee and were held in contempt of Congress. The industry stood by as they were thrown to the wolves. A Committee for the First Amendment, chaired by John Huston, was formed to protest against the HUAC's infringement of the constitutional rights of the Hollywood Ten, but proved a broken reed when it came under pressure itself. In November the Association of Motion Picture producers pledged that the industry would not 'knowingly employ a Communist or a member of any party or group which advocates the overthrow of the Government of the United States by force or by any illegal or uncontrolled method'. Thus began the dreaded 'blacklist', on which were placed the names of writers, directors and actors who were suspected of the slightest traces of left-wing sympathies. Notable casualties included actors Edward G Robinson, Larry Parks, Marsha Hunt and Gale Sondergaard. The 'blacklist' eventually played a baleful part in the death of John Garfield, from a heart attack, in 1952.

The director and producer among the Hollywood Ten were, respectively, Edward Dmytryk and Adrian Scott, two of RKO's top talents. Ironically, they had been responsible for *Crossfire,* the studio's biggest financial and critical success of the year. *Crossfire* was an example of Hollywood's new-found social conscience, a hard-hitting assault on anti-Semitism in which liberal-minded cop Robert Young unravels the mystery of the brutal murder of Jewish veteran

Larry Parks

Marsha Hunt

Gregory Peck, Celeste Holm and John Garfield in
Gentleman's Agreement (Fox)

Richard Webb, Jane Greer and Dickie Moore in *Out of
the Past* (GB *Build My Gallows High*) (RKO)

Richard Ney in *Ivy* (Univ)
▽ Lizabeth Scott in *Dead Reckoning* (Col)

Sam Levene. The killer is a serving soldier, Robert Ryan, a psychopathic bully and sadist.

While exploring this previously uncharted territory the studios had to move with some circumspection. In the novel on which *Crossfire* was based the victim had been a homosexual, but this subject was still way out of bounds. An air of 'punches being pulled' also hangs about Elia Kazan's *Gentleman's Agreement* (Twentieth Century-Fox), another attack on anti-Semitism in which crusading writer Gregory Peck poses as a Jew to discover at first hand the prejudice directed against the Jewish community. The Academy voted *Gentleman's Agreement* the Best Film of the Year and Kazan the Best Director.

The year produced a rich crop of *films noirs*. In Henry Hathaway's *Kiss of Death*, (Twentieth Century-Fox) Richard Widmark made a stunning debut as the fearsome, giggling hood Tommy Udo, pushing crippled Mildred Dunnock down a flight of stairs and terrorising small-time stoolie Victor Mature. RKO's *Out of the Past* (GB *Build My Gallows High*), moodily directed by Jacques Tourneur, established Robert Mitchum's sleepily laconic film persona and gave Jane Greer a special place in the femmes fatales' hall of fame. The genre even infiltrated the Western with Warner Brothers' *Pursued,* again with Robert Mitchum and directed by Raoul Walsh, a brooding film full of landscapes of the mind, hauntingly photographed by James Wong Howe.

It was a year when deadly dames did their worst. In Warners' *Nora Prentiss,* nightclub singer Ann Sheridan led happily married doctor Kent Smith fatally astray. Joan Fontaine murdered her husband and framed her lover in *Ivy* (Universal) but came to a messy end at the bottom of a lift shaft. In *Born to Kill* (GB *Lady of Deceit*), (RKO) mercenary bitch Claire Trevor threw in her lot with hoodlum Lawrence Tierney. Ruthless floozie Janis Carter enticed out-of-work engineer Glenn Ford into a bank heist in Columbia's *Framed* (GB *Paula*).

In Columbia's *Dead Reckoning* Lizabeth Scott was the lethal lady Humphrey Bogart had to reckon with as he tried to solve the murder of a wartime buddy. Scott was one of the most distinctive of the decade's leading ladies, husky of voice and decidedly masculine in manner, and this is one of her most hypnotic performances, coolly sexy and unscrupulous, but not quite unscrupulous enough for Bogie.

Humphrey Bogart was re-united with Lauren Bacall in Delmer Daves' *Dark Passage,* as an escaped convict who undergoes plastic surgery to emerge looking like, well, Humphrey Bogart. The first 40 minutes of the film are a bravura technical achievement, filmed entirely from Bogart's point of view in a manner reminiscent of *The Lady in the Lake* (1946).

Claude Rains had been one of Warner's most reliable stars since 1935, and for consistent flair in supporting roles, notably with Bette Davis, he had few equals. His last under contract to the studio, and his tenth with director Michael

Curtiz, was *The Unsuspected* in which he was silkily persuasive as the deranged radio producer Victor Grandison, living out one of his own murder stories.

Susan Hayward hit her stride in *Smash-Up, The Story of a Woman* (GB *A Woman Destroyed*), tautly directed by the excellent Stuart Heisler, playing a torch singer who gives up husband Lee Bowman for the booze in a female re-run of *The Lost Weekend* (1945).

Susan Hayward

The bottle lay in wait for Tyrone Power at the end of Twentieth Century-Fox's *Nightmare Alley*, directed by Edmund Goulding. In a determined effort to change his blandly romantic image, Power played a swindling carnival barker who shoots to the top as a fashionable mind-reader before the inevitable descent to a terrible fate – employment as a fairground 'geek', tearing the heads off live chickens in a bran-pit for a bottle of liquor a day.

Power had begged for the part in *Nightmare Alley*, but the studio had hedged its bets with *Captain from Castile*, a handsome actioner set in the days of the Spanish conquistadores and the kind of vehicle with which Power's fans were more familiar. Audiences were also familiar with Kathleen Winsor's best-seller *Forever Amber,* a property on which Darryl F Zanuck lavished $6 million, with a lacklustre Linda Darnell cast as the seventeenth-century adventuress at the court of Charles II. The result was a gaudy, broken-backed epic which lacked the earthy drive of the original. *Forever Amber* was, perhaps, an aberrational project for a studio now increasingly committed to 'quality' films. The only player to survive the shambles was George Sanders as a languid Charles II gazing sceptically at Darnell's creamy cleavage.

Jessica Tandy and Linda Darnell in *Forever Amber* (Fox)

There was never a dull moment in Cecil B DeMille's *Unconquered,* a tuppence-coloured eighteenth-century Western with Gary Cooper and Paulette Goddard opening up Virginia and Howard da Silva as a juicy villain in league with the Indians.

Ronald Colman won the Best Actor Oscar in 1947 for *A Double Life* (Universal) as a Shakespearean actor who succumbs to schizophrenia and assumes the character of the role he is playing, in this case Othello, with fatal results for his off-stage Desdemona, Shelley Winters.

Loretta Young was the surprise winner of the year's Best Actress Oscar for her performance in RKO's *The Farmer's Daughter* as the Swedish farm girl who leaves the land for a career in politics. This was an unexceptionable Capraesque comedy-romance, co-starring Joseph Cotten, and the Oscar was presumably a reward for Young's determined maintenance of a clonking Swedish accent throughout.

William Powell

A far wittier satire on politics was *The Senator Was Indiscreet* (GB *Mr Ashton Was Indiscreet*), George S Kaufman's only film as a director, which starred William Powell as an irredeemably fatuous politician whose lost diaries cause a scandal. One of the film's best lines, 'There's a rule in our state – if you can't beat 'em, bribe 'em', caused Senator Joe

Harold Lloyd in *Mad Wednesday* (RKO)

Marilyn Nash in *Monsieur Verdoux* (UA)

Peter Lawford and Jimmy Durante in *It Happened in Brooklyn* (MGM)

Larry Parks, Adele Jergens and Rita Hayworth in *Down to Earth* (Col)

McCarthy to denounce *The Senator was Indiscreet* as 'traitorous' and 'un-American'. Edmund Gwenn carried off the Best Supporting Actor Award in another delightful comedy, Twentieth Century-Fox's *The Miracle on 34th Street* (GB *The Big Heart*), playing 'Kris Kringle', the department store Santa Claus who might just be the real thing.

At Universal Claudette Colbert had a big hit with *The Egg and I,* as a sophisticated lady coming to terms with life on husband Fred MacMurray's chicken farm. *The Egg and I* also prominently featured Marjorie Main and Percy Kilbride as Ma and Pa Kettle, whose success in the film led to a money-spinning series of their own.

In *Mad Wednesday* (HH) Harold Lloyd returned to the screen in Preston Sturges' sadly botched attempt to re-create the days of 'thrill comedy'. Lloyd acquired a silly name, Harold Diddlebock, a silly suit and a lion on a lead, but of thrills there were very few and of comedy none.

Charles Chaplin also returned with *Monsieur Verdoux* (United Artists), a black comedy – and box-office failure – in which he played a dapper little wife murderer, second cousin to Adolphe Menjou's cynical seducer Pierre in Chaplin's masterly *A Woman of Paris* (1923). Monsieur Verdoux was full of Chaplin's deep misogyny, the result of broken marriages and paternity suits, and presented the mirror image of the Tramp's sentimental vision of women.

Frank Sinatra and Jimmy Durante were teamed in MGM's *It Happened in Brooklyn,* in which Sinatra came badly unstuck when attempting to sing 'La Ci Darem La Mano', from Don Giovanni, with Kathryn Grayson. In contrast Jimmy Durante was completely at home in MGM's *This Time for Keeps.* Several of the movie's numbers came from the swimming pool, as this was an Esther Williams aquacaper, and Durante was immaculate in white top hat and tails marooned in the middle of the studio tank warbling 'Inka Dinka Doo'.

In *Down to Earth,* Columbia revived the character of Mr Jordan – this time played by the urbane Roland Culver – who despatches a ravishing Terpsichore (Rita Hayworth) back to Earth to star in a musical comedy show. Every bit as absurd, but with fewer excuses, was MGM's *Song of Love,* an unintentionally comic account of the relationship between Johannes Brahms (Robert Walker) and Clara Schumann (Katharine Hepburn). Paul Henreid and Henry Daniell weighed in as Robert Schumann and Franz Liszt. Universal entered the Celebrated Composer stakes with *Song of Scheherezade,* in which dancer Yvonne De Carlo inspired Jean-Pierre Aumont's Rimsky-Korsakov to write the song of the title. This was a gloriously garish extravaganza.

In 1945 MGM had signed up the coolly graceful Deborah Kerr as the next Greer Garson. Two years later she made her Hollywood debut as the love interest for Clark Gable in *The Hucksters,* a lively satire on Madison Avenue stolen by Sydney Greenstreet as the egomaniacal king of the Beautie Soap empire. Robert Rossen made his directing debut with

Columbia's *Johnny O'Clock,* a tightly scripted thriller with Dick Powell in superb form as a hardboiled gambler.

Rossen followed *Johnny O'Clock* with *Body and Soul* (UA), a fierce study of a boxing champion corrupted by success. John Garfield played the fighter with an intense dumb eloquence, and the superb photography was by James Wong Howe, who shot some of the fight sequences on roller skates. Packing a similar punch was Jules Dassin's *Brute Force* (Universal), an explosive prison-break drama starring Burt Lancaster.

Joseph Pevney and Lilli Palmer in *Body and Soul* (UA)

In MGM's *Cynthia* (GB *The Rich Full Life*), directed by Robert Z Leonard, Elizabeth Taylor blossomed into a beautiful young teenager, making her first date with James Lydon, better known as Henry Aldrich. They both turned up in Warners' *Life With Father,* Michael Curtiz' affectionate screen version of the Broadway play about a New York family in the 1880s.

The year saw the death of master director Ernst Lubitsch, sophisticated purveyor of that elusive quality dubbed 'the Lubitsch touch'; opera star Grace Moore, who had appeared in a number of films, the best of which was Victor Schertzinger's charming *One Night of Love* (1934); and cowboy star and character actor Harry Carey.

In prestige terms British cinema continued to command commercial and critical attention. Powell and Pressburger's *Black Narcissus* was an erotic masterpiece, pulsing with colour and with a remarkable score by Brian Easdale. And in *Brighton Rock,* (US *Young Scarface*), directed by John Boulting, Richard Attenborough gave a mesmeric performance as Graham Greene's teenage hoodlum Pinkie.

Elizabeth Taylor and Jimmy Lydon in *Cynthia* (MGM)

Costume melodramas continued to attract big audiences. Ealing's contribution to the cycle was *The Loves of Joanna Godden,* a turn-of-the-century sheepfarming saga with Googie Withers; and Alberto Cavalcanti's adaptation of *Nicholas Nickleby,* an ambitious film which collapsed under the weight of the novel's myriad characters and subplots.

Ealing was more at home in the drab, buttoned-up world of postwar austerity Britain, unforgettably evoked in Robert Hamer's thriller *It Always Rains on Sunday,* which vividly conveys the pinched, glum mood of the period and provided Googie Withers with another powerful role as a married woman whose past comes back to haunt her in the form of escaped convict John McCallum.

Compared with their American equivalents, Britain's postwar crime barons were very small potatoes, operating in a semi-operatic world of sloppy pubs and steamed-up cafés linked by bomb sites (for ritual violence) and railway stations (for quick thefts). These were the standing sets for the postwar 'crime wave', celebrated in films like *They Made Me a Fugitive* (US *I Became a Criminal*), in which former RAF pilot Trevor Howard is drawn into a gang of Soho racketeers; and the entertainingly lurid *Good-Time Girl,* in which Jean Kent described a downward spiral from night-club hostess to unwilling accomplice in murder.

Grace Moore
▽ Googie Withers and John McCallum, stars of *It Always Rains on Sunday* (EaS)

Jeanette Tregarthen, Emrys Jones and Flora Robson in
Holiday Camp (G'boro)

Maurice Chevalier and Marcelle Derrien in *Le Silence est
d'Or* (GB *Man About Town*) (FrF)

Suzy Delair

Murder even stalked the British at play in Gainsborough's *Holiday Camp,* a marvellous compendium of British social life in the late 1940s directed at a cracking pace by Ken Annakin. As the camp's inmates go about their pleasures with characteristically native doggedness, bogus squadron leader Dennis Price stalks his female prey on the windswept sand-dunes. The stars of *Holiday Camp* were Jack Warner and Kathleen Harrison, playing a working-class couple, the Huggetts, who later became South London's answer to Ma and Pa Kettle.

In France, Henri-Georges Clouzot returned to film-making with *Quai des Orfèvres*, a stylish murder mystery set in the seedy world of the music hall with Suzy Delair and Louis Jouvet starring as a down-at-heel detective. Maurice Chevalier made a comeback after eight years in René Clair's *Le Silence est d'Or,* playing a raffish old-time movie director. In grimmer mood was René Clement's *Les Maudits (The Damned)* in which a gang of diehard Nazis flee by U-boat to South America at the end of the war.

Roberto Rossellini's *Germania Anno Zero (Germany, Year Zero)* was the sombre tale of the degradation and suicide of a young boy (Edmund Möschke) in the ruins of postwar Berlin. The German film industry was beginning to struggle to its feet. In the Russian-occupied zone the newly formed Defa (Deutsche Film Aktiengesellschaft) inherited the old Ufa organisation, the Neubabelsburg and Johannistal studios, and the Agfa laboratories along with the Agfacolor process. Prominent in their output were a number of films set in the devastated capital. A typical example was Kurt Maetzig's *Ehe im Schatten (Marriage in the Shadows)*, based on the story of the famous Jewish actor Gottschalk who, together with his Jewish wife, committed suicide in Nazi Germany.

In the Western zone production was licensed at Munich's Geiselgasteig studios and at the old Tempelhof studios in Berlin. Among the films dealing with recent German history and her present plight was Wolfgang Liebeneiner's *Liebe '47 (Love '47)* in which a young woman's faith in Hitler is shattered but her faith in humanity restored when she falls in love with a man suffering from war wounds.

In Japan the film industry had been thoroughly purged as part of the 'demilitarisation' policy of the Supreme Command of the Allied Forces in the Pacific (SCAP). In the aftermath of the war SCAP ordered the burning of negatives and prints of over 200 Japanese films which dealt with such outlawed subjects as militarism, feudal loyalty, ritual suicide and the oppression of women. In line with SCAP's ambitious programme to impose a Western-style democracy on the Japanese, their film-makers were encouraged to tackle upbeat themes, particularly the emancipation of women. This produced a masterpiece, Teinosuke Kinugasa's *Joyu (Actress)*, the story of the Japanese stage star Sumako Matsui (Isuzu Yamada), whose radical views and choice of career after two failed marriages made her Japan's first truly liberated woman.

Dennis Hoey, Ann Doran, Louise Currie and Kent Taylor in *Second Chance* (Fox)

Richard Basehart

Philip Reed and Hillary Brooke in *I Cover Big Town* (Par)

Film Favourites 1947

From now until the end of the decade it was very much the mixture as before — musicals, thrillers, films based on old classics such as *Anna Karenina* (LF) and modern best-sellers like Ernest Hemingway's *The Macomber Affair* (UA) were all the order of the day. Audiences still packed the cinemas.

Robert Hutton and Martha Vickers in *Love and Learn* (WB)

Hugh Beaumont, Cathy O'Donnell and Mark Daniels in *Bury Me Dead* (EL)

Michael Denison, Dulcie Gray and Josephine Stuart in *My Brother Jonathan* (ABPC)

Victor Mature and Coleen Gray in *Kiss of Death* (Fox)

Douglas Fairbanks Jr and Maureen O'Hara in *Sinbad the Sailor* (RKO)

Barbara Hale and Bill Williams in *A Likely Story* (RKO)

Alan Curtis and Terry Austin in *Philo Vance's Gamble* (PRC)

Henry Fonda and Barbara Bel Geddes in *The Long Night* (RKO)

Paulette Goddard and Michael Wilding in *An Ideal Husband* (LF)

Burgess Meredith and Dulcie Gray in *Mine Own Executioner* (LF)

Fritz Leiber, Andy Devine and Roy Rogers in *Bells of San Angelo* (Rep)

▽ Vanessa Brown in *The Foxes of Harrow* (Fox)

William Marshall, Jane Frazee, Kenny Baker and James Ellison in *Calendar Girl* (Rep)

▽ Joan McCracken and June Allyson in *Good News* (MGM)

Vivien Leigh and Ralph Richardson in *Anna Karenina* (LF)

Brian Donlevy, Yvonne De Carlo and Charles Kullman in *Song of Scheherazade* (Univ)

Maxwell Reed and Patricia Roc in *The Brothers* (Tr)

Joyce Reynolds and Robert Hutton in *Always Together* (WB)

◁ Guy Madison in *Honeymoon* (GB *Two Men and a Girl*) (RKO)

Maurice Chevalier

Dany Robin and Maurice Chevalier in *Le Silence est d'Or* (GB *Man About Town*) (Pat/RKO)

Tommy Dorsey, Janet Blair, Jimmy Dorsey and William Bakewell in *The Fabulous Dorseys* (UA) ▽

Jean Gillie, Robert Preston, Joan Bennett and Gregory Peck in *The Macomber Affair* (UA)

Gale Sondergaard, Robert Warwick, Maria Montez and Philip Reed in *Pirates of Monterey* (Univ) ▽

1

2

3

Picture Gallery for 1947

4

5

6

7

1. Marvin Miller, George Raft and June Havoc in *Intrigue* (UA)
2. Humphrey Bogart and Lizabeth Scott in *Dead Reckoning* (Col)
3. Aĺan Curtis and Sheila Ryan in *Philo Vance's Secret Mission* (PRC)
4. Albert Dekker and Alan Carney in *The Pretender* (Rep)
5. Vera Ralston and Robert Paige in *The Flame* (Rep)
6. Dolores Del Rio in *The Fugitive* (RKO)
7. Chill Wills, Ken Farrell, Edward Norris and Sheila Ryan in *Heartaches* (PRC)
8. Frank Puglia, Joan Chandler, Zachary Scott, Ronald Reagan and Alexis Smith in *Stallion Road* (WB)
9. Alexis Smith and Ronald Reagan in *Stallion Road* (WB)

8 ◁
▷ 9

1. Don Defore star of *It Happened on Fifth Avenue* (AA)
2. Gale Storm and Don Defore in *It Happened on Fifth Avenue* (AA)
3. Barbara Stanwyck and Humphrey Bogart in *The Two Mrs Carrolls* (WB)
4. Dennis O'Keefe and Hedy Lamarr in *Dishonored Lady* (UA)
5. Eleanor Parker and Ronald Reagan in *The Voice of the Turtle* (WB)
6. William Bendix and Alan Ladd in *Calcutta* (Par)
7. Nancy Coleman and Michael O'Shea (std together) in *Violence* (MoP)
8. Clifton Young, Kent Smith, Ann Sheridan and Don McGuire in *Nora Prentiss* (WB)
9. Ilka Gruning, Steve Brodie and Audrey Long in *Desperate* (RKO)

8
▷
9

1. Rory Calhoun and Julie London in *The Red House* (UA)

2. Allene Roberts and Lon McCallister in *The Red House* (UA)

3. Edward G Robinson and Judith Anderson in *The Red House* (UA)

4. John Ireland and Sheila Ryan in *Railroaded* (EL)

5. Hugh Beaumont and Sheila Ryan in *Railroaded* (EL)

6. Joel McCrea and Preston Foster in *Ramrod* (UA)

7. Don Defore and Joel McCrea in *Ramrod* (UA)

8. John Lund and Betty Hutton in *The Perils of Pauline* (Par)

9. John Lund and Betty Hutton in *The Perils of Pauline* (Par)

10. Rhonda Fleming and Robert Mitchum in *Out of the Past* (GB *Build My Gallows High*) (RKO)

11. Gale Sondergaard, Maria Montez, Philip Reed and Rod Cameron in *Pirates of Monterey* (Univ)

12. Kirk Douglas in *Out of the Past* (GB *Build My Gallows High*) (RKO)

Alan Ladd

Tyrone Power in *Captain from Castile* (Fox)

1. Leif Erickson in *Blonde Savage* (EL)
2. Tyrone Power and John Sutton in *Captain from Castile* (Fox)
3. June Lockhart, Mark Daniels and Cathy O'Donnell in *Bury Me Dead* (EL)
4. June Lockhart and Hugh Beaumont in *Bury Me Dead* (EL)
5. Stewart Granger in *Captain Boycott* (I/IP)
6. Gus Schilling and James Ellison in *Calendar Girl* (Rep)
7. J Carrol Naish and Vera-Ellen in *Carnival in Costa Rica* (Fox)
8. James Ellison, Jane Frazee, William Marshall and Kenny Baker in *Calendar Girl* (Rep)
9. Vera-Ellen and Dick Haymes in *Carnival in Costa Rica* (Fox)
10. Dick Haymes, Celeste Holm, Cesar Romero and Vera-Ellen in *Carnival in Costa Rica* (Fox)

1. Art Smith and Wanda Hendrix in *Ride the Pink Horse* (Univ)
2. Holmes Herbert in *The Swordsman* (Col)
3. Anthony Hulme in *The Three Weird Sisters* (BN)
4. George Macready in *The Swordsman* (Col)
5. Robert Walker in *Song of Love* (MGM)
6. Henry Daniell in *Song of Love* (MGM)
7. Paul Henreid in *Song of Love* (MGM)
8. Evelyn Brent and Gilbert Roland in *Robin Hood of Monterey* (MoP)
9. Louis Jean Heydt (l) and Paul Kelly (r) in *Spoilers of the North* (Rep)
10. Chris-Pin Martin, Gilbert Roland and Travis Kent in *Robin Hood of Monterey* (MoP)

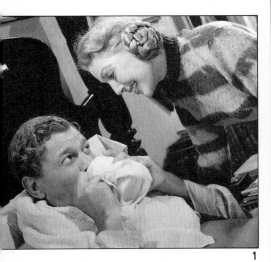

1

David O Selznick certainly knew a good play when he saw one. With Ingrid Bergman in mind, he bought the rights to the Swedish play on which *The Farmer's Daughter* (RKO) was based. Ingrid Bergman was unable to take on the title role and it was handed to Loretta Young who, seizing the splendid opportunity with commendable foresight and ability, won for her performance the Oscar award for Best Actress.

1. Joseph Cotten and Loretta Young
2. Ethel Barrymore and Joseph Cotten
3. Loretta Young and Charles Bickford
4. Joseph Cotten and Loretta Young
5. Ethel Barrymore, Joseph Cotten and Charles Bickford
6. Rhys Williams (I) and Loretta Young
7. Loretta Young
8. Art Baker, Charles Bickford and Ethel Barrymore

3

4

5

6

7

◁ 8

359

1. Dennis Price
2. William Wright and Terry Austin in *Philo Vance Returns* (PRC)
3. Ann Sothern and Barry Nelson in *Undercover Maisie* (MGM)
4. Louis Calhern
5. Clark Gable, Adolphe Menjou and Kathryn Card in *The Hucksters* (MGM)
6. Marcel Pagliero and Simone Signoret in *Dedee D'Anvers* (US *Dedee*) (FrF)
7. John Kellogg (std), Lee J Cobb and Dick Powell in *Johnny O'Clock* (Col)
8. Pat Clark
9. Don Beddoe in *Behind Green Lights* (Fox)

1

After his meritorious war service, Douglas Fairbanks Jr returned to the screen in the swashbuckling *Sinbad The Sailor* (RKO)

Once again, so reminiscent of his athletic father, Doug romped through this Technicolor extravaganza with fantastic leaps and bewildering swordplay, all to the discomfiture of Walker Slezak and Anthony Quinn and the admiration of Maureen O'Hara

2

3

1. George Tobias and Douglas Fairbanks Jr
2. Douglas Fairbanks Jr
3. John Miljan, Douglas Fairbanks Jr and George Tobias
4. Douglas Fairbanks Jr, Walter Slezak and Anthony Quinn
5. Douglas Fairbanks Jr
6. Douglas Fairbanks Jr
7. Maureen O'Hara and Anthony Quinn
8. Maureen O'Hara and Douglas Fairbanks Jr

4

6

7

5

8

1

2

4

6

5

7

8

3

9

10

11

1. Robert Paige, Ted Donaldson, Daisy and Noreen Nash in *The Red Stallion* (EL)

2. Robert Paige, Noreen Nash, Pierre Watkin and Jane Darwell in *The Red Stallion* (EL)

3. Robert Paige and Noreen Nash in *The Red Stallion* (EL)

4. Fred MacMurray in *Singapore* (Univ)

5. John Eldredge, Margot Grahame, Walter Abel, and Dorothy Christy in *The Fabulous Joe* (HR)

6. Fred MacMurray in *Singapore* (Univ)

7. Selena Royle, Van Johnson, Dean Stockwell, Janet Leigh and Thomas Mitchell in *The Romance of Rosy Ridge* (MGM)

8. Pamela Kellino in *The Upturned Glass* (Tr)

9. Richard Widmark and Victor Mature in *Kiss of Death* (Fox)

10. Regis Toomey, John Litel, Bonita Granville and Don Castle in *The Guilty* (MoP)

11. Don Castle and Bonita Granville in *The Guilty* (MoP)

1

2

3

4

5

1. Leo G Carroll in *Time Out of Mind* (Univ)
2. Linda Christian, Van Heflin and Lana Turner in *Green Dolphin Street* (MGM)
3. Richard Haydn in *The Foxes of Harrow* (Fox)
4. Barton MacLane, John Warburton, Wallace Scott and Patricia Morison in *Tarzan and the Huntress* (RKO)
5. Martha Vickers and Dane Clark in *That Way With Women* (WB)
6. Howard da Silva, Mike Mazurki and Paulette Goddard in *Unconquered* (Par)
7. Cara Williams in *Boomerang* (Fox)
8. Anne Jeffreys in *Riff-Raff* (RKO)
9. Vincent Price, Edmond O' Brien and Fritz Leiber in *The Web* (Univ)
10. Jason Robards and Virginia Owen in *Thunder Mountain* (RKO)
11. Laraine Day, Judith Anderson and Cedric Hardwicke in *Tycoon* (RKO)
12. Robert Young in *They Won't Believe Me* (RKO)

6

7

9

8

11

12

1. Joan Leslie and Tom Conway in *Repeat Performance* (EL)

2. Joan Leslie and Louis Hayward in *Repeat Performance* (EL)

3. Diana Lynn and Sonny Tufts in *Easy Come, Easy Go* (Par)

4. Albert Basserman, Isobel Elsom, Reginald Denny and Ida Lupino in *Escape Me Never* (WB)

5. Gig Young and Eleanor Parker in *Escape Me Never* (WB)

6. Sally Gray and Trevor Howard in *They Made Me a Fugitive* (US *I Became a Criminal*) (G/All)

7. Catherine McLeod and John Carroll in *The Fabulous Texan* (Rep)

8. Robert Lowery (l), Vince Barnett (2nd l), Hillary Brooke and Charles Lane (r) in *Big Town* (Par)

9. Spencer Tracy and Katharine Hepburn in *The Sea of Grass* (MGM)

10. Stephen Dunne and Thurston Hall in *The Son of Rusty* (Col)

11. Stephen Dunne and Ted Donaldson in *The Son of Rusty* (Col)

12. Marlene Dietrich in *Golden Earrings* (Par)

12 ▷

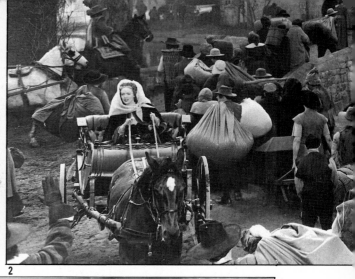

1

2

3

The novel *Forever Amber* by Kathleen Winsor was already one of the all-time best-sellers when it was filmed by Twentieth Century-Fox. In 1947 the erotic episodes of the book had to be toned down to meet the stringent demands of the film censors and so the movie became just another romantic costume drama with, in the event, a rather unsuitable tragic ending.

1. Linda Darnell and Richard Haydn
2. Linda Darnell
3. Cornel Wilde and Linda Darnell
4. George Sanders, Alma Kruger, Edmond Breon, Linda Darnell and Richard Haydn
5. Richard Greene and Linda Darnell
6. John Russell and Linda Darnell
7. Linda Darnell
8. Richard Greene, Cornel Wilde and Linda Darnell
9. Richard Greene (l) and Cornel Wilde (r)
10. Linda Darnell and Richard Greene
11. Richard Greene, Linda Darnell and Cornel Wilde

4

5

6

7

8

9
10

11

1

2

3

4

5

6

1. Brenda Marshall
2. Andy Russell
3. Peter Lawford
4. Dick Simmons
5. Janis Paige, Dennis Morgan and Jane Wyman in *Cheyenne* (WB)
6. Maxwell Reed and Patricia Roc in *The Brothers* (Tr)
7. Jane Wyman, Bruce Bennett and Janis Paige in *Cheyenne* (WB)
8. Howard Duff in *Brute Force* (Univ)
9. Lawrence Tierney and Ted North in *The Devil Thumbs a Ride* (RKO)
10. Barbara Stanwyck, Richard Basehart and John Ridgely in *Cry Wolf* (WB)

7

8

9

10

1. Andy Parker and the Plainsmen in *Black Hills* (PRC)
2. Phyllis Calvert and James Donald in *Broken Journey* (G'boro)
3. Henry Wilcoxon and Joan Barclay in *Dragnet* (SCG)
4. Darryl Hickman and Jan Ford in *The Devil on Wheels* (PRC)
5. Glenn Ford and Jim Bannon in *Framed* (GB *Paula*) (Col)
6. Mary Anderson and Helmut Dantine in *Whispering City* (EL)
7. Ricky Jordan
8. John Carradine
9. Bruce Bennett

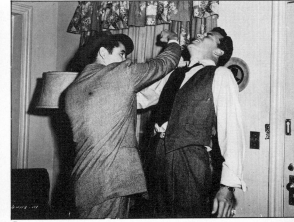

367

1. Ella Raines
2. Marc Lawrence
3. Clayton Moore
4. Gail Russell
5. Peggy Ryan
6. Don Terry
7. Marjorie Lord
8. Harold Lloyd
9. Charles Coburn
10. Albert Dekker
11. Tom Kennedy
12. Eve Arden
13. Lon McCallister
14. Cesar Romero
15. Carol Andrews
16. Charles Butterworth

1
2
3
4
5
6
7
8
9
10
11
12
13
14
15
16

The Secret Life of Walter Mitty (SG) was another highly successful Sam Goldwyn movie starring the ubiquitous Danny Kaye. Diffident and retiring to a degree, Walter Mitty mentally projects himself into a number of heroic rolls ranging from a Mississippi river-boat gambler to a surgeon whose skill with the scalpel enables him to perform miracle cures. This was one of Danny Kaye's best in which he took full advantage of the superb opportunities offered for his amazing versatility.

1. Danny Kaye
2. Danny Kaye and Henry Corden
3. Gordon Jones, Danny Kaye, Ann Rutherford, Thurston Hall, Fay Bainter and Florence Bates
4. Virginia Mayo
5. Gordon Jones (I) and Danny Kaye
6. Danny Kaye and Nat Carr
7. Lumsden Hare, Danny Kaye and Virginia Mayo

2

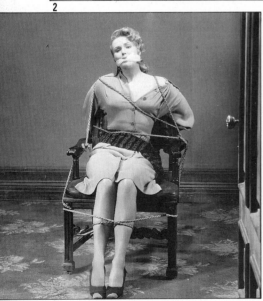

3

4

5

6
▷
7

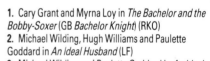

1. Cary Grant and Myrna Loy in *The Bachelor and the Bobby-Soxer* (GB *Bachelor Knight*) (RKO)
2. Michael Wilding, Hugh Williams and Paulette Goddard in *An Ideal Husband* (LF)
3. Michael Wilding and Paulette Goddard in *An Ideal Husband* (LF)
4. Paulette Goddard and Constance Collier in *An Ideal Husband* (LF)
5. Edward Chapman
6. Lloyd Gough
7. Roland Culver
8. Clifford Evans
9. Audrey Long and Lawrence Tierney in *Born to Kill* (RKO)
10. William Marshall, Stephanie Bachelor and Grant Withers in *Blackmail* (Rep)
11. Ricardo Cortez and William Marshall in *Blackmail* (Rep)
12. Esther Howard in *Born to Kill* (RKO)

1

2

3

1. Dewey Robinson, Robert Hutton and Joyce Reynolds in *Always Together* (WB)

2. Robbin Winan, Jean Moorhead, Sharyn Moffett and George McDonald in *Banjo* (RKO)

3. David Farrar and Flora Robson in *Black Narcissus* (Univ)

4. Cary Grant and Loretta Young in *The Bishop's Wife* (SG)

5. Marshall Thompson

6. Karin Booth

7. Phillip Terry, June Clayworth, Ralph Edwards and Donald MacBride in *Beat the Band* (RKO)

8. Derek Bond

9. Kieron Moore and Vivien Leigh in *Anna Karenina* (LF)

10. Ralph Richardson and Vivien Leigh in *Anna Karenina* (LF)

11. John Hodiak and George Murphy in *The Arnelo Affair* (MGM)

4

5

7

8

9

11

◁ 10

1. Mickey Rooney and Ann Blyth in *Killer McCoy* (MGM)
2. Betty Grable, Frank Dawson and Dick Haymes in *The Shocking Miss Pilgrim* (Fox)
3. Betty Grable, Arthur Shields, Allyn Joslyn, Charles Kemper and Lillian Bronson in *The Shocking Miss Pilgrim* (Fox)
4. Joan Fontaine and Patric Knowles in *Ivy* (Univ)
5. Lillian Bronson and Allyn Joslyn in *The Shocking Miss Pilgrim* (Fox)
6. Tom Drake and Franklin Pangborn in *I'll Be Yours* (Univ)
7. Martha Stewart and Mark Stevens in *I Wonder Who's Kissing Her Now?* (Fox)
8. June Haver and Mark Stevens in *I Wonder Who's Kissing Her Now?* (Fox)
9. Peter Whitney and Joseph Schildkraut in *Northwest Outpost* (Rep)

◁ 9

Ronald Colman

Linda Darnell in *Forever Amber* (Fox)

1. Richard Ney and Vanessa Brown in *The Late George Apley* (Fox)
2. Richard Haydn, in *The Late George Apley* (Fox)
3. Richard Ney in *The Late George Apley* (Fox)
4. Edna Best and Ronald Colman in *The Late George Apley* (Fox)
5. Richard Haydn, Ronald Colman and Edna Best in *The Late George Apley* (Fox)
6. Michael O'Shea and Jeff Donnell in *Mr. District Attorney* (Col)
7. Peggy Cummins (l) in *Moss Rose* (Fox)
8. Margaret Johnston and Kieron Moore in *A Man About the House* (BL)
9. Milburn Stone, Leonard East and William Brooks in *The Michigan Kid* (Univ)

9 ▷

1. Dennis Morgan in *My Wild Irish Rose* (WB)
2. Ben Blue, Dennis Morgan and George O'Brien in *My Wild Irish Rose* (WB)
3. Dennis Morgan in *My Wild Irish Rose* (WB)
4. Dennis Hoey, Ann Doran, Louise Currie and Kent Taylor in *Second Chance* (Fox)
5. Ann Richards, Tom Conway, Franchot Tone and Clarence Kolb in *Lost Honeymoon* (EL)

1. Martha Scott and John Mills in *So Well Remembered* (All/RKO)
2. Trevor Howard and John Mills in *So Well Remembered* (All/RKO)
3. Patricia Roc and John Mills in *So Well Remembered* (All/RKO)
4. Tyrone Power, Coleen Gray and Mike Mazurki in *Nightmare Alley* (Fox)
5. Marjorie Lord in *New Orleans* (UA)
6. Sally Gray and Eric Portman in *The Mark of Cain* (TC)
7. Derek Bond in *Nicholas Nickleby* (EaS)
8. Dorothy Patrick and Arturo de Cordova in *New Orleans* (UA)
9. Maureen O'Hara in *Miracle on 34th Street* (Fox)

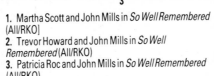

◁ 7

9 ▷

1. Cameron Mitchell (c) and Van Johnson in *High Barbaree* (MGM)
2. Elisha Cook Jr in *The Long Night* (RKO)
3. Henry Stephenson, Helen Walker, Cornel Wilde and Tommy Cook in *The Homestretch* (Fox)
4. Leon Errol and Joe Kirkwood Jr in *The Knockout* (MoP)
5. Marcelle Derrien in *Le Silence est d'Or* (US *Man About Town*) (RKO/Pat)
6. Martha Vickers, Robert Hutton, Janis Paige and Jack Carson in *Love and Learn* (WB)
7. Dulcie Gray and Burgess Meredith in *Mine Own Executioner* (LF)
8. Jack Carson and Robert Hutton in *Love and Learn* (WB)
9. Kieron Moore and Barbara White in *Mine Own Executioner* (LF)
10. Dulcie Gray and Kieron Moore in *Mine Own Executioner* (LF)

9 ◁
▷
10

1. Guy Madison in *Honeymoon* (RKO)
2. Guy Madison in *Honeymoon* (RKO)
3. Lina Romay and Franchot Tone in *Honeymoon* (RKO)
4. James Millican and Brenda Joyce in *Stepchild* (PRC)
5. Virginia Hunter
6. Robert Douglas
7. Brenda Joyce and Donald Woods in *Stepchild* (PRC)
8. Jeanne Crain
9. Gus Schilling and Jackie Cooper in *Stork Bites Man* (UA)
10. Audrey Totter, star of *Lady in the Lake* (MGM)

379

1. Phyllis Thaxter in *Living In a Big Way* (MGM)
2. Joan Hopkins in *The First Gentleman* (US *Affairs of a Rogue*) (Col)
3. Eddie Bracken and Priscilla Lane in *Fun On A Weekend* (UA)
4. Irene Dunne, William Powell, Jimmy Lydon, Martin Milner, Derek Scott and Johnnie Calkins in *Life With Father* (WB)
5. Burt Lancaster, Wendell Corey, Lizabeth Scott, Kristine Miller and Kirk Douglas in *I Walk Alone* (Par)
6. George Sanders, Lucille Ball and Cedric Hardwicke in *Lured* (GB *Personal Column*) (UA)
7. Cedric Hardwicke, Mildred Natwick and Jessica Tandy in *A Woman's Vengeance* (Univ)
8. Joan Crawford, Dana Andrews and Henry Fonda in *Daisy Kenyon* (Fox)
9. Donald Barry, Lynne Roberts and Paul Stanton in *That's My Gal* (Rep)
10. Robert Mitchum and Robert Young in *Crossfire* (RKO)

◁ **9**

1

2

3

4

5

1. Dane Clark in *Deep Valley* (WB)
2. Humphrey Bogart in *Dark Passage* (WB)
3. Earle Hodgins and William Boyd in *The Marauders* (UA)
4. John Hodiak and Sylvia Sidney in *Love From a Stranger* (GB *A Stranger Walked In*) (EL)
5. Constance Bennett and Joan Caulfield in *The Unsuspected* (WB)
6. Don Castle, Terry Austin, Frank Orth and Johnny Sands in *Born To Speed* (PRC)
7. Robert Lowery and Charles King in *Killer at Large* (PRC)
8. Gene Autry, Bobby Blake and Carol Thurston in *The Last Round-Up* (Col)
9. Jean Porter with Jerry Wald and his Orchestra in *Little Miss Broadway* (Col)

6

7

8

▽ 9

1. Anthony Quinn (c) and Doris Lloyd in *The Imperfect Lady* (GB *Mrs Loring's Secret*) (Par)
2. Ray Milland, Teresa Wright, Virginia Field and Anthony Quinn in *The Imperfect Lady* (GB *Mrs Loring's Secret*) (Par)
3. Joan McCracken, Ray McDonald and Robert Strickland in *Good News* (MGM)
4. Peter Lawford and June Allyson in *Good News* (MGM)
5. Jimmy Dorsey, Janet Blair and Tommy Dorsey in *The Fabulous Dorseys* (UA)
6. Joan Greenwood and John Mills in *The October Man* (TC)
7. Gilbert Roland and Warren Douglas in *High Conquest* (MoP)
8. John Blythe and Flora Robson in *Holiday Camp* (G'boro)
9. Jack Warner in *Holiday Camp* (G'boro)
10. Hazel Brooks in *Body and Soul* (UA)

1. Douglas Fairbanks Jr in *The Exile* (Univ)
2. Robert Coote and Douglas Fairbanks Jr in *The Exile* (Univ)
3. Rachel Kempson in *A Woman's Vengeance* (Univ)
4. Nigel Bruce in *The Exile* (Univ)
5. Douglas Fairbanks Jr and Nigel Bruce in *The Exile* (Univ)
6. Robert Lowery, Jane Withers and Charles Coleman in *Danger Street* (Par)
7. Joan Fulton
8. Eddie Dean and George Chesebro in *Shadow Valley* (PRC/EL)
9. Richard Conte in *The Other Love* (UA)
10. Joan Greenwood and Richard Attenborough in *The Man Within* (US *The Smugglers*) (PFS)

◁10

383

1. Mary Young and Bill Williams in *A Likely Story* (RKO)
2. Bill Williams and Sam Levene in *A Likely Story* (RKO)
3. Barbara Hale, Lanny Rees and Bill Williams in *A Likely Story* (RKO)
4. Tamara Desni in *The Hills of Donegal* (Bch)
5. Jimmy Wakeley and Douglas Fowley in *Ridin' Down the Trail* (MoP)
6. Marjorie Mars in *Take My Life* (Cine/IP)
7. Philip Reed, Don Taylor (on floor), Gloria Grahame and Keenan Wynn in *Song of the Thin Man* (MGM)
8. Tommy Ivo, Brenda Joyce, Donald Woods and Terry Austin in *Stepchild* (PRC)
9. Walter Abel

1. Anne Gwynne
2. Ian Hunter and Margaret Lockwood in *The White Unicorn* (US *Bad Sister*) (JC)
3. Arthur Treacher (l) and Andy Devine (r) in *Slave Girl* (Univ)
4. Charles Kullman and Eve Arden in *Song of Scheherazade* (Univ)
5. Brian Donlevy, Yvonne De Carlo and Charles Kullman in *Song of Scheherazade* (Univ)
6. Dennis O'Keefe and Mary Meade in *T-Men* (EL)
7. Helena Carter
8. Wallace Ford and Dennis O'Keefe in *T-Men* (EL)
9. Adele Mara in *Web of Danger* (Rep)
10. Michael Redgrave and Nancy Coleman in *Mourning Becomes Electra* (RKO)
11. Leo Genn in *Mourning Becomes Electra* (RKO)

1

2

3

4

5

1. Peggy Wynn, Roscoe Ates and Eddie Dean in *The Wild Country* (PRC)
2. Andy Devine and Jon Hall in *The Vigilantes Return* (Univ)
3. Allan Lane in *Oregon Trail Scouts* (Rep)
4. Michael O'Shea in *The Last of the Redmen* (Col)
5. Gene Autry and Lynne Roberts in *Robin Hood of Texas* (Rep)
6. Al 'Fuzzy' St John, Lash LaRue and John Merton in *Cheyenne Takes Over* (PRC)
7. Stephanie Bachelor and Roy Rogers in *Springtime in the Sierras* (Rep)
8. Johnny Mack Brown and Riley Hill in *Flashing Guns* (MoP)

6

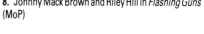

7

8

1. Roy Rogers, Paul Harvey and James Taggert in *Heldorado* (Rep)
2. Roy Rogers and Barry Mitchell in *Heldorado* (Rep)
3. Jimmy Wakely and Henry Hall in *Song of the Wasteland* (MoP)
4. Jimmy Wakely (l) in *Six-Gun Serenade* (MoP)
5. Raymond Hatton (c) and Johnny Mack Brown in *Gun Talk* (MoP)
6. Allan Lane and Bobby Blake in *Homesteaders of Paradise Valley* (Rep)
7. Johnny Mack Brown in *Valley of Fear* (MoP)
8. Margaret Lindsay in *Louisiana* (MoP)
9. Lynne Roberts and Gene Autry in *Saddle Pals* (Rep)
10. Warren Mills, Noel Neil (3rd), and Freddie Stewart in *Vacation Days* (MoP)

1

2

3

4

5

6

7

8

9

10

1. Phyllis Calvert and Robert Hutton in *Time Out of Mind* (Univ)

2. Ray Collins, Allen Jenkins, William Powell and Charles D Brown in *The Senator Was Indiscreet* (GB *Mr Ashton Was Indiscreet*) (Univ)

3. Norma Varden, Ray Milland and Teresa Wright in *The Trouble With Women* (Par)

4. James Ellison in *The Ghost Goes Wild* (Rep)

5. Robert Cummings in *The Lost Moment* (Univ)

6. Lon McCallister and Peggy Ann Garner in *Bob, Son of Battle* (aka *Thunder in the Valley*) (Fox)

7. Eduardo Ciannelli, Jacqueline White and Phillip Terry in *Seven Keys to Baldpate* (RKO)

8. Lizabeth Scott and Burt Lancaster in *Desert Fury* (Par)

9. Paulette Goddard and Fred MacMurray in *Suddenly It's Spring* (Par)

10. Angela Lansbury, Karolyn Grimes and George Sanders in *The Private Affairs of Bel Ami* (UA)

CHAPTER NINE

1948

NEW BATTLES TO FIGHT

Lew Ayres in *Johnny Belinda* (WB)

Lauren Bacall and Humphrey Bogart in *Key Largo* (WB)

Cinema still clung to its position as the principal form of popular entertainment, but television was beginning to present a serious challenge to its supremacy. In the United States the sale of TV sets quadrupled.

During the summer MGM's President, Nicholas Schenck, persuaded RKO's head of production, the former MGM producer and scriptwriter Dore Schary, to rejoin his old studio as head of production. Schary left behind a studio thrown into confusion by Howard Hughes' purchase of just under a million shares in a move described as 'the biggest motion picture transaction since Twentieth-Century took over Fox films'. It was as if RKO had been taken over by a combination of Dr Mabuse and Charles Foster Kane.

RKO faced a more immediate problem. Rising star Robert Mitchum was arrested on a drugs charge and sentenced to 60 days in jail. (Two years later the verdict was set aside). However, far from wrecking his career, the scandal cemented his 'Go to hell' image, and by the end of the decade he was one of the ailing studio's biggest assets.

Warner Brothers had three prestige successes with *Johnny Belinda, Key Largo* and *The Treasure of the Sierra Madre.* Jane Wyman won the year's Best Actress Oscar for her moving performance as the deaf-mute victim of rape in *Johnny Belinda,* directed by Jean Negulesco. Wyman studied for the role at a school for the dumb and placed plastic plugs in her ears on set. Her performance is a model of underplaying and a singular triumph for a previously anodyne actress.

Claire Trevor won the Best Supporting Actress Oscar for her performance as gangster Edward G Robinson's pathetic drunken moll in *Key Largo,* directed by John Huston. Huston was also at the helm of *The Treasure of the Sierra Madre,* in which his father Walter picked up the Best Supporting Actor

Humphrey Bogart, Walter Huston and Tim Holt in *The Treasure of the Sierra Madre* (WB)

389

Van Heflin in *Act of Violence* (MGM)

Ted De Corsia (wearing hat) in *The Naked City* (Univ)

Olivia de Havilland and Mark Stevens in *The Snake Pit*
(Fox)

Oscar as the grizzled, quirky old-timer prospecting for gold in Tampico with Humphrey Bogart and Tim Holt. Skilfully adapted from the novel by the mysterious B Traven, and shot on location in Mexico, *The Treasure of the Sierra Madre* gave Bogart one of the best roles of his career as the shifty drifter, Fred C Dobbs, who disintegrates under the irreconcilable pressures of loyalty and greed. Jack Warner hated the film, insisting that Bogart survive the final reel - a demand which Huston ignored. Nevertheless, the film was voted Best Picture by the New York critics and Huston the Best Director, and the Academy added the Best Screenplay and Director Awards to Walter Huston's Oscar.

Montgomery Clift made his debut in MGM's *The Search*, directed by Fred Zinnemann, a sympathetic study of displaced children in the US-occupied Germany. Echoes of the war continued to reverberate at home. In Zinnemann's *Act of Violence*, (MGM) crippled Robert Ryan erupted into Van Heflin's quiet suburban life to settle an old prisoner-of-war camp score. In Twentieth Century-Fox's breezy romantic comedy *Apartment for Peggy*, newly wed veteran William Holden continued his education under the GI Bill of Rights with the help of benevolent college professor Edmund Gwenn.

In Universal's adaptation of Arthur Miller's play *All My Sons*, Edward G Robinson was the war profiteer harbouring a terrible secret from his family.

In the late 1940s the Soviet Union had replaced Nazi Germany as the principal international villain. The first in a depressing cycle of Cold War melodramas was Twentieth Century-Fox's *The Iron Curtain*, directed by William Wellman and allegedly based on the story of Igor Gouzenko, a cypher clerk in the Soviet Embassy in Ottawa who defected to the West. Dana Andrews played the defector and Gene Tierney his wife – the most unlikely Russians since the Barrymores were let loose in *Rasputin and the Empress* (1932).

The never-ending war against crime took a documentary turn in Universal's *The Naked City*, produced by ex-newsman Mark Hellinger and directed with great vigour by Jules Dassin. Introduced in hectoring journalese by Hellinger, and filmed entirely on location in and around Manhattan, *The Naked City* followed a Homicide Squad manhunt led by Barry Fitzgerald as the leprechaun-like Lieutenant Muldoon.

The Naked City owed something to old-style racket-busting journalism, something to Italian neo-realism and something to semi-documentary predecessors like Anthony Mann's excellent *T-Men* (1947). But its rasping attempt to bring authenticity to the crime film served as a model for a string of pacy thrillers – *The Undercover Man* (1949); *The Street With No Name, He Walked By Night* – all of which emphasised police procedure and atmospheric location shooting.

Olivia de Havilland gave the performance of the year in Anatole Litvak's *The Snake Pit* (Twentieth Century-Fox),

Fred Astaire and Judy Garland in *Easter Parade* (MGM)

Judy Garland

playing an intelligent woman hovering on the edge of complete mental collapse in an overcrowded state mental asylum. Leo Genn and Mark Stevens provide rather stolid support as gently romantic psychiatrist and loyal husband, but the film remains an innovatory study of madness.

Michael Redgrave was completely potty in Fritz Lang's *The Secret Beyond the Door* (Universal), displaying a distinctly unhealthy interest in murder, turning his home into a museum of famous homicides and deciding to make wife Joan Bennett the latest exhibit. That marriage could be a dangerous affair was demonstrated in another Anatole Litvak film, *Sorry Wrong Number* (Paramount), an out-and-out sheet-chewer in which Barbara Stanwyck emoted furiously as the bedridden neurotic who overhears a telephone conversation in which husband Burt Lancaster is hatching a plan to kill her.

An undignified fate is in store for Universal's monster gallery in *Abbott and Costello Meet Frankenstein*, a joyless attempt to breathe new life into the comedy duo's flagging popularity.

Paramount's *The Paleface*, directed by Norman Z McLeod, was one of Bob Hope's best comedies of the 1940s, despatching him Way out West as Painless Potter the cowardly dentist, encountering Calamity Jane Russell's big guns.

William Powell had the title role in *Mr Peabody and the Mermaid* (Universal), finding fishy lady Ann Blyth on the end of his line. *Mr Blandings Builds His Dream House* (RKO) was a charming throwback to the 1930s, with just a touch of *The Egg and I* (1947), in which Cary Grant and Myrna Loy encountered myriad complications when they decided to build a rural retreat in Connecticut.

Frank Capra directed MGM's *State of the Union* (GB *The World and His Wife*). This Tracy–Hepburn vehicle was a satire on politics in which the two stars play an estranged couple who try to patch up their differences when idealistic aircraft tycoon Tracy is persuaded to run for President by power-hungry newspaper proprietor Angela Lansbury and smooth fixer Adolphe Menjou. The film is propelled along by its stars and an unusually good performance from Van Johnson as a cheerfully cynical aide, but its neatly sentimental resolution leaves one longing for the smoke-filled rooms and backstairs chicanery of the real political world.

Clifton Webb had a big hit with Twentieth Century-Fox's *Sitting Pretty*, playing the caustic Lynn Belvedere, bachelor and self-declared genius, placed in charge of Robert Young and Maureen O'Hara's unruly brood and achieving miracles of discipline.

Swimming hard against this tide of American cheerfulness was Billy Wilder's *A Foreign Affair*, set in the ruins of Berlin through which US Army jeeps race to the strains of 'Isn't It Romantic?' Sadly the film subsides into a kind of sub-Lubitsch love triangle between American soldier John Lund, chanteuse Marlene Dietrich and starchy visiting

Barbara Stanwyck (on bed) and Burt Lancaster (r) in *Sorry, Wrong Number* (Par)

William Powell and Irene Hervey in *Mr Peabody and the Mermaid* (Univ)

Paul Langton, Steve Cochran and Virginia Mayo in *A Song is Born* (RKO)

Lola Albright in *Easter Parade* (MGM)

Van Heflin, Gig Young, Lana Turner and Gene Kelly in *The Three Musketeers* (MGM)

▽ Ingrid Bergman in *Joan of Arc* (RKO)

Congresswoman Jean Arthur. But there are some gleefully black touches in its unblinking picture of the occupiers and the occupied, all sucked into the gravitational pull of the black market and a world away from Capra's saccharine Utopianism.

A pert young Doris Day made her debut in a Warner musical, *Romance on the High Seas* (GB *It's Magic*), sweetly singing 'It's Magic'. Howard Hawks turned his hand to a misfiring musical remake of his own *Ball of Fire* (1941), now called *A Song is Born* and starring Danny Kaye and Virginia Mayo in the roles originally played by Gary Cooper and Barbara Stanwyck.

MGM's *Easter Parade*, directed by the dependable Charles Walters, was Judy Garland's only film with Fred Astaire, who returned to the screen after a two-year 'retirement' to replace an injured Gene Kelly. The result was one of the most charming of all backstage romances, crammed with Irving Berlin standards and classic routines, including Garland and Astaire's 'A Couple of Swells' and Astaire's innovative 'Stepping Out With My Baby', which simultaneously combined slow and normal motion.

Garland was teamed with Gene Kelly in MGM's *The Pirate*, produced by Arthur Freed and directed by Vincente Minnelli, a frenetic, fantastical vehicle for Kelly's braggadoccio as the strolling player masquerading as a Caribbean buccaneer.

Arthur Freed also presided over *Words and Music*, directed by Norman Taurog, a largely fictitious biopic of the composer Rodgers (Tom Drake, quite dreadful) and Hart (Mickey Rooney, characteristically bumptious). The highlight was Gene Kelly and Vera-Ellen dancing the 10-minute ballet 'Slaughter on Tenth Avenue'.

Kelly then donned a doublet and rapier as the most athletic of all D'Artagnans in MGM's handsome *The Three Musketeers*, with Lana Turner as a virtually inanimate Milady de Winter.

No expense was spared on RKO's *Joan of Arc*, a Walter Wanger production, starring Ingrid Bergman as the Maid of Orleans and based on the Maxwell Anderson drama, Joan of Lorraine, in which Bergman had played on Broadway. The expenditure of $5.6 million secured sumptuous sets, a cast of several thousand, some natty designer armour for Bergman and two-and-a-half hours of ennui.

Alan Ladd took the title role in Paramount's serviceable Western *Whispering Smith*, a part originally played by an even stonier-faced star, William S Hart.

Columbia's *The Strawberry Roan* was Gene Autry's first in colour and a big hit in spite of the fact that its storyline bore more than a passing resemblance to Roy Rogers' *My Pal Trigger* (1946). More inventively, elements of 'The Tempest' were borrowed for William Wellman's *Yellow Sky* (Twentieth Century-Fox), in which a gang of bank robbers led by a repentant Gregory Peck and a ruthless Richard Widmark stumble across a Death Valley ghost town inhabited by an old man (James Barton) and his granddaughter (Anne Baxter).

The Western was no longer confined to simple-minded shoot-'em-ups. RKO's shadow-drenched *Blood on the Moon*, directed by Robert Wise, was set firmly in *film noir* territory, underlined by the casting of laconic Robert Mitchum as a hired gun who switches sides to protect Barbara Bel Geddes against his former friend Robert Preston. In the low-budget *I Shot Jesse James* (Lippert), Samuel Fuller made a remarkable directing debut, hacking away at a Western legend in frenzied close-up.

For lovers of the classical Western there was Howard Hawks' *Red River*, the story of the first cattle drive over the Chisholm Trail; and John Ford's *Fort Apache*, the first in his great 'cavalry trilogy'.

Unclassifiable but exploding with primitive vitality was King Vidor's rip-roaring melodrama *The Fountainhead* (Warners), based on a surreal Ayn Rand novel and starring Gary Cooper as a rogue genius of an architect, loosely based on Frank Lloyd Wright, who does not shrink from blowing up his own buildings when he feels that his vision has been compromised by philistine patrons.

Alfred Hitchcock ventured into colour for the first time in Warners' *Rope*, celebrated for its ten-minute takes and the implicitly homosexual relationship between its two sadistic young killers, cruelly calculating John Dall and his panicking catamite Farley Granger. James Mason made his Hollywood debut in MGM's *Caught*, directed by Max Ophüls, whose *Letter from an Unknown Woman* (Universal) was one of the decade's most finely wrought tearjerkers.

Nicholas Ray made a notable directing debut with *They Live By Night* (RKO), coaxing touching performances from Farley Granger and Cathy O'Donnell as the doomed young couple fleeing helplessly from their past. Screenwriter Abraham Polonsky's first film as a director was the powerful *Force of Evil* (MGM), a driving B-thriller delivered in blank verse and starring John Garfield as a bent lawer making his way in the numbers racket.

On 27 July David Wark Griffith died at Hollywood's Knickerbocker Hotel, an embittered alcoholic spectator of the industry which he had dominated until the growth of the studio system thrust him on to the sidelines. In the Soviet Union the silent cinema's greatest propagandist, Sergei M Eisenstein, died of a heart ailment. The second part of his final masterpiece, *Ivan the Terrible*, had been suppressed by Stalin two years earlier, and was not released until 1958. Other deaths included Warren William – Columbia's suave Lone Wolf – Dame May Whitty, King Baggott – who had collaborated with William S Hart on the masterly *Tumbleweeds* (1925) – C Aubrey Smith and Carole Landis, who in a fit of depression took her own life. Reviewing a Columbia B, *Ladies of the Chorus*, Motion Picture Herald declared that its young blonde leading lady, a certain Marilyn Monroe, was 'promising'.

In Britain Laurence Olivier scored a signal triumph with his *Hamlet*, which won Academy Awards as Best Picture, for

Joanne Dru and Hank Worden in *Red River* (UA)

Joan Fontaine and Louis Jourdan in *Letter from an Unknown Woman* (Univ)

Farley Granger and Cathy O'Donnell in *They Live by Night* (RKO)

Moira Shearer and Leonide Massine in *The Red Shoes* (IP)

Jack Hawkins and Bobby Henrey in *The Fallen Idol* (US *Lost Illusion*) (LF)

▽ Enzo Staiola and Lamberto Maggiorani in *Ladri di Biciclette* (GB *Bicycle Thieves*) (PDS-ENIC)

Olivier's performance (Best Actor), for Roger Furse's art direction and for Carmen Dillon's set decoration. However, as so often in the history of the British film industry, the success of a single film obscured a financial crisis, exacerbated by the American Motion Picture Association's decision to retaliate against the *ad valorem* tax with an embargo on the export of new films to Britain.

The success at the box-office of Herbert Wilcox's *Spring in Park Lane* confirmed its independent producer-director's belief that in the late 1940s British audiences wanted 'films about nice people'. The nice people were Michael Wilding and Anna Neagle, decorating a featherweight romance, conducted to the sound of popping champagne corks, in which Wilding played a peer masquerading as a footman.

Among the outstanding British films of the year were Powell and Pressburger's *The Red Shoes*, a remarkable ballet fantasy throbbing with colour and saturated with emotions moving in time with the rhythms of the soundtrack; and Carol Reed's *The Fallen Idol*, his first collaboration with Graham Greene.

David Lean followed *Great Expectations* (1946) with another Dickens film, *Oliver Twist*. The assurance and sweep were there, but accompanied by indications that Lean was becoming the prisoner of his own technical virtuosity. Alec Guinness' portrayal of Fagin created such fury among Jewish groups in the United States that the film was not shown there until 1951.

In France one of the greatest of screen clowns, Jacques Tati, made his feature film debut in *Jour de Fête*, as a village postman deciding to adopt 'American' methods to speed up delivery.

The Japanese actor Toshiro Mifune made a big impression in Akira Kurosawa's *Yoidore Tenshi* (*Drunken Angel*) as a tubercular gangster given a temporary reprieve by an alcoholic doctor (Takashi Shimura). It was the beginning of a long and fruitful association between actor and director.

In Italy Silvana Mangano sprang from the earth like a sexy, proletarian Rita Hayworth in Giuseppe de Santis' *Riso Amaro* (*Bitter Rice*), a neo-realist exposé of the exploitation of rice workers which owed much of its international success to its erotic content.

Luchino Visconti's *La Terra Trema* was the first in an uncompleted trilogy whose strikingly romantic compositions were at odds with its theme, the grinding poverty of a small Sicilian fishing village.

Neo-realism was now threatened by its own success. When Vittorio De Sica was raising money for *Ladri di Biciclette* (*Bicycle Thieves*), he received a generous offer from David O Selznick, who was prepared to back the film if Cary Grant was cast in the role of the bill-sticker who loses his bicycle, his means of livelihood. De Sica rejected this intriguing proposition and used a workman, Lamberto Maggiorani, who had brought his child to be auditioned for the part of the bill-sticker's son (played in the film by Enzo Staiola). The result was an enduring masterpiece.

Jose Ferrer in *Joan of Arc* (RKO)

John Wayne, Montgomery Clift and Walter Brennan in *Red River* (UA)

Joan Davis and Eddie Cantor in *If You Knew Susie* (RKO)

Film Favourites 1948

This was another year of successful films, many still very popular today on television – John Wayne in *Red River,* (UA) Gene Kelly in *The Three Musketeers* (MGM) and Sydney Greenstreet in *The Woman in White* (WB) and *Ruthless* (EL) among them. Television, though, was beginning to make its mark.

Pedro Armendariz and Maria Elena Marques in *The Pearl* (RKO)

Ann Sothern and Jeanne Crain in *A Letter to Three Wives* (Fox)

Louis Hayward, Diana Lynn and Zachary Scott in *Ruthless* (EL)

Philip Friend and Teresa Wright in *Enchantment* (RKO)

Ward Bond and Richard Long in *Tap Roots* (Univ)

Douglas Fairbanks Jr in *That Lady in Ermine* (Fox)

Robert Arthur and Burl Ives in *Green Grass of Wyoming* (Fox)

Gig Young and Gene Kelly in *The Three Musketeers* (MGM)

Akim Tamiroff, Mike Mazurki and Marguerite Chapman in *Relentless* (Col)

Melvyn Douglas, Phyllis Calvert and Philip Friend in *My Own True Love* (Par)

Oscar Levant and Dan Dailey in *You Were Meant For Me* (Fox)

Lana Morris and Cecil Parker in *The Weaker Sex* (TC)

Sam Wanamaker and Lilli Palmer in *My Girl Tisa* (WB)   Paul Henreid and Joan Bennett in *Hollow Triumph* (EL)   Gig Young and Eleanor Parker in *The Woman in White* (WB)

▽ Dennis Price in *The Bad Lord Byron* (Tr)   John Mills in *Scott of the Antarctic* (EaS)

Anna Sten, Robert Cummings and Hedy Lamarr in *Let's Live a Little* (EL)

Dona Drake, Dan Duryea, Whit Bissell and Fredric March in *Another Part of the Forest*
▽ (Univ)

6

7

2

Picture Gallery for 1948

3

8

4

5

6

1. Noel Neill, Warren Mills, June Preisser and Freddie Stewart in *Campus Sleuth* (MoP)
2. Jose Iturbi in *Three Daring Daughters* (GB *The Birds and the Bees*) (MGM)
3. Robert Mitchum
4. Jane Hylton
5. Monte Hale and James Burke in *The Timber Trail* (Rep)
6. Faith Brook and Michael Rennie in *Uneasy Terms* (BN)
7. Yvonne De Carlo in *Black Bart* (Univ)
8. Dennis O'Keefe, Louis Hayward and Louise Allbritton in *Walk a Crooked Mile* (Col)

◁ 7

1

2

3

In *A Southern Yankee* (GB *My Hero*) (MGM) – a US Civil War comedy – neither side was helped to victory by bellhop Red Skelton's efforts to become a daring spy. Apart from that, this was the usual crazy fun that Red always managed to pack into his movies.

1. Art Baker and Red Skelton
2. Red Skelton
3. Brian Donlevy and Arlene Dahl
4. Brian Donlevy and John Ireland
5. Red Skelton and Joyce Compton
6. Brian Donlevy, Red Skelton and John Ireland
7. Red Skelton and Art Baker

4

5

6

7

1. Ann Todd and Gregory Peck in *The Paradine Case* (DS)
2. Terry Moore in *The Return of October* (Col)
3. Helena Carter and Lloyd Gough in *River Lady* (Univ)
4. George Raft and Marilyn Maxwell in *Race Street* (RKO)
5. Dan Duryea and Yvonne de Carlo in *River Lady* (Univ)
6. Lena Horne
7. Joyce Reynolds, Don McGuire and Janis Paige in *Wallflower* (WB)
8. Joan Leslie
9. Phil Brown and Robert Newton in *Obsession* (US *The Hidden Room*) (IS)
10. Florence Bates, Rod Cameron and Lloyd Gough in *River Lady* (Univ)

402

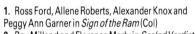

1. Ross Ford, Allene Roberts, Alexander Knox and Peggy Ann Garner in *Sign of the Ram* (Col)

2. Ray Milland and Florence Marly in *Sealed Verdict* (Par)

3. Susan Peters and Alexander Knox in *Sign of the Ram* (Col)

4. Allene Roberts, Alexander Knox, Peggy Ann Garner, Ross Ford, Diana Douglas, Dame May Whitty and Susan Peters in *Sign of the Ram* (Col)

5. Nigel Patrick in *Noose* (US *The Silk Noose*) (ED)

6. Carole Landis, Nigel Patrick and Joseph Calleia in *Noose* (US *The Silk Noose*) (ED)

7. Marshall Reed, Tom London, Lash LaRue and Al 'Fuzzy' St John in *Mark of the Lash* (WA)

8. John Lund and Gail Russell in *Night Has a Thousand Eyes* (Par)

9. Peter Bull and Joan Greenwood in *Saraband for Dead Lovers* (US *Saraband*) (EaS)

10. Joan Greenwood, Peter Bull, Françoise Rosay and Frederick Valk in *Saraband for Dead Lovers* (US *Saraband*) (EaS)

403

1

2

3

4

5

1. Tim Holt, Nan Leslie and Jason Robards Sr in *Western Heritage* (RKO)
2. James Cardwell
3. Scott Brady
4. Milada Mladova in *The Siren of Atlantis* (UA)
5. Brenda Joyce
6. Robert Cummings and Anna Sten in *Let's Live a Little* (EL)
7. Virginia Grey, Philip Reed and Barton MacLane (all stg left) in *Unknown Island* (FCL)
8. Mary Field, Dick Haymes and Albert Sharpe in *Up in Central Park* (Univ)
9. Barry Sullivan in *Smart Woman* (AA)
10. Constance Bennett in *Smart Woman* (AA)
11. Deanna Durbin and Dick Haymes in *Up in Central Park* (Univ)
12. Barry Sullivan and Constance Bennett in *Smart Woman* (AA)

6

7

8

9

11

12

10

404

1. Dona Drake in *So This is New York* (UA)
2. Dennis Morgan and Jack Carson in *Two Guys From Texas* (WB)
3. Danny Kaye, Virginia Mayo, Tommy Dorsey and Charlie Barnet (r) in *A Song is Born* (RKO)
4. Danny Kay, O Z Whitehead, Benny Goodman and Ludwig Stossell in *A Song is Born* (RKO)
5. Henry Morgan, Virginia Grey and Dona Drake in *So This is New York* (UA)
6. Don Castle
7. Edwige Feuillere
8. Anthony Caruso, Dennis Morgan, Tom D'Andrea, Eduardo Ciannelli and William Conrad in *To the Victor* (WB)
9. Eddie Dean, Jennifer Holt and Lee Bennett in *The Tioga Kid* (PRC)

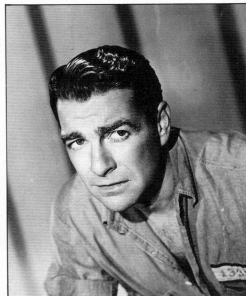

◁ **7**

9 ▷

1. Robert Stack, Wanda Hendrix and John Lund in *Miss Tatlock's Millions* (Par)

2. Ilka Chase and Richard Haydn in *Miss Tatlock's Millions* (Par)

3. Kirk Douglas and Laraine Day in *My Dear Secretary* (UA)

4. Ray Teal

5. Andy Clyde, Rand Brooks (white hat), Don Haggerty, Elaine Riley and William Boyd in *Sinister Journey* (UA)

6. Edgar Barrier in *To the Ends of the Earth* (Col)

7. John Sutton (I), Lois Butler and Skip Homeier in *Mickey* (EL)

8. James Davis and Bette Davis in *Winter Meeting* (WB)

9. Marshall Reed, Bill Kennedy, Johnny Mack Brown, Raymond Hatton and Virginia Carroll in *Triggerman* (MoP)

10. David Street

9
▷◁
10

1

2

3

1. Elyse Knox, Don Castle, Rory Mallinson and Regis Toomey in *I Wouldn't Be In Your Shoes* (MoP)
2. Regis Toomey in *I Wouldn't Be In Your Shoes* (MoP)
3. Don Castle and Elyse Knox in *I Wouldn't Be In Your Shoes* (MoP)
4. Lita Baron, Johnny Weissmuller, Virginia Grey and Rick Vallin in *Jungle Jim* (Col)
5. Orson Welles in *Macbeth* (Rep)
6. Dorothy Lamour in *Lulu Belle* (Col)
7. Ellen Drew in *The Man From Colorado* (Col)
8. Glynis Johns in *Miranda* (G'boro)
9. Burt Lancaster and Joan Fontaine in *Kiss the Blood Off My Hands* (Univ)

4

5

6

7

8 ▷

9

407

1. Mickey Rooney and Marilyn Maxwell in *Summer Holiday* (MGM)
2. Paul Fix
3. Max Baer
4. David Farrar in *The Small Back Room* (US *Hour of Glory*) (LF)
5. Katharine Hepburn and Adolphe Menjou in *State of the Union* (GB *The World and His Wife*) (MGM)
6. Ian Hunter, Michael Rennie and Madeleine Carroll in *High Fury* (UA)
7. Mae Clarke and Robert Livingston in *Daredevils of the Clouds* (Rep)
8. Johnny Mack Brown, Bill Kennedy and Milburn Morante in *Overland Trails* (MoP)
9. Farley Granger and Cathy O'Donnell in *They Live By Night* (RKO)
10. William Henry
11. Dub Taylor, Jimmy Wakely and Pierce Lyden in *The Rangers Ride* (MoP)

1. Robert Lowery, Lyle Talbot, Pamela Blake and Dan Seymour in *Highway 13* (SGP)
2. Diane Hart and Maureen O'Hara in *Britannia Mews* (US *The Forbidden Street*) (Fox)
3. Jane Wyatt, Dick Powell and Lizabeth Scott in *The Pitfall* (UA)
4. Virginia Mayo in *Smart Girls Don't Talk* (WB)
5. Johnny Mack Brown in *Hidden Danger* (MoP)
6. Lynne Roberts and Warren Douglas in *Lightnin' in the Forest* (Rep)
7. Dan Dailey and Barbara Lawrence in *Give my Regards to Broadway* (Fox)
8. Valerie Hobson and Amy Veness in *Blanche Fury* (Cine/IP)
9. Joel McCrea and Charles Bickford in *Four Faces West* (UA)

1. Denis O'Dea, Jack Hawkins, Bobby Henrey and Bernard Lee in *The Fallen Idol* (US *Lost Illusion*) (LF)
2. Joan Davis (l), Eddie Cantor and Bobby Driscoll (r) in *If You Knew Susie* (RKO)
3. Micheline Presle and Fernand Gravet in *Foolish Husband* (SIR)
4. John Kellogg and Barry Sullivan in *Bad Men of Tombstone* (AA)
5. Stephen Murray

6. Van Heflin in *Act of Violence* (MGM)
7. Van Heflin and Robert Ryan in *Act of Violence* (MGM)
8. Rita Hayworth in *The Lady From Shanghai* (Col)
9. Tim Holt, Gary Gray and Richard Martin in *Gun Smugglers* (RKO)

◁ **9**

1

2

3

Hollywood has always excelled in films dealing with small town life. *The Inside Story* (Rep) was a typical comedy of the genre with wit and invention, and with a warmly human atmosphere underlying the laughs. Several well-known actors such as Allen Jenkins, Roscoe Karns and Florence Bates were there to support Charles Winninger and Gene Lockhart while Marsha Hunt and William Lundigan competently handled the love interest.

1. Gail Patrick and Robert Shayne
2. Marsha Hunt and Charles Winninger
3. Gene Lockhart and Charles Winninger
4. Allen Jenkins, Florence Bates and William Haade
5. William Lundigan and Marsha Hunt
6. Robert Shayne, Gail Patrick, William Lundigan and Marsha Hunt
7. Roscoe Karns, Allen Jenkins, William Haade and Charles Winninger
8. Hobart Cavanaugh and Charles Winninger
9. Will Wright and Florence Bates

4

5

6

7

8
▷
▷
9

1

2

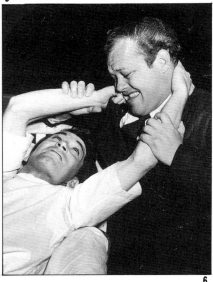

3

4

7

5

6

1. Jackie Cooper (fg) and Jackie Coogan (c) in *French Leave* (MoP)
2. Barbara Stanwyck and Charles Coburn in *B F's Daughter* (MGM)
3. Eddie Albert and Gale Storm in *The Dude Goes West* (AA)
4. Barbara Stanwyck and Van Heflin in *B F's Daughter* (MGM)
5. Margaret Leighton in *Bonnie Prince Charlie* (LF)
6. Richard Conte (l) in *Cry of the City* (Fox)
7. Betty Hutton (r) in *Dream Girl* (Par)
8. Virginia Field and Patric Knowles in *Dream Girl* (Par)
9. Whitfield Connor in *Tap Roots* (Univ)
10. Wylie Watson, Gordon Jackson, Joan Greenwood and Bruce Seton in *Whisky Galore* (US *Tight Little Island*) (EaS)

8

9

10

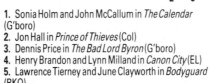

1. Sonia Holm and John McCallum in *The Calendar* (G'boro)

2. Jon Hall in *Prince of Thieves* (Col)

3. Dennis Price in *The Bad Lord Byron* (G'boro)

4. Henry Brandon and Lynn Milland in *Canon City* (EL)

5. Lawrence Tierney and June Clayworth in *Bodyguard* (RKO)

6. Ernie Adams and Edward Norris (c) in *Trapped by Boston Blackie* (Col)

7. Anne Revere, Dean Stockwell and Dana Andrews in *Deep Waters* (Fox)

8. Cesar Romero, Ed Begley, Dean Stockwell, Dana Andrews and Art Baker in *Deep Waters* (Fox)

9. Vera Ralston, George Brent, Gus Schilling, Ross Elliott, Constance Bennett and Walter Reed in *Angel On the Amazon* (GB *Drums Along the Amazon*) (Rep)

10. Walter Reed, Constance Bennett, Gus Schilling and Ross Elliott in *Angel On the Amazon* (GB *Drums Along the Amazon*) (Rep)

Hamlet (TC) was a winner all the way for it won an Oscar award for Best Film, Best Black-and-white Photography, Best Art Direction and Best Costume Design. Laurence Olivier rounded off these accolades with the award for Best Actor. He also directed and produced this filmic triumph of William Shakespeare's play.

1

2

4

3

5 ▷

1. Laurence Olivier
2. Stanley Holloway
3. Eileen Herlie and Laurence Olivier
4. Norman Wooland
5. Eileen Herlie, Laurence Olivier, Basil Sydney and Terence Morgan
6. Eileen Herlie, Basil Sydney and Felix Aylmer
7. Jean Simmons, Terence Morgan and Felix Aylmer
8. Norman Wooland, Jean Simmons, Eileen Herlie and Basil Sydney
9. Felix Aylmer
10. Laurence Olivier
11. Basil Sydney and Laurence Olivier
12. Tony Tarver and Patrick Troughton (The Queen and King in the play within a play).
13. Laurence Olivier and Jean Simmons

6

7

8

9

10

11

▽ 13

12 ◁

1

2

3

4

5

6

7

Looking back it must have been with reasonable confidence that the producers of *Scott of the Antarctic* (EaS) foresaw during its filming that it would be selected as the Royal Command Performance Film of 1948 – and so it transpired. The script wrung the last ounce of emotion out of the disappointment of Scott and his gallant companions when they arrived at the South Pole only to find the tent and flag left behind by Roald Amundsen and his Norwegian team. There then follows the heart-breaking return journey and the tragic ending of the British expedition.

1. John Mills
2. John Mills and James Robertson Justice
3. Clive Morton
4. Reginald Beckwith
5. Anne Firth and Harold Warrender
6. John Mills
7. Harold Warrender
8. James Robertson Justice
9. Kenneth More
10. Harold Warrender, Reginald Beckwith, Derek Bond, John Mills and James Robertson Justice
11. Christopher Lee
12. Diana Churchill
13. Derek Bond

8

9

10

12

13

◁ 11

417

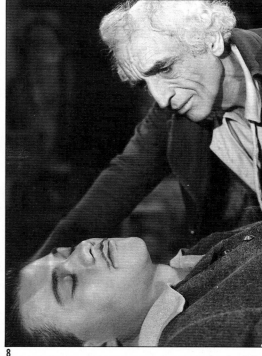

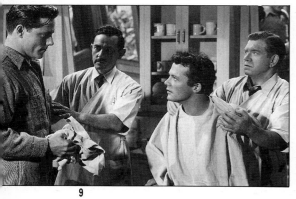

1. Akim Tamiroff and Mike Mazurki in *Relentless* (Col)
2. Robert Young, Mike Mazurki, Marguerite Chapman, Willard Parker and Akim Tamiroff in *Relentless* (Col)
3. Celeste Holm and Olivia de Havilland in *The Snake Pit* (Fox)
4. George Tobias (c) in *Adventures of Casanova* (EL)
5. Arturo de Cordova in *Adventures of Casanova* (EL)
6. Olivia de Havilland and Mark Stevens in *The Snake Pit* (Fox)
7. John Sutton, Lloyd Corrigan and Nestor Paiva in *Adventures of Casanova* (EL)
8. Fritz Leiber and Turhan Bey in *Adventures of Casanova* (EL)
9. Robert Karnes (l), Lon McCallister (c) and Matt McHugh in *Scudda Hoo! Scudda Hay!* (Fox)
10. Robert Karnes and June Haver in *Scudda Hoo! Scudda Hay!* (Fox)

418

10 ▷

1

2

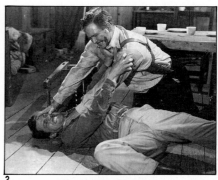

3

4

5

6

7

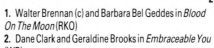

8

9

10

1. Walter Brennan (c) and Barbara Bel Geddes in *Blood On The Moon* (RKO)
2. Dane Clark and Geraldine Brooks in *Embraceable You* (WB)
3. John Carroll and Barton MacLane in *Angel in Exile* (Rep)
4. Dick Powell in *Rogues Regiment* (Univ)
5. John Lund and Jean Arthur in *A Foreign Affair* (Par)
6. Ray Milland, Maureen O'Sullivan, Elsa Lanchester and Lloyd Corrigan in *The Big Clock* (Par)
7. Ray Milland, Rita Johnson and Elsa Lanchester in *The Big Clock* (Par)
8. Ray Milland in *The Big Clock* (Par)
9. Henry Morgan and Ray Milland in *The Big Clock* (Par)
10. Wallace Beery in *Alias a Gentleman* (MGM)

1. John Hoyt in *Winter Meeting* (WB)
2. Joan Bennett and Michael Redgrave in *Secret Beyond the Door* (Univ)
3. Clifton Webb in *Sitting Pretty* (Fox)
4. John Wayne in *Wake of the Red Witch* (Rep)
5. Adele Mara and Gig Young in *Wake of the Red Witch* (Rep)
6. Gail Russell and John Wayne in *Wake of the Red Witch* (Rep)
7. Adele Jergens, Donna DeMario and Michael Duane in *The Woman from Tangier* (Col)
8. Joe Sawyer, Harry Cheshire and Thomas Jackson in *Here Comes Trouble* (UA)
9. Gerald Perreau, Ardda Lynwood, Larry Olsen, Dale Belding and Eilene Janssen in *Who Killed Doc Robbin?* (UA)
10. Dick Powell in *Station West* (RKO)
11. Peggy Cummins and Robert Arthur in *Green Grass of Wyoming* (Fox)

10

9

11

1. Anne Jeffreys in *Return of the Badmen* (RKO)
2. Robert Ryan in *Return of the Badmen* (RKO)
3. Robert Ryan and Anne Jeffreys in *Return of the Badmen* (RKO)
4. Douglas Fairbanks Jr in *That Lady in Ermine* (Fox)
5. Douglas Fairbanks Jr, Walter Abel, Edmund McDonald and Betty Grable in *That Lady in Ermine* (Fox)
6. Whit Bissell, Reginald Gardiner and Betty Grable in *That Lady in Ermine* (Fox)
7. Douglas Fairbanks Jr and Betty Grable in *That Lady in Ermine* (Fox)
8. Lucile Watson and Gene Tierney in *That Wonderful Urge* (Fox)
9. Taylor Holmes, Porter Hall and Tyrone Power (std at table), Gene Tierney and Gene Lockhart in *That Wonderful Urge* (Fox)

In *The Three Musketeers* (MGM) Gene Kelly, as a whirlwind D'Artagnan, abandoned the dance for the duel. He and the three Musketeers, Athos (Van Heflin), Porthos (Gig Young) and Aramis (Robert Coote) fought gallantly in the service of the King (Frank Morgan) and Queen (Angela Lansbury). June Allyson provided the romance while Vincent Price as Cardinal Richelieu and Lana Turner as Milady were suitably menacing.

1. Angela Lansbury and Gene Kelly
2. Gene Kelly
3. Byron Foulger, Gene Kelly, Van Heflin, Robert Coote and Gig Young.
4. Vincent Price and Lana Turner
5. June Allyson and Keenan Wynn
6. Frank Morgan
7. June Allyson and John Sutton
8. Gig Young, Van Heflin, Lana Turner, Gene Kelly and Robert Coote

5

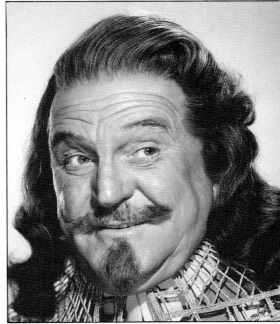

4

6

7
8

1. Robert Barrat in *Joan of Arc* (RKO)
2. Hurd Hatfield in *Joan of Arc* (RKO)
3. George Zucco in *Joan of Arc* (RKO)
4. Ingrid Bergman and Mary Currier in *Joan of Arc* (RKO)
5. Grant Withers, William Elliott and Bruce Cabot in *The Gallant Legion* (Rep)
6. Glenn Langan and Victor Mature in *Fury at Furnace Creek* (Fox)
7. Ralph Byrd, Denise Darcel and George Reeves in *Thunder in the Pines* (Lip)
8. Arnold D Moss in *The Loves of Carmen* (Col)
9. Harry Shannon and Cary Grant in *Mr Blandings Builds His Dream House* (RKO)
10. Glenn Ford in *The Loves of Carmen* (Col)

9
▷
▷
10

George Montgomery

STRIKE IT RICH

ALLIED ARTISTS presents

A JACK WRATHER PRODUCTION

Slippy McGEE

A Republic Picture

1. John Wayne, Shirley Temple, Henry Fonda and John Agar in *Fort Apache* (RKO)

2. Henry Fonda, George O'Brien, John Wayne and Grant Withers in *Fort Apache* (RKO)

3. George O'Brien (l), Anna Lee, Shirley Temple, Pedro Armendariz, John Wayne and Henry Fonda in *Fort Apache* (RKO)

4. Larry Parks in *The Gallant Blade* (Col)

5. Dan Dailey and Nancy Guild in *Give My Regards to Broadway* (Fox)

6. Warner Baxter (c), in *The Gentleman from Nowhere* (Col)

7. Robert Ryan and Dale Robertson in *The Boy With Green Hair* (RKO)

8. Lee J Cobb in *Call Northside 777* (Fox)

9. Jeffrey Lynn and Don Taylor in *For the Love of Mary* (Univ)

◁ 7

427

1

2

3

4

5

Easter Parade (MGM) was another of Fred Astaire's froth-light musicals backed up harmoniously by Irving Berlin's melodies. 'We're A Couple Of Swells', sung and danced by Judy and Fred still comes echoing down the years. The film is famous if only for that number.

1. Fred Astaire, Peter Lawford and Judy Garland
2. Fred Astaire
3. Fred Astaire
4. Judy Garland
5. Ann Miller and Fred Astaire
6. Fred Astaire and Judy Garland
7. Judy Garland and Peter Lawford
8. Jimmy Bates and Fred Astaire
9. Judy Garland and Fred Astaire

7

8

◁ 6

9 ▷

1. Barbara Murray, Naunton Wayne (stdg), Stanley Holloway and Betty Warren in *Passport to Pimlico* (EaS)
2. Eleanor Parker and Gig Young in *The Woman in White* (WB)
3. Alexis Smith and Eleanor Parker in *The Woman in White* (WB)
4. Marcia Mae Jones (l) in *Street Corner* (WIS)
5. Peggy Knudsen, John Miljan and Samuel S Hinds in *Perilous Waters* (MoP)
6. Audrey Long and Don Castle in *Perilous Waters* (MoP)
7. Ethel Barrymore, Cecil Kellaway and Jesse White in *Portrait of Jennie* (GB *Jennie*) (DS)
8. Akim Tamiroff and Sam Wanamaker in *My Girl Tisa* (WB)
9. Sam Wanamaker and Lilli Palmer in *My Girl Tisa* (WB)
10. Oscar Levant and Dan Dailey in *You Were Meant For Me* (Fox)
11. Jeanne Crain and Dan Dailey in *You Were Meant For Me* (Fox)

9
10

11

1. Billy De Wolfe and Mona Freeman in *Isn't It Romantic* (Par)
2. Veronica Lake and Billy De Wolfe in *Isn't It Romantic* (Par)
3. Richard Martin and Nan Leslie in *Guns of Hate* (RKO)
4. Tony Barrett and Steve Brodie in *Guns of Hate* (RKO)
5. Tim Holt in *Guns of Hate* (RKO)
6. Jan Sterling in *Johnny Belinda* (WB)
7. Jan Sterling and Stephen McNally in *Johnny Belinda* (WB)
8. Stephen McNally in *Johnny Belinda* (WB)

7 ▷

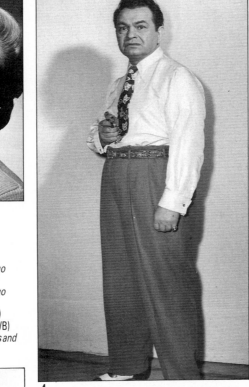

1. Gloria Jean (c) in *An Old-Fashioned Girl* (EL)
2. Philip Reed
3. Virginia Christine in *Night Wind* (Fox)
4. Edward G Robinson in *Key Largo* (WB)
5. Lauren Bacall and Humphrey Bogart in *Key Largo* (WB)
6. Lauren Bacall and Humphrey Bogart in *Key Largo* (WB)
7. Bob Hope and Jane Russell in *The Paleface* (Par)
8. Tom D'Andrea and Errol Flynn in *Silver River* (WB)
9. Ann Sothern with the Blackburn Twins in *Words and Music* (MGM)

◁ 7

8

9 ▷

1. Wendell Corey in *Man-Eater of Kumaon* (Univ)
2. Luba Malina in *Mexican Hayride* (Univ)
3. Howard Freeman, Skip Homeier and Barbara Brown in *Arthur Takes Over* (Fox)
4. Barry Fitzgerald in *The Naked City* (Univ)
5. Esther Williams and Jimmy 'Schnozzle' Durante in *On An Island With You* (MGM)
6. Sheila Ryan and Richard Fraser in *The Cobra Strikes* (EL)
7. Dane Clark and Gail Russell in *Moonrise* (Rep)
8. Richard Fraser, Leslie Brooks, Philip Ahn and Sheila Ryan in *The Cobra Strikes* (EL)
9. Morris Carnovsky and Joanne Page in *Man Eater of Kumaon* (Univ)
10. James Craig, Joan Leslie and Jack Oakie in *Northwest Stampede* (EL)

1

2

3

4

5

6

7

8

1. Fredric March and Florence Eldridge in *Another Part of the Forest* (Univ)
2. Edmond O'Brien and Dan Duryea in *Another Part of the Forest* (Univ)
3. Ann Blyth and Fredric March in *Another Part of the Forest* (Univ)
4. Whit Bissell, Edmond O'Brien, Dan Duryea, Dona Drake and Don Beddoe in *Another Part of the Forest* (Univ)
5. Dona Drake and Dan Duryea in *Another Part of the Forest* (Univ)
6. Robert Beatty (c) in *Against the Wind* (EaS)
7. Leo Pessin and Joan Fontaine in *Letter From An Unknown Woman* (Univ)
8. Jack Lambert, George Montgomery, Rod Cameron, Ruth Roman and Chris-Pin Martin in *Belle Starr's Daughter* (Fox)
9. Tony Martin in *Casbah* (Univ)
10. Yvonne de Carlo and Tony Martin in *Casbah* (Univ)

10

◁ 9

1

2

3

4

5

6

7

8

9

10

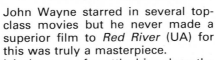

John Wayne starred in several top-class movies but he never made a superior film to *Red River* (UA) for this was truly a masterpiece.

It is the story of a cattle drive along the newly discovered Chisholm Trail and the conflict between an arrogant cattle baron, John Wayne, and his adopted son (Montgomery Clift). Their quarrel is intensified by the rancher's harsh treatment of his crew. *Red River* was a Western de luxe mounted on a magnificent scale.

1. John Wayne and Coleen Gray
2. Montgomery Clift and Joanne Dru
3. John Ireland, Montgomery Clift and Joanne Dru
4. Joanne Dru and Hank Worden
5. Harry Carey, Walter Brennan, Montgomery Clift, Paul Fix, Hank Worden and Ray Hyke
6. Montgomery Clift
7. John Ireland
8. Noah Beery Jr, Montgomery Clift, Harry Carey Jr, John Ireland, John Wayne and Walter Brennan
9. John Wayne
10. Joanne Dru and John Wayne
11. Montgomery Clift and Harry Carey
12. Walter Brennan, John Wayne and Mick Kuhn
13. Ray Hyke, Walter Brennan, John Wayne, Paul Fix and Montgomery Clift

11

12

13

1.   Keefe Brasselle   11.   Richard Long
2.   Dana Andrews   12.   Googie Withers
3.   Ian Hunter   13.   Sir Cedric Hardwicke
4.   Gordon Jones   14.   Martha Scott
5.   Richard Quine   15.   Susan Shaw
6.   Richard Denning   16.   Bruce Cowling
7.   Rory Calhoun   17.   Richard Attenborough
8.   Robert Sterling   18.   Bill Conrad
9.   Bill Goodwin   19.   Howard Freeman
10.   Edward Everett Horton

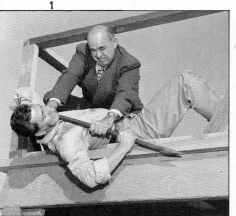

1. Richard Denning, Sheila Ryan, Mary Beth Hughes and Larry 'Buster' Crabbe in *Caged Fury* (Par)

2. Ralph Byrd in *Jungle Goddess* (LIP)

3. William Eythe and Nestor Paiva in *Mr Reckless* (Par)

4. Marsha Hunt in *Raw Deal* (EL)

5. Larry 'Buster' Crabbe and Richard Denning in *Caged Fury* (Par)

6. Catherine McLeod, Tito Renaldo, William 'Wild Bill' Elliott and Joseph Schildkraut in *Old Los Angeles* (Rep)

7. Jacqueline White and Walter Reed in *Mystery In Mexico* (RKO)

8. Sheila Sim and Richard Attenborough in *The Guinea Pig* (US *The Outsider*) (Pilgrim)

9. Francis Lederer, Gene Raymond and Osa Massen in *Million Dollar Weekend* (EL)

10. Jacqueline White and William Lundigan in *Mystery in Mexico* (RKO)

10
◁

◁ 8

1

2

3

4

5

6

7

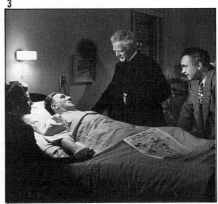

8

1. Percy Helton and John Payne in *Larceny* (Univ)
2. Dan Duryea and John Payne in *Larceny* (Univ)
3. John Payne and Shelley Winters in *Larceny* (Univ)
4. Claire Trevor and William Bendix in *The Babe Ruth Story* (AA)
5. William Bendix, Lennie Bremen and Claire Trevor in *The Babe Ruth Story* (AA)
6. Claire Trevor, William Bendix, Charles Bickford and Sam Levene in *The Babe Ruth Story* (AA)
7. Edwige Feuillere in *Woman Hater* (TC)
8. Frances Gifford
9. Stuart Erwin, Rod Cameron and Don Castle in *Strike It Rich* (AA)
10. Richard Hart
11. Jimmy Wakely, Patsy Moran and Mildred Coles in *Song of the Drifter* (MoP)

9

10 ▷

11

438

1. Diana Dors, Michael Dear and John Howard Davies in *Oliver Twist* (Cineguild)

2. John Howard Davies and Michael Dear in *Oliver Twist* (Cineguild)

3. Mary Clare and Francis L Sullivan in *Oliver Twist* (Cineguild)

4. Bobby Driscoll in *So Dear To My Heart* (RKO)

5. Ann Blyth

6. Robert Beatty

7. Jeanne Cagney in *The Time Of Your Life* (UA)

8. James Barton, Gregory Peck, Charles Kemper, Robert Arthur, Anne Baxter, Harry Morgan, John Russell and Richard Widmark in *Yellow Sky* (Fox)

9. Lucille Bremer

1

2

3

4

5

6

7

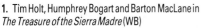

8

9

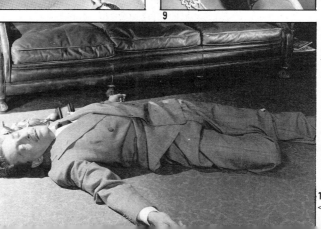

1. Tim Holt, Humphrey Bogart and Barton MacLane in
The Treasure of the Sierra Madre (WB)
2. Walter Huston, Humphrey Bogart and Tim Holt (r) in
The Treasure of the Sierra Madre (WB)
3. Humphrey Bogart and Bobby Blake in *The Treasure of
the Sierra Madre* (WB)
4. Roy Roberts and Scott Brady in *He Walked by Night*
(EL)
5. Felice Ingersoll in *He Walked By Night* (EL)
6. Richard Denning, Virginia Grey and Philip Reed in
Unknown Island (FCP)
7. Virginia Grey and Richard Denning in *Unknown Island*
(FCP)
8. Peggy Knudsen
9. Jane Greer
10. Robert Hutton and Janis Paige in *Wallflower* (WB)
11. Leon Ames in *The Velvet Touch* (RKO)

10

11

1. Mai Zetterling
2. Pedro Amendariz and Maria Elena Marques in *The Pearl* (RKO)
3. James Lydon
4. Hazel Brooks in *Arch of Triumph* (UA)
5. Paul Henreid in *Hollow Triumph* (EL)
6. Steve Brown, Peggy McIntyre, Oscar Homolka and Barbara Bel Geddes in *I Remember Mama* (RKO)
7. Wanda Hendrix and Melvyn Douglas in *My Own True Love* (Par)
8. Irene Dunne, Rudy Vallee, Oscar Homolka and Steve Brown in *I Remember Mama* (RKO)
9. Paul Henreid and Joan Bennett in *Hollow Triumph* (EL)
10. Robert Shayne, George Nokes and Brenda Joyce in *Shaggy* (Par)
11. Brenda Joyce, George Nokes, Robert Shayne and Ralph Sanford in *Shaggy* (Par)

1. Louis Hayward and Diana Lynn in *Ruthless* (EL)
2. William Gargan and Richard Crane in *Waterfront at Midnight* (Par)
3. Richard Travis, Mary Beth Hughes and Richard Crane in *Waterfront at Midnight* (Par)
4. Douglas Dick (c), Loretta Young and Robert Cummings (r) in *The Accused* (Par)
5. Stanley Holloway
6. Nan Leslie
7. Shepperd Strudwick
8. Martha Vickers and Zachary Scott in *Ruthless* (EL)
9. Evelyn Keyes and Farley Granger in *Enchantment* (RKO)
10. Teresa Wright and Shepperd Strudwick in *Enchantment* (RKO)
11. Naunton Wayne in *Quartet* (G'boro)

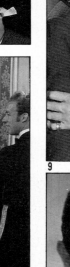

11 ▷

442

Betty Grable

J Farrell MacDonald, Pedro Armendariz, Ward Bond, Victor McLaglen and Henry Fonda in *Fort Aparche* (RKO)

1. Jeanne Crain and Kirk Douglas in *A Letter to Three Wives* (Fox)
2. Jeffrey Lynn and Jeanne Crain in *A Letter to Three Wives* (Fox)
3. Linda Darnell and Paul Douglas in *A Letter to Three Wives* (Fox)
4. James Craig in *The Man from Texas* (EL)
5. Lee J Cobb and Tyrone Power in *The Luck of the Irish* (Fox)
6. Anne Baxter in *The Luck of the Irish* (Fox)
7. Cecil Kellaway in *The Luck of the Irish* (Fox)
8. J M Kerrigan and Anne Baxter in *The Luck of the Irish* (Fox)
9. James Craig, Reed Hadley and Lynn Bari in *The Man from Texas* (EL)
10. Richard Crane
11. Bill Owen and Ursula Jeans in *The Weaker Sex* (TC)
12. Cecil Parker, Ursula Jeans and Derek Bond in *The Weaker Sex* (TC)

Jeanne Crain

James Edwards and Lloyd Bridges in *Home of the Brave*
(UA)

CHAPTER TEN

1949
BIG CHANGES LOOMING

MGM celebrated its silver jubilee with a blaze of publicity. The studio crept back into profit, but the future looked increasingly uncertain.

During the course of the year the Hollywood majors – MGM, Paramount, Warner Brothers, Twentieth Century-Fox and RKO – agreed with the US government to split their theatre organisations from the production-distribution side of the business. The implementation of the Supreme Court's divestiture decree sealed the fate of the vertically integrated studio system, which had guaranteed the profitability of the majority of films.

Having tackled anti-Semitism in 1948, Hollywood now turned its attention to the colour question. In Twentieth Century-Fox's *Pinky*, directed by Elia Kazan, Jeanne Crain played a college-educated coloured girl so light-skinned that she can pass for white and romance white doctor William Lundigan. The casting of a white star in the title role – which insulated white audiences against the shock of seeing a black-white embrace – was symptomatic of the spirit of compromise in which the film was made.

Similar evasions were made in *Lost Boundaries*, produced by Louis de Rochemont and directed by Alfred Werker. Another white actor, Mel Ferrer, played a light-skinned coloured doctor accepted unquestioningly as white in a small New Hampshire town. All is revealed when he attempts to enlist in the Navy. The high-minded citizens of his home town eventually rally to the hapless medic but the effect, as the critic Richard Winnington observed, was calculated to 'improve White conceit and preserve the colour bar'.

At MGM Clarence Brown's *Intruder in the Dust*, had an intensity uncharacteristic of the studio's bland, glossy image. Juano Hernandez gave a performance of great dignity as an elderly Southern black falsely accused of murder and threatened with lynch law. His contempt for his accusers is so great that he declines to defend himself, and it falls to a small band of liberal-minded whites to save him.

Trading heavily on its 'progressiveness' was United Artists' *Home of the Brave*, directed by Mark Robson, in which James Edwards was a black soldier in the Pacific war whose hysterical paralysis is traced back to an incident in combat when a trusted white friend calls him a 'yellow-bellied nigger'. (In the play on which the film was based the victim had been Jewish.) Tough but concerned psychiatrist Jeff Corey, a group of conscience-stricken buddies, and a 'happy' ending in which Edwards becomes a well-adjusted bartender, lend the film a tidy glibness typical of its writer Carl Foreman and producer Stanley Kramer.

As memories of World War II began to recede, the war film made a comeback. William Wellman's *Battleground* (MGM) was a gritty account of the Battle of the Bulge which focused a single platoon of the US 101st Airborne Division. As in *The Story of GI Joe* (1945), this was the war from the foot-soldier's point of view with no mock heroics and Van Johnson wryly amusing as a scrounging rifleman continually frustrated in his efforts to scramble eggs in his helmet.

At the beginning of Twentieth Century-Fox's *Twelve O' Clock High*, directed by Henry King, the passage of time is conveyed by Dean Jagger's sentimental return to a deserted airfield 'somewhere in England'. In flashback Jagger recalls a hard-driving CO (Gregory Peck) who restores the morale of a battle-fatigued USAAF bomber group at the cost of his own mental breakdown. Peck gave a riveting performance, well-supported by stalwarts Millard Mitchell, Hugh Marlowe, Paul Stewart, Gary Merrill and Jagger, who won the year's Best Supporting Actor Oscar as his calm, pipe-sucking subordinate.

Republic's *Sands of Iwo Jima*, directed by Allan Dwan, starred John Wayne as the hard-bitten Sergeant John M Stryker slugging his way through the Pacific until his pitiless progress is halted by a Japanese sniper. Somehow the Allies manage to finish the war without him. *Sands of Iwo Jima* is a surging uncomplicated actioner, pushed along with Dwan's unfailing gusto, and a forerunner of the flag-wagging war films of the early 1950s which fed on the militarism revived by the Korean War.

The Academy voted Robert Rossen's *All the King's Men* (Columbia) the year's Best Picture, as did the New York critics. Broderick Crawford won the Best Actor Oscar for his blistering performance as Willie Stark, a corrupt political demagogue whose character was a thinly disguised amalgam of the Louisiana 'Kingfisher' Huey Long and Columbia's brutal, bullying boss Harry Cohn. It was a part so perfectly tailored to Crawford's belligerent loudmouth style that it provided one of those infrequent examples of actor and character becoming completely one. *All the King's Men* also won Mercedes McCambridge – making her debut – the Best Supporting Actress Oscar and gave John Ireland the best role of his career as the jaundiced newspaper-man who narrates the story.

Warners' *Flamingo Road* was a full-blooded version of the

John Kellogg in *Twelve O'Clock High* (Fox)

Dean Jagger

Joanne Dru and John Ireland in *All The King's Men* (Col)

Ruth Roman in *Champion* (UA)

Louis Jourdan and Jennifer Jones in *Madame Bovary* (MGM)

Ralph Richardson and Olivia de Havilland in *The Heiress* (Par)

Robert Ryan in *The Set-Up* (RKO)

Joan Crawford plot No. 1: determined girl from the wrong side of the tracks claws her way to the top, sacrificing love and happiness to stay there. Just like Joan herself. Here she was a tough carnival dancer matching wits with malignant small-town Caesar Sydney Greenstreet, a mink stole over her shoulders and a gun in her hand. Barbara Stanwyck had more on which to bite in Robert Siodmak's *The File on Thelma Jordan*, as the shady lady drawing DA Wendell Corey into a web of murder and deceit. There's an unforgettable moment when Stanwyck sighs, 'Maybe I'm a dame and just don't know it', after she kisses Corey for the first time.

In Raoul Walsh's *White Heat* another Warner star, James Cagney, returned to his gangster past as the mother-fixated psychopath Cody Jarrett. This was a superbly choreographed performance, moving from apparent tranquility to the manic, reeling overdrive of one of Cody Jarrett's 'headaches'. 'Top of the world, Ma!' Cagney shrieks just before he perishes in the flash of a gigantic petrol tank explosion.

Kirk Douglas took the title role in Mark Robson's *Champion* (United Artists), an adaptation of Ring Lardner's story of the rise and fall of a cocksure boxer whose savage fight scenes belied its sentimental centre. Robert Wise's *The Set-Up* provided an overly schematic but infinitely bleak picture of the underbelly of the fight game, with Robert Ryan reining himself in as the punched-out pug Stoker Thompson, savagely beaten up for refusing to take a dive.

MGM levered three heavyweight literary adaptations off the production line. Jennifer Jones took the title role in *Madame Bovary*, directed by Vincente Minnelli, which has a distracting framing device in which Flaubert (a walrus-moustached James Mason) is tried for corrupting morals and sets out to justify his anti-heroine's behaviour.

Robert Siodmak's *The Great Sinner* (MGM), was based on fragments of Dostoievsky's life and work, notably 'The Gambler', with Gregory Peck unequal to the task of conveying doomed obsession and literary genius and Ava Gardner out of place as a Russian countess, or rather Hollywood's idea of one.

That Forsyte Woman was cobbled up from John Galsworthy's family saga and anonymously directed by the English Compton Bennett. It was quintessential MGM – lush, star-filled and full of longueurs.

Paramount turned to Henry James in *The Heiress*, based on the Broadway adaptation of his 'Washington Square' and directed by William Wyler. Olivia de Havilland's beauty defied her dowdy make-up as the repressed spinster wooed by fortune hunter Montgomery Clift. Her acutely observed performance won her a deserved Best Actress Oscar.

Cecil B DeMille ransacked the Old Testament in *Samson and Delilah* (Paramount), starring Victor Mature as the Biblical strongman and Hedy Lamarr as his devious mate. Nature created Mature for the role of Samson, threatening to burst out of his fetching array of thongs, mangling a stuffed lion and toppling a pasteboard temple.

A new comic team, Dean Martin and Jerry Lewis, made their debut in Paramount's *My Friend Irma*, starring Marie Wilson as the klutzy lady of the title. Universal launched Marjorie Main and Percy Kilbride in *Ma and Pa Kettle*, the first in the popular hayseed series. The studio also had a hit with *Francis*, directed by Arthur Lubin, the first in a moneyspinning series featuring a loquacious mule and his harassed human friend Donald O' Connor.

Shirley Temple returned to Twentieth Century-Fox after a nine-year absence, but took second billing to Clifton Webb, repeating his success in *Sitting Pretty* (1948), with *Mr Belvedere Goes to College*. Tracy and Hepburn were teamed again in George Cukor's *Adam's Rib* (MGM) as the married lawyers at professional loggerheads during the trial of ineffably dumb broad Judy Holliday for husband-shooting.

Howard Hawks' *I Was a Male War Bride* (GB *You Can't Sleep Here*) (Twentieth Century-Fox) was a classic comedy of humiliation in which smooth French officer Cary Grant was obliged to take a roundabout route to marrying spunky US servicewoman Ann Sheridan, spending much of the film in fetching drag. Sheridan was one of the decade's most engaging leading ladies and her sense of enjoyment in *I Was a Male War Bride* leaps off the screen.

Comedy honours of the year went to Joseph L Mankiewicz's *A letter to Three Wives* (Twentieth Century-Fox), an acid-tinged dissection of married life in which he displayed his flair for the skilful manipulation of complicated plotting and the deployment of intelligently barbed dialogue. The Academy awarded Mankiewicz two Oscars, for his Screenplay and Direction.

Oliver Hardy made a rare solo appearance in Republic's *The Fighting Kentuckian*, in which fur trapper John Wayne buckled down to the thankless task of romancing the frosty queen of the lot, Vera Ralston. Wayne was more at home in the masculine knockabout of John Ford's *She Wore a Yellow Ribbon* (RKO), rescuing the film from its sentimental excesses with the melancholy edge he gave his performance as Captain Nathan Brittles, on the eve of retirement.

The biggest grossing film of the year was Columbia's *Jolson Sings Again*, much of which is devoted to the making of *The Jolson Story* (1946). At one point Larry Parks appears in double-exposure as himself and Al Jolson. Bing Crosby strolled through an old Will Rogers vehicle, *A Connecticut Yankee in King Arthur's Court* (GB *A Yankee in King Arthur's Court*) (Paramount). Judy Garland's infectious sense of comedy was skilfully exploited in MGM's *In The Good Old Summertime*, a musical remake of *The Shop Around The Corner* (1940), co-starring Van Johnson. Buster Keaton turned up in a cameo, demonstrating that he had lost none of his magical sense of comic timing. Danny Kaye burlesqued his way through Warners' *The Inspector-General*, which was very loosely based on Gogol's black comedy. Mario Lanza made his debut in MGM's *That Midnight Kiss*, as a singing truck-driver romancing

Marie Wilson

Marjorie Main

Donald O'Connor and Patricia Medina in *Francis* (Univ)

Larry Parks and Barbara Hale in *Jolson Sings Again* (Col)

Arthur Kennedy, Bobbie Driscoll and Barbara Hale in *The Window* (RKO)

Joseph Cotten in *The Third Man* (LF)

Alida Valli in *The Third Man* (LF)

opera-struck heiress Kathryn Grayson.

Fred Astaire and Ginger Rogers were reunited after a ten-year gap in MGM's *The Barkleys of Broadway.*

A decade of musicals reached its climax with MGM's landmark *On the Town.* Gene Kelly and Stanley Donen were given an artistic free rein to create the musical, which had its origins in a Jerome Robbins ballet 'Fancy Free' and a subsequent Broadway show scored by Leonard Bernstein. The slim storyline – three sailors' adventures on a 24-hour leave in New York – looks back to *Anchors Aweigh* (1945), but *On the Town's* balletic inspiration, location shooting, and seemingly spontaneous integration of song, dance and story, propelled the genre into its final flowering in the early 1950's. Kelly was at his exuberantly brash best, falling in love with Vera-Ellen when he sees her on a poster as the subway's Miss Turnstile; Frank Sinatra was perfectly cast as his bashful buddy; and Ann Miller, gutsy trouper of a score of musicals, seized her chance to tap all and sundry into submission as a man-eating anthropologist.

Warners' *Always Leave Them Laughing* celebrated comedian Milton Berle's rise to become 'Mr Television', a harbinger of many a career founded on small-screen success. Television's steady diet of domestic comedies, cop thrillers and Westerns had traditionally been the staples of the B-movie, for so long the forcing ground of new talent and the pasture on which fading stars were put out to graze. But the Bs were now under threat, not only from television but also from the cost of colour film, changing patterns of distribution and falling audiences. Nevertheless, a clutch of classic second features – among them *Gun Crazy, The Big Steal, The Window* and *DOA.* – ensured that the B-movie went down with all guns blazing.

Tony Curtis made an impression as a teenage hoodlum in Universal's *City Across the River.* In *Love Happy* (UA) Marilyn Monroe complained to a leering Groucho Marx that men were following her around. Johnny Weissmuller was replaced as Tarzan by Lex Barker.

Four significant Hollywood figures passed away: Richard Dix, the durable stern-jawed hero; Wallace Beery, who died shortly after completing MGM's *Big Jack*; and directors Sam Wood and Victor Fleming.

In Britain the collaboration between Carol Reed and Graham Greene, reached a peak in *The Third Man,* a romantic thriller set in postwar Vienna and dominated by Orson Welles' Harry Lime, the Citizen Kane of the occupied city's black market in penicillin. Meanwhile Citizen Rank's empire was plunged into crisis. His debts approached £16 million and an accountant, John Davis, was called in to institute a sweeping programme of financial retrenchment.

Associated British replied to Rank's cutback with the announcement of a co-production deal with Warners. Director Vincent Sherman and stars Ronald Reagan and Patricia Neal were imported for Associated Britain's *The Hasty Heart,* a wartime melodrama in which Richard Todd played a hospitalised Scots soldier who discovers that he has only a few weeks to live. Other Hollywood studios were using up some of the assets frozen by British postwar restrictions. MGM filmed *Edward, My Son* and *Conspirator* in England, and established their own studio at Boreham Wood.

Richard Burton made his screen debut in *The Last Days of Dolwyn* (US *Woman of Dolwyn*). Ealing capitalised on the success of their Australian outback drama *The Overlanders* (1946) with another robust Antipodean 'Western', *Eureka Stockade* (US *Massacre Hill*), in which a heavily bearded Peter Finch had a substantial role. This encouraged Finch to come to London, where Ealing cast him as a homicidal maniac in an episode in *Train of Events*, one of the most polished examples of the 'portmanteau' films so popular in Britain in the late 1940's.

Ealing Studios produced the three classic comedies with which its name will always be associated. In Henry Cornelius' *Passport to Pimlico*, a London street discovers that it is part of the ancient dukedom of Burgundy. Alexander Mackendrick's *Whisky Galore* (US *Tight Little Island*) was based on a Compton Mackenzie tale in which a small Hebridean island's whisky famine is ended when a steamer loaded with a huge export consignment runs aground. Robert Hamer's *Kind Hearts and Coronets* is one of the masterpieces of British postwar cinema, with feline Dennis Price murdering his way to a dukedom in a supremely elegant black comedy. In a virtuoso feat of acting Alex Guinness played the eight victims, contriving to give them all a life of their own.

After completing Alfred Hitchcock's *Under Capricorn* (1948), Ingrid Bergman travelled to Italy to make Roberto Rossellini's *Stromboli* (God's Land), playing an unhappy wife escaping to the island of the title.

Bergman was disillusioned with her own marriage and fell in love with Rossellini, bearing his child. This sent Hollywood into characteristically hypocritical convulsions and led to a six-year exile for Bergman.

In France Jean-Pierre Melville made an impressive directing debut with *Le Silence de la Mer*, a downbeat film based on a clandestine wartime best-seller in which an aristocratic German officer in Occupied France (Howard Venon) wins over his hosts, an old man and his niece, before being ordered to the Eastern Front. On the strength of this film Melville was assigned *Les Enfants Terribles*, based on the Cocteau novel which Cocteau himself described as inhabiting 'the no-man's-land between life and death.'

In Japan Akira Kurosawa joined forces with Toshiro Mifune in *Nora Ina* (Stray Dog). Mifune played a detective pursuing his stolen gun through the lower depths of Tokyo. He finally catches up with the thief in a paddyfield, and after the climactic fight they are both so plastered with mud that 'good' and 'bad' are interchangeable. This excellent film posing questions about who is really on the side of law and justice, looks forward to Kurosawa's *Rashomon* (1950), which thrust Japanese cinema on to the international stage.

Richard Burton

Peter Finch

Valerie Hobson in *Kind Hearts and Coronets* (EaS)

Dennis Price and Audrey Fildes in *Kind Hearts and Coronets* (EaS)

Barry Fitzgerald, Ann Blyth and Bing Crosby in *Top o' the Morning* (Par)

The end of a decade and already Hollywood was realizing that the hey-day of the big cinema chains might be over. Stereophonic sound, wide screens and 3-D were all to be tried out to woo back audiences but eventually, the little television screen was to win out. Even so, Hollywood fought back vigorously

Victor Jory and Joel McCrea in *South of St Louis* (WB)

Olivia de Havilland and Montgomery Clift in *The Heiress* (Par)

Barbara Bel Geddes and James Mason in *Caught* (MGM)

George Raft, Bill Williams and Ella Raines in *A Dangerous Profession* (RKO)

Celeste Holm and Loretta Young in *Come to the Stable* (Fox)

Marc Lawrence

◁ Boyd Irwin, Patricia Medina and Helena Carter in *The Fighting O'Flynn* (Univ)

Lloyd Gough, Raymond Massey, Peter Miles (boy), Pat Flaherty and Arthur Franz in *Roseanna McCoy* (SG)

Barbara Britton and Dennis O'Keefe in *Cover-Up* (UA)

Lon McCallister and Preston Foster in *The Big Cat* (EL)

Richard Conte and Gene Tierney in *Whirlpool* (Fox)

Max Baer and Robert Young in *Bride for Sale* (RKO)

Jeff Corey, James Edwards, Steve Brodie and Douglas Dick in *Home of the Brave* (UA)

Will Kuluva in *Abandoned* (Univ)
Sam Wanamaker and Lea Padovani in *Give Us This Day*
(US *Salt and the Devil*) (EL) ▷

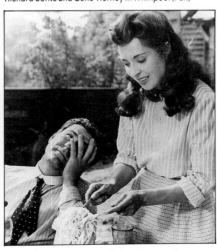

Ray Walker

453

Ross Ford, Edmund Gwenn, Lumsden Hare, Geraldine Brooks and Alan Webb in *Challenge to Lassie* (MGM)

Edward Brophy and Robert Lowery in *Arson Inc* (LIP)

Don Kohler, June Storey, Richard Lane and Lois Collier in *Miss Mink of 1949* (Fox)

Mischa Auer
    Robert Sterling and Gloria Grahame in ▷
Roughshod (RKO)

Virginia McDowall, George Sanders, Jeanne Crain and Martita Hunt in
The Fan (GB *Lady Windermere's Fan*) (Fox)
▽ Ray Milland and Ted De Corsia in *It Happens Every Spring* (Fox)

John Sutton in *The Fan* (GB *Lady Windermere's Fan*) (Fox)

        Robert Hutton ▷

Picture Gallery for 1949

1. David Bruce (l) in *Prejudice* (NEO)
2. Claire Trevor
3. Fernandel
4. George Cole
5. Fernand Gravet
6. Dane Clark
7. Chris-Pin Martin
8. John Carradine (std) and Dean Jagger in *C-Man* (FCL)
9. Van Johnson

◁ 8

9

455

1. Sally Forrest
2. Joseph Cotten
3. Veronica Lake
4. Donald Houston
5. Jean Gabin
6. Ruth Hussey
7. Janet Blair
8. Allyn Joslyn
9. Martin Kosleck
10. Arlene Dahl
11. Edmond O'Brien
12. Richard Travis
13. Barbara Bel Geddes
14. June Allyson
15. Walt Disney
16. Noel Coward

Winton C Hoch won the 1949 Oscar for Best Colour Cinematography for his work on *She Wore a Yellow Ribbon* (RKO). It is generally recognised that this, the second of John Ford's famous cavalry epics, was without doubt one of the most beautiful Westerns ever filmed. Hoch lavished all his skill on the magnificent scenery of Monument Valley, the awe-inspiring dawns and sunsets with troopers riding doggedly along against the skylines. The film, too was one of John Wayne's triumphs. He rose splendidly to the challenge of the character role of Captain Nathan Brittles on the verge of retirement in the immediate aftermath of the massacre of Custer and his men at the Little Big Horn.

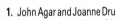

1. John Agar and Joanne Dru
2. Mildred Natwick, Victor McLaglen and Joanne Dru
3. John Wayne, Harry Carey Jr, Ben Johnson, John Agar and George O'Brien
4. John Wayne and Joanne Dru
5. Harry Carey Jr, Joanne Dru and John Agar
6. John Wayne, Joanne Dru and John Agar

◁ 5

6 ▷

1

2

3

4

5

6

7

1. Richard Widmark in *Down to the Sea in Ships* (Fox)

2. Jim Backus

3. Stewart Granger in *Adam and Evelyne* (TC)

4. Frank Lackteen (l), Carole Donne and Tom Neal in *Amazon Quest* (FCL)

5. Robert Young, Max Baer and Claudette Colbert in *Bride for Sale* (RKO)

6. Howard da Silva and Charles McGraw in *Border Incident* (MGM)

7. Robert Young and Claudette Colbert in *Bride for Sale* (RKO)

8. William Lundigan and Virginia Bruce in *Assignment in China* (aka *State Department - File 649*) (FCL)

9. John Penrose and Dennis Price in *Kind Hearts and Coronets* (EaS)

10. Richard Jaeckel, Peter Fernandez, Stephen McNally, Al Ramsen and Mickey Knox in *City Across the River* (Univ)

11. Martha Sherrill and Robert Lowery in *Call of the Forest* (LIP)

8

9

10
▷
▷
11

1

2

3

4

5

6

8

1. Huntz Hall and Leo Gorcey in *Hold That Baby* (MoP)
2. Ellen Drew and John Payne in *The Crooked Way* (UA)
3. Charles Evans (r) in *The Crooked Way* (UA)
4. Lee J Cobb, Adele Jergens, Stephen Dunne and Lois Maxwell in *Dark Past* (Col)
5. Lynne Baggett
6. Martha Vickers and Philip Reed in *Daughter of the West* (FCL)
7. Walter Brennan and Joe Sawyer in *Curtain Call at Cactus Creek* (GB *Take the Stage*) (Univ)
8. James Mitchell, John Archer and Joel McCrea in *Colorado Territory* (WB)
9. Randolph Scott, John Ireland, Louise Allbritton and Noah Beery Jr in *The Doolins of Oklahoma* (Col)
10. James J Griffith and Donald Woods in *Daughter of the West* (FCL)
11. Douglas Fairbanks Jr (mkd), Henry Brandon (ptg) and Otto Waldis in *The Fighting O'Flynn* (Univ)

7

9

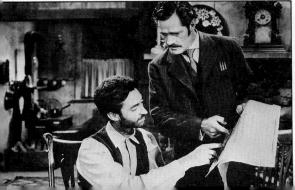

10
11

1. William Bendix and Allen Martin Jr in *Johnny Holiday* (UA)
2. Vera-Ellen and Paul Valentine in *Love Happy* (UA)
3. Ralph Richardson in *The Heiress* (Par)
4. Montgomery Clift, Miriam Hopkins and Olivia de Havilland in *The Heiress* (Par)
5. Ralph Richardson, Montgomery Clift, Olivia de Havilland and Miriam Hopkins in *The Heiress* (Par)
6. Ralph Richardson, Vanessa Brown and Olivia de Havilland in *The Heiress* (Par)
7. Montgomery Clift and Olivia de Havilland in *The Heiress* (Par)
8. Johnny Weissmuller and Myrna Dell in *The Lost Tribe* (Col)
9. Michael Denison, Dulcie Gray and Josephine Stuart in *My Brother Jonathan* (ABPC)
10. Janet Leigh and June Allyson in *Little Women* (MGM)

Two scenes from *Samson and Delilah* (Par) (top) Victor Mature

461

Humphrey Bogart

1. June Holden
2. Jinx Falkenburg
3. Lew Ayres
4. Anna Sten
5. Peter Glenville
6. Celeste Holm
7. Marilyn Nash
8. Gloria Grahame
9. Charles Drake
10. Gloria Henry
11. Shelley Winters
12. Alida Valli
13. David Farrar
14. Zena Marshall
15. Jane Harker

1. Suzette Delair in *Pattes Blanches* (FrF)
2. Raimu in *L'Homme au Chapeau Rond* (US *The Eternal Husband*) (FrF)
3. Charles Starrett and Smiley Burnette in *Frontier Outpost* (Col)
4. George Slocum, Margia Dean, Tom Neal and Jack Holt (all stdg), and John Cason, Don Barry Holly Bane and Byron Foulger (all std) in *Red Desert* (LIP)
5. Andy Clyde, Tris Coffin and Whip Wilson in *Riders of the Dark* (MoP)
6. Dan Duryea and Dorothy Lamour in *Manhandled* (Par)
7. Esther Williams, Gene Kelly and Tom Dugan in *Take Me Out to the Ball Game* (MGM)
8. John Gregson
9. Rona Anderson
10. Laurence Harvey
11. Peter Finch
12. Richard Burton
13. Victor Mature
14. Leo Genn in *No Place for Jennifer* (ABPC)
15. Raymond Lovell
16. Bing Crosby

13
▷◁
14

15
▷◁
16

1. John McCallum
2. Patricia Dainton
3. Patricia Knight
4. Charles Victor
5. Sonia Holm
6. Dan Dailey
7. Christine Norden
8. Jacques Sernas
9. Judy Campbell
10. John Bentley
11. Claire Bloom
12. Anne Vernon
13. Robert Stack
14. Mary Morris
15. John Mills and John Howard Davies in *The Rocking Horse Winner* (TC)
16. Maria Denis in *Private Angelo* (Pil)
17. George Raft and Marie Windsor in *Outpost in Morocco* (UA)
18. Mai Zetterling in *The Romantic Age* (US *Naughty Arlette*) (Pin)

1. Carol Raye
2. Pamela Bramah
3. Mary Hatcher
4. Ilka Chase
5. Janet Leigh
6. Jean Peters
7. Ann Richards
8. Sylvia Sidney
9. Nancy Walker
10. Siobhan McKenna
11. Margot Grahame
12. K T Stevens
13. Viveca Lindfors
14. Annabella
15. Agnes Moorehead
16. Coleen Gray
17. Virginia Huston

1. Allan Jeayes
2. Dewey Robinson
3. Serge Reggiani
4. Walter Hudd
5. Leslie Dwyer
6. Brian Roper
7. Allen Jenkins
8. Stuart Erwin
9. Roddy McDowall
10. Montgomery Clift
11. Leon Errol
12. Kent Smith
13. Anthony Steel
14. David Bruce
15. Edward Ashley
16. Michael Rennie
17. Jimmy 'Schnozzle' Durante

1

2

3

4

5

6

7

8

9

1. Barry Sullivan, Darryl Hickman, Alexis Smith and Clark Gable in *Any Number Can Play* (MGM)
2. Frank Morgan, Clark Gable and Charles Arnt in *Any Number Can Play* (MGM)
3. Valerie Hobson in *The Interrupted Journey* (BL)
4. Virginia Mayo and James Cagney in *White Heat* (WB)
5. Hank Worden
6. Paul Kelly, Joan Tetzel, Barbara Stanwyck and Wendell Corey in *The File on Thelma Jordan* (Par)
7. Felix Aylmer and Wanda Hendrix in *Prince of Foxes* (Fox)
8. Murvyn Vye in *A Connecticut Yankee in King Arthur's Court* (Par)
9. Silvana Mangano (r) in *Bitter Rice*
10. George Sanders

10 ▷

468

2

3

4

5

6

1. Bobby Howes
2. Michael Gough
3. David Tomlinson
4. Andrea Lea
5. Norman Lloyd
6. Peter Reynolds
7. Alec Guinness
8. Rosalyn Boulter
9. Buster Keaton
10. George Montgomery
11. Kirk Douglas
12. Beatrice Campbell
13. Red Skelton
14. Walter Huston
15. Ronald Colman
16. Oscar Levant

7

8

9

10

11

13
▷ ◁
14

12

15
◁

16

469

2

3

4

1

5

6

7

8

1. William Holden in *Streets of Laredo* (Par)
2. Geraldine Brooks
3. Howard Duff
4. Dorothy Hart
5. Celeste Holm and Loretta Young in *Come to the Stable* (Fox)
6. Robert Hutton and Jean Wallace in *The Man On The Eiffel Tower* (RKO)
7. Franchot Tone (r) in *The Man On The Eiffel Tower* (RKO)
8. Burgess Meredith (r) in *The Man On The Eiffel Tower* (RKO)
9. Robert Cummings
10. Helen Gilbert
11. Wendell Corey
12. Lizabeth Scott and Victor Mature in *Easy Living* (RKO)

9

10 ▷
▽ ◁
11

◁ **12**

1. Moira Lister
2. Jack Raine, Eleanor Summerfield and Terrence de Marney in *No Way Back* (Con)
3. Arlene Dahl and Jess Barker in *Reign of Terror* (EL)
4. Jean Hagen
5. Charles Starrett and Paula Raymond in *Challenge of the Range* (Col)
6. Valentina Cortesa and Richard Conte in *Thieves Highway* (Fox)
7. Carol Marsh
8. Barbara Murray
9. John Agar
10. Jeff Donnell
11. Charley Grapewin, Coleen Gray and Mark Stevens in *Sand* (Fox)
12. Coleen Gray and Mark Stevens in *Sand* (Fox)

10
11

 12

1. Burl Ives
2. John Lund
3. Louise Allbritton
4. Joseph Tomelty
5. Jane Barrett
6. Lana Morris
7. Charles Smith
8. Michael Denison
9. Jack Hawkins
10. John Ireland
11. Richard Erdman
12. Patricia Plunkett
13. Richard Conte
14. Philip Dorn
15. Felix Aylmer
16. Frank Jenks
17. Frank McHugh
18. Ludwig Stossel
19. Marjorie Gateson

1

2

3

4

1. Hedy Lamarr and Victor Mature in *Samson and Delilah* (Par)
2. Julia Faye, Victor Mature and Hedy Lamarr in *Samson and Delilah* (Par)
3. Hedy Lamarr and Russ Tamblyn in *Samson and Delilah* (Par)
4. Victor Mature in *Samson and Delilah* (Par)
5. George Sanders (I) and Hedy Lamarr in *Samson and Delilah* (Par)
6. John Garfield
7. Nina Foch in *The Undercover Man* (Col)
8. Pamela Britton

5

6

7

8

Ginger Rogers and Fred Astaire in the *Barkleys of Broadway* (MGM)

1

2

3

1. Joseph Cotten and Bette Davis in *Beyond the Forest* (WB)
2. Andy Clyde and Whip Wilson in *Range Land* (MoP)
3. Betty Lynn and Robert Arthur in *Mother Is A Freshman* (Fox)
4. Robert Preston, Susan Hayward and Lloyd Gough in *Tulsa* (EL)
5. Mark Stevens and June Haver in *Oh, You Beautiful Doll* (Fox)
6. Marcia Mae Jones and Edward Brophy in *Arson Inc* (LIP)
7. Arthur Hunnicutt, Dennis O'Keefe and Charlotte Greenwood in *The Great Dan Patch* (UA)
8. Douglas Fowley and Marcia Mae Jones in *Arson Inc* (LIP)
9. Robert Lowery and Anne Gwynne in *Arson Inc* (LIP)

4

5

6

7
◁
▷
8

9
▷

1. Edmund Gwenn
2. Audrey Totter
3. Ronald Shiner
4. Gregory Peck
5. Yolande Donlan
6. Clinton Sundberg
7. Elizabeth Sellars
8. Lucile Watson
9. Denise Darcel
10. Lizabeth Scott
11. Craig Stevens
12. Barbara Hale
13. Valerie Hobson
14. Paul Douglas
15. Maurice Denham
16. Van Heflin
17. Gale Storm
18. Don Taylor
19. Al (Lash) LaRue
20. Jan Sterling

1

1. Bobby Driscoll in *The Window* (RKO)
2. Edgar Buchanan and Howard Duff in *Red Canyon* (Univ)
3. John Calvert and Ben Welden in *Search for Danger* (FC)
4. Valentina Cortese and Richard Conte in *Thieves Highway* (Fox)
5. Susan Hayward and Dana Andrews in *My Foolish Heart* (RKO)
6. Peggy Cummins and Richard Greene in *That Dangerous Age* (US *If This Be Sin*) (LF)
7. Arthur Kennedy, Ella Raines, John Ireland (Stdg) and Randolph Scott in *The Walking Hills* (Col)
8. Joan Bennett and James Mason in *The Reckless Moment* (Col)

2

3

5

6

8

◁ 7

John Wayne in *The Fighting Kentuckian* (Rep)

1. Betty Underwood and Bill Williams in *A Dangerous Profession* (RKO)

2. Roland Winters, George Raft and Robert Gist in *A Dangerous Profession* (RKO)

3. Vera Ralston and John Howard in *The Fighting Kentuckian* (Rep)

4. Jennifer Jones and Van Heflin in *Madame Bovary* (MGM)

5. Oliver Hardy and John Wayne in *The Fighting Kentuckian* (Rep)

6. Van Heflin in *Madame Bovary* (MGM)

7. Joanne Dru and John Ireland in *All The King's Men* (Col)

8. John Derek, John Ireland and Broderick Crawford in *All The King's Men* (Col)

9. John Ireland and Broderick Crawford in *All The King's Men* (Col)

10. Houseley Stevenson and John Ireland in *All The King's Men* (Col)

1

3

5

6

7

8

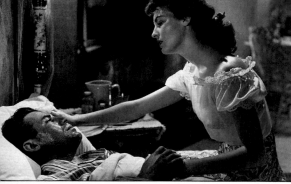

10

11

2

1. Richard Greene and Madeleine Carroll in *The Fan* (Fox)
2. Alan Ladd
3. Kent Smith and Patricia Neal in *The Fountainhead* (WB)
4. Richard Greene, George Sanders and John Sutton in *The Fan* (Fox)
5. Ray McDonald in *Flame of Youth* (Rep)
6. Rhonda Fleming
7. Mark Stevens and Betsy Drake in *Dancing In The Dark* (Fox)
8. Helen Spring, Art Baker, Ann E Todd, Barbara Britton and Dennis O'Keefe in *Cover-Up* (UA)
9. Gale Robbins
10. John Hodiak and Ava Gardner in *The Bribe* (MGM)
11. Nancy Guild and Frank Latimore in *Black Magic* (UA)

1

2

3

4

5

6

1. Mary Anderson	10. Jim Davis
2. Frank Lovejoy	11. Sabu
3. Lois Collier	12. Tim Holt
4. Pedro Armendariz	13. Burt Lancaster
5. Richard Egan	14. Sheila Sim
6. Joe Kirkwood	15. Anne Baxter
7. Mildred Dunnock	16. Wanda Hendrix
8. Ava Gardner	17. Luther Adler
9. Lauren Bacall	18. John Carroll

7

8

9

10

11

12

13

14

15
◁
▷
16

17
◁
▷
18

1. Barbara Bel Geddes and James Mason in *Caught* (MGM)
2. James Mason in *Caught* (MGM)
3. Gary Cooper in *Task Force* (WB)
4. Dan Duryea and Lizabeth Scott in *Too Late For Tears* (UA)
5. Alan Young (l), Clifton Webb (std) and Tom Drake in *Mr Belvedere Goes To College* (Fox)
6. Philip Reed in *Indian Scout* (UA)
7. Franchot Tone and Marc Lawrence (stg) in *Jigsaw* (UA)
8. Ray Milland and Jean Peters in *It Happens Every Spring* (Fox)
9. James Stewart
10. Jimmy Hanley
11. Joanne Dru

484

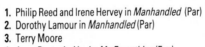

1. Philip Reed and Irene Hervey in *Manhandled* (Par)
2. Dorothy Lamour in *Manhandled* (Par)
3. Terry Moore
4. Anne Baxter in *You're My Everything* (Fox)
5. Jimmie Davis and Veda Ann Borg in *Mississippi Rhythm* (MoP)
6. Doris Day
7. Laura Elliot and George Reeves in *Special Agent* (Par)
8. Albert Dekker (c) in *Tarzan's Magic Fountain* (RKO)
9. Robert Hutton in *The Younger Brothers* (WB)
10. Gene Tierney and Charles Bickford (c) in *Whirlpool* (Fox)
11. Janis Paige and Wayne Morris in *The Younger Brothers* (WB)

1. Humphrey Bogart (r) in *Knock On Any Door* (Col)
2. Susan Perry in *Knock On Any Door* (Col)
3. Myrna Dell and Glenn Ford in *Lust for Gold* (Col)
4. George Chandler and John Derek in *Knock On Any Door* (Col)
5. Audie Murphy (c) and Ray Teal in *Bad Boy* (AA)
6. Merril McCormick and Del Cambre in *Arctic Fury* (PLY)
7. Leif Erickson, Barbara Stanwyck and Stephen McNally in *The Lady Gambles* (Univ)
8. Skip Homeier, Forrest Tucker, Irving Bacon (std), Lon McCallister and Preston Foster in *The Big Cat* (EL)
9. Peggy Ann Garner and Lon McCallister in *The Big Cat* (EL)
10. Harry Woods and Joseph Crehan (c) in *Alias the Champ* (Rep)

◁ **10**

1

2

3

4

5

6

7

8

9

1. Peggy Ann Garner and Johnny Sheffield in *Bomba, the Jungle Boy* (MoP)

2. Jack Haley and Joan Davis in *Make Mine Laughs* (RKO)

3. Monte Hale in *Prince of the Plains* (Rep)

4. Farley Granger and Joan Evans in *Roseanna McCoy* (SG)

5. Paul Hurst (l), Monte Hale and Shirley Davis in *Prince of the Plains* (Rep)

6. Marshall Thompson, Gigi Perreau, Aline MacMahon, Peter Miles and Raymond Massey in *Roseanna McCoy* (SG)

7. Robert Armstrong, Ben Johnson, Nestor Paiva and Terry Moore in *Mighty Joe Young* (RKO)

8. John Lund and Paulette Goddard in *Bride of Vengeance* (Par)

9. William Hartnell (Sgt) and Dennis Price (std) in *The Lost People* (G'boro)

10. Macdonald Carey (l), Charles Dayton, Donald Randolph and Raymond Burr in *Bride of Vengeance* (Par)

◁**10**

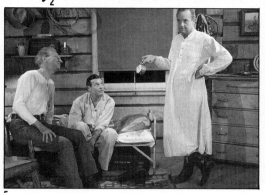

1. Gail Davis, Roy Rogers and Andy Devine in *The Far Frontier* (Rep)
2. Bob Cason, Charles Starrett (std), Ethan Laidlaw, Robert Wilke and Fred Sears in *Laramie* (Col)
3. John Payne in *El Paso* (Par)
4. Robert Wilke, Monte Hale and Roy Barcroft in *San Antone Ambush* (Rep)
5. Olin Howland, Richard Arlen and Grady Sutton in *Grand Canyon* (LIP)
6. Reed Hadley (hatless) and Victor Kilian (sheriff r) in *Rimfire* (LIP)
7. Tim Holt, Richard Martin and Lois Andrews in *Rustlers* (RKO)
8. Joel McCrea and Zachary Scott in *South of St Louis* (WB)
9. Paul Maxey and Victor Jory in *South of St Louis* (WB)
10. Douglas Kennedy, Zachary Scott and Joel McCrea in *South of St Louis* (WB)
11. Zachary Scott and Bob Steele (r) in *South of St Louis* (WB)

1

2

3

4

5

6

1. Roy Rogers on Trigger in *Susanna Pass* (Rep)

2. Marshall Reed and Robert Lowery in *The Dalton Gang* (Don Barry Prod)

3. Claude Jarman Jr and Robert Sterling in *Roughshod* (RKO)

4. Myrna Dell and Shawn McGlory in *Roughshod* (RKO)

5. Damian O'Flynn (l) and Gene Autry (r) in *Riders of the Whistling Pines* (Col)

6. Myrna Dell, Gloria Grahame, James Bell and Robert Sterling in *Roughshod* (RKO)

7. Tom Steele, Monte Hale and Ted Mapes in *Outcasts of the Trail* (Rep)

8. Bill Elliott, Adrian Booth, Jack Holt, Hank Bell and Andy Devine in *The Last Bandit* (Rep)

9. Gene Autry in *The Cowboy and the Indians* (Col)

10. Jason Robards, John Dehner, Charles Starrett and Jock Mahoney in *Horsemen of the Sierras* (Col)

7   ▽ 9

8

10

489

1. Maureen O'Hara
2. Edward Arnold, Katherine Alexander, Patricia Neal and Ronald Reagan in *John Loves Mary* (WB)
3. Edmund Gwenn in *Challenge to Lassie* (MGM)
4. Lumsden Hare and Donald Crisp in *Challenge to Lassie* (MGM)
5. Phillip Terry
6. John Payne in *Captain China* (Par)
7. Lea Padovani in *Give Us This Day* (US *Salt and the Devil*) (P)
8. Sam Wanamaker and Lea Padovani in *Give Us This Day* (US *Salt and the Devil*) (P)
9. Hugh Marlowe
10. Paul Douglas and Linda Darnell in *Everybody Does It* (Fox)

1

1. Gigi Perreau
2. George Raft and Nina Foch in *Johnny Allegro* (Col)
3. Nina Foch in *Johnny Allegro* (Col)
4. George Raft, George Macready and Matt McHugh in *Johnny Allegro* (Col)
5. Olga San Juan, Margaret Hamilton, Betty Grable, Al Bridge, Cesar Romero, Hugh Herbert and Chris Pin Martin in *The Beautiful Blonde From Bashful Bend* (Fox)
6. Natalie Wood, Betty Lynn, Fred MacMurray and Maureen O'Hara in *Father Was a Fullback* (Fox)
7. Charles Coburn, Ella Raines, Clarence Kolb and Brian Donlevy in *Impact* (UA)
8. James Edwards, Lloyd Briges and Frank Lovejoy in *Home of the Brave* (UA)
9. Jeff Corey and James Edwards in *Home of the Brave* (UA)
10. Steve Brodie, Lloyd Bridges and Frank Lovejoy in *Home of the Brave* (UA)

4

3

5

6

7

8

9
10

1. Charles Ruggles (bearded) and Minerva Urecal in *The Lovable Cheat* (FCL)

2. Ludwig Donath and Tamara Shayne in *Jolson Sings Again* (Col)

3. Keefe Brasselle and Anne O'Neal in *Not Wanted* (FCL)

4. Barbara Hale and Larry Parks in *Jolson Sings Again* (Col)

5. Claude Jarman Jr and Jeanette MacDonald in *The Sun Comes Up* (MGM)

6. Ella Raines and William Bishop in *The Walking Hills* (Col)

7. Peter Finch in *Train of Events* (EaS)

8. Michael Whalen, Adele Jergens and Glenn Langan in *Treasure of Monte Cristo* (LIP)

9. Jon Hall in *Zamba* (EL)

1. Gail Russell and Sabu in *Song of India* (Col)
2. Sabu, Gail Russell and Turhan Bey in *Song of India* (Col)
3. Ron Randell in *Omoo Omoo* (SGP)
4. Gail Russell, Robert H Barrat, Turhan Bey and Anthony Caruso in *Song of India* (Col)
5. Stephen McNally (c) and Hugh French in *Sword in the Desert* (Univ)
6. Peggy Ryan and Ray McDonald in *Shamrock Hill* (EL)
7. Dale Robertson
8. William Demarest
9. Linda Darnell and Richard Widmark in *Slattery's Hurricane* (Fox)
10. Linda Darnell and John Russell in *Slattery's Hurricane* (Fox)
11. George Tobias and Robert Ryan in *The Set Up* (RKO)

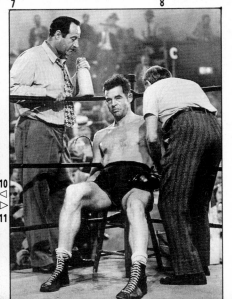

MANHATTAN
ANGEL
A COLUMBIA PICTURE

COLUMBIA
PICTURES
presents
CORNEL WILDE
SHOCKPROOF
with PATRICIA KNIGHT

BASED ON FILES OF THE U.S. DEPT. OF JUSTICE

ILLEGAL ENTRY

A UNIVERSAL-INTERNATIONAL PICTURE

M-G-M present

TENSION

STARRING

RICHARD BASEHART · AUDREY TOTTER
CYD CHARISSE · BARRY SULLIVAN

A METRO-GOLDWYN-MAYER PICTURE

Robert Taylor had shed his glamour-boy image when he starred in MGM's action-packed Western *Ambush*. This gritty film was based on a best-selling book penned by renowned Luke Short. Opposite Taylor was Arlene Dahl in all her blonde beauty while John McIntire was superb as a grizzled old pathfinder, wise in the cunning ways of the ruthless Apache Indians. The veteran director Sam Wood, responsible for so many movie winners, regrettably died shortly after completing this, his last and very successful film.

1. John McIntire and Robert Taylor
2. Robert Taylor and Arlene Dahl

1

2

ABBREVIATIONS AND LOBBY CARDS

P	Plantaganet	G'boro	Gainsborough	PLY	Plymouth
RKO	RKO Radio Pictures	Cine	Cineguild	c	centre
Univ	Universal	TFI	Tricolore Films Inc	Std	Seated
Cine/IP	Cineguild/Independent Producers	I	Individual	r	right
Par	Paramount	A/IP	Archers/Independent Producers	l	left
DS	David Selznick	Emb	Embassy	Sgt	Sergeant
MGM	Metro Goldwyn Mayer	FrF	French Film	Stdg	Standing
UA	United Artists	JLP	Jules Levey Productions	aka	also known as
WB	Warner Brothers	Exc	Excelsior Film Productions	mkd	masked
EaS	Ealing Studios	HuS	Hunt Stromberg	ptg	pointing
Fox	Twentieth Century-Fox	PP	Pennant Pictures	fg	foreground
Rep	Republic	Boc	Boca Productions	S	Sitting
Col	Columbia	Box	Sydney Box		
Coy	Colony	EL	Eagle Lion		
HR	Hal Roach	Tr	Triton		
ES	Edward Small	AA	Allied Artists		
MoP	Monogram Productions	G/All	Gloria Alliance	**LOBBY CARDS**	
SG	Samuel Goldwyn	SCG or SGP	Screen Guild Productions	*Seven Miles from Alcatraz 141*	
SIR	Siritzky	BL	British Lion	*The Purple V 141*	
WaW	Walter Wanger	All/RKO	Alliance/RKO	*San Diego I Love You 213*	
Penn	Pennant	RKO/Pat	RKO/Pathe	*Sweet and Low-Down 213*	
JRP	Jack Raymond Productions	PFS	Production Film Service	*Objective Burma 231*	
BN	British National	Bch	Butchers	*Henry V 231*	
Unv	University Film Products	JC	John Corfield	*Mr Emmanuel 267*	
PRC	Producers Releasing Corporation	IS	Independent Sovereign	*Woman Who Came Back 267*	
SeP	Select Productions	ED	Edward Dryhurst	*Strike It Rich 426*	
TC	Two Citys	WA	Western Adventures	*Slippy McGee 426*	
LF	London Films	FCL	Film Classics	*I Was a Male War Bride 479*	
ABPC	Associated British Picture Corporation	LIP	Robert L Lippert	*Easy Living 479*	
NF	Niksos Films	Pil	Pilgrim	*Manhattan Angel 494*	
CF	Charter Films	Pin	Pinnacle	*Shockproof 494*	
IP	Independent Producers	Con	Concanen	*Illegal Entry 495*	
HH	Howard Hughes	FC	Four Continents	*Tension 495*	

INDEX OF FILM TITLES

When a film title is mentioned in the introduction of any chapter, its page number is printed in Roman (upright type). When a title appears under a picture, the page number is printed in italics. Some films were released under different titles in America and Great Britain. The different versions are indexed separately.

INDEX OF PERSONNEL